Villages on Wheels

Villages on Wheels

A Social History of the Gathering to Zion

Stanley B. Kimball
and Violet T. Kimball

GREG KOFFORD BOOKS
SALT LAKE CITY, UTAH
2011

Greg Kofford Books
P.O. Box 1362
Draper, UT 84020
www. koffordbooks.com

2015   14   13   12   11   5   4   3   2   1

Library of Congress Cataloging-in-Publication Data

Kimball, Stanley Buchholz, author.
  Villages on wheels : a social history of the gathering to Zion /
Stanley B. Kimball and Violet T. Kimball.
      pages cm
  Includes index.
  ISBN 978-1-58958-119-7
  1. Church of Jesus Christ of Latter-day Saints--History. 2. Mor-
mon Church--History. 3. Mormon pioneers--History. 4. Mormon
Pioneer National Historic Trail--History. 5. Frontier and pioneer
life--West (U.S.)--History. I. Kimball, Violet T., author. II. Title.
  BX8611.K54 2011
  289.3'7309034--dc23
                          2011038532

In Memoriam
Stanley B. Kimball

Contents

Preface

This has been a bittersweet project. My husband, Stanley B. Kimball, Mormon Trails historian, began to talk and make notes about his "magnum opus" about 1990. He outlined the book, which he wanted to title *Villages on Wheels*, in about ten single-spaced sections with suggestions of what a social history should include. He then wrote a draft and incorporated some of the material from many of the papers he had presented at Sunstone Symposiums and at annual meetings of the Mormon History Association.

Many times he agonized over whether "social history" was not too broad a trail classification to try to write about; but with characteristic optimism, he plowed ahead. By 1997, he had been diagnosed with stomach cancer, but he continued his normal routine. Then a new enemy invaded in 1998, more deadly than the first: multiple myeloma. Chemotherapy left him too sick to do any writing, so he sent his draft off to a university and we began to pack for our retirement in St. George, Utah. We moved in September 2001 during a too-brief remission.

Constantly on Stan's mind was this unfinished project. One day when he was fretting about the manuscript, I assured him that I would finish it myself—which was a classic "fools rush in" statement if there ever were one. I'm a photojournalist\writer and have enjoyed accompanying Stan on some of his trail explorations. I am not a historian nor a trail expert, but traveling along those dusty ruts on at least four occasions makes me an admirer of what those brave and hardy men, women, and children accomplished. Stan's faith in me glowed in his eyes, though. He seized my hand, kissed it, and whispered "Oh, thank you, thank you." He hit the trail to his own eternal destination on May 15, 2003.

Four months after his death, I began to gather material to see what that pledge was going to do to my life. I found a copy of his original draft on a floppy disk, but I could not open it until computer experts Chase Kimball and Clayton Hunt succeeded after spending several weeks trying one thing after another. Finally, by the first anniversary of his passing, I had a fair knowledge of what was ahead of me.

After a few ten-hour days, the first chapter began to take shape almost magically. I rewrote from Stanley's draft, bringing in new material and ideas. A few of my chapters were not in the original material. I spread hundreds of journals, both photocopied and published, and spread them out—on the floor, on every table in the house, and on card tables set up to hold my multiplying sources. Soon my king-sized bed was covered with even more documents. I slept perched on the edge.

What the pioneers would call the "hand of Providence" was present in a lot of the material I searched for and the words I typed afterwards. More than once, I prayed for wisdom to know what to do and moaned aloud at what remained to be done. "What would Stanley do?" became my mantra. It seemed at times that someone was whispering the name of a journal I should check—and there I would find the exact quotation I needed.

I became a recluse, telling friends I was on a two-year mission. My timing was good. In early May 2005, just two years after Stan's passing, I had a workable draft and sent it out to two readers while I continued to correct, add new material, and re-read more journals.

At one point, I contemplated replacing Stanley's choice of a title, "Villages on Wheels," with "Journey of Obedience," which I noticed was a theme in many accounts. Many immigrants commented on the advice that they were given about the importance of immigrating—particularly that gathering to Zion was as important as baptism, a critical sign of obedience. British artist Frederick Piercy, who crossed the ocean and the plains in 1853, likewise called it "a journey of obedience." But "Villages on Wheels" won out.

I feel that Stanley knows how I have captured "the power of place and the spirit of locale," which was his own phrase and which so aptly fits his experience. To a lesser extent, it also fits mine. While

Stanley's forte was the physical aspect of the trail, mine was more the social history and the people involved in that process. Fulfilling my promise to Stanley has been a spiritual, emotional, and physical journey that pushed me into new territory. Perhaps it is fitting, after all, that I finished what Stanley began about 1990.

Editorial Procedures

To make it easier for ordinary readers to enter the experience of those who made the journey of obedience in their villages on wheels, I have chosen to weave the narrative from the documents and quotations but without the scholarly apparatus of citations. For several reasons, we—first Stan and then I—have chosen to use a narrative—or storytelling—style, with little or no scholarly apparatus, such as footnotes. *History* comes from the Greek *historia* meaning narrative, a tale or a story. We aim to write a "true" history, written to convey more than names, places, and dates. But we provide the names of those cited and let the Saints tell their own stories in most of this book. The vast majority of our sources are located in three archives: the LDS Church History Library of the Church of Jesus Christ of Latter-day Saints in Salt Lake City; the L. Tom Perry Special Collections at the Harold B. Lee Library, Brigham Young University, Provo, Utah; and the Western Americana Archives of the J. Willard Marriott Library, University of Utah, Salt Lake City.

We have done minor editing—for example, adding terminal punctuation and initial capitalization where necessary, other punctuation necessary for clarification, and correcting spelling if the original spellings might be confusing. We changed a few third-person accounts to first person. In many cases, we worked from photocopies of holograph documents, in others from published accounts. We visited every Mormon and Oregon/California Trail Center in the United States plus many universities.

In preparation for my own move to Georgia in June 2007, I donated Stan's papers—a whopping six crammed-full filing cabinets—to the University of Utah and the LDS Church History Library. Most of his books, maps, and records dealing with the Mormon Trail were given to the LDS Church History Library, while most of his private collection and personal correspondence went to the

University of Utah. This collection included his private correspondence with LDS Church authorities, including about seventy letters
to President Spencer W. Kimball, for instance. I am glad that they
found homes where other scholars will be able to consult them.

After my manuscript was accepted by Greg Kofford Books, I
moved from St. George, Utah, to Macon, Georgia, in 2007 to be
near my children and grandchildren. At that point, I brought only
about twenty-five Church and trail books, my personal filing cabinet,
and a box of journals. I was "finished" with writing. But of course,
when I started to do my final editing, I panicked. I needed *all* of my
research material. I spent three hours one night trying to find what
instrument William Clayton played in Pitts's Brass Band. (It was the
violin. I could not find that in Clayton's own famous journal which
I have.)

Fortunately, I remembered that I had several CDs with lots of
Church and trail history. They helped enormously. I couldn't help
contrasting the life I was writing about 160 years ago, with my computer, Google, and instant messaging. Who would have had a harder
time adjusting if we could swap lifestyles: Vilate Kimball, Heber C.
Kimball's first wife, or I?

As I finish the final editing, my mind is more and more on the
past and I find comfort in reading again the heroic accounts of the
pioneers' journey. I find that my admiration of their feat is greater
than ever. I hope this book imparts some of this feeling to the reader.

This book was not written to be faith promoting, though I think
it will be. It was also not written to prove a point or justify Mormon
history. It is a factual history, sometimes dark, but more often heroic.
I have tried to be an unbiased observer. Stanley is not here to save me
from major blunders; but if there are any, I hope the readers will not
judge me by the standard to which they could have held him. It has
truly been a labor of love. As Sir Winston Churchill wrote: "History
. . . stumbles along the trail of the past, trying to reconstruct its scene,
to revive its echoes and kindle . . . the passion of former days."

Acknowledgements

I have been blessed with a wonderful family and friends who have
rendered moral support and supplied me with precious, unpublished

sources. Howard D. Lowe of St. George read the entire manuscript and wrote encouraging comments about how the material impressed him. Jacqueline Rice Jensen loaned me family journals that proved to be a good addition to what I already had. Some of her ancestors had made that pre-1869 trek and were already included in the book.

My children were helpful, especially Kay Kimball and April Hunt, who read and edited several chapters. Michael Landon of the Church Historian's Office graciously agreed to read my draft because of his admiration for Stanley. He is both a history and a trail buff. He knew exactly what I needed to bring the book into better focus and sharpen the writing, and recommended additional sources to consult.

Nedra Anderson, editor extraordinaire, spent many hours of her Christmas season in 2004 working on my manuscript. I was thrilled with her expert guidance and consider her one of the Three Nephites from Mormon legend, who appear when desperately needed. My thanks also to Lavina Fielding Anderson, who edited my final version and proved once again that she is Utah's best.

Violet T. Kimball
Macon, Georgia, 2011

Introduction

We might say of Israel, behold a city on wheels, for the commotion of the Camp of Israel much resembles the bustle of a business city.
—Guy M. Keysor, Iowa, 1846

Close to the beginning of the twentieth century, Finley Peter Dunne, an American journalist and humorist, created the Irish philosopher, "Mr. Dooley," who famously commented:

> "I know histhry isnh't thrue, Hinnessy, because it ain't like what I see ivry day in Halsted Sthreet. If any wan comes along with a histhry iv Greece or Rome that'll show me th' people; fightin', gettin' dhrunk, makin' love, gettin' married, owin' the grocery man an' bein' without hard-coal, I'll believe they was a Greece or Rome, but not befure. Historyans is like doctors. They . . . tells ye what a counthry died iv. But I'd like to know what it lived iv.

Mr. Dooley was issuing a plea for the social history of ordinary people, which, in his opinion, was the interesting and exciting part of human existence. All human activities are either political, social, cultural, or economic, but the social has often been slighted and overshadowed by political and economic history.

Social history is the story of social institutions, customs, and laws—the history of life in its fundamental fullness and routine. It is the heartbeat, the routine cycles of birth, growth, work, marriage, reproduction, good times, tragedies, intimacy, illness and death—the history of the masses. It includes courtship, weddings, childbearing, working, playing, praying, relating to others, relocating, dressing, eating, and dying. The common people get the attention and sympathy, not the drum and trumpet or crown and constitutional history. We know much about Mormon leaders; this history reveals the heroism and humanity of common men and women, and also includes the four-legged heroes of the trek west, the draft animals. It covers faith, society, work and trading, intimacy, recreation, disease and death, discipline, and the human dimension or "dark side." It also includes interaction with "Gentiles" (as Mormons called non-Mormons), Indians, and blacks. Blacks have not been treated extensively in trail history, nor has the role that draft animals played in the westward movement. These are two unique contributions of this volume.

The purpose of this book is to tell the story of typical Mormons' pilgrimage to the valleys of the Rocky Mountains. Their travels began in a first move in 1831 from New York and Pennsylvania, then on to Ohio, Missouri, and Illinois. However, my emphasis is on the great exodus from Nauvoo, Illinois, to the Great Salt Lake starting in 1846. The book ends in 1869 when the railroad reached Promontory Summit in northern Utah. Emigrants could then come by railroad nearly all the way. This social history shows what the Mormons "lived in" and believed in. They died from the same things everyone else did.

Before the Exodus

The energy that propelled the Mormons from Nauvoo into the Iowa prairies in February 1846 had been building for fourteen years, since the organization of the Church of Jesus Christ of Latter-day Saints in 1830 in New York. It is a saga of heroic and tragic proportions with heroes, heroines, visions, villains, tragedy, faith, fanaticism, evil spirits, heavenly visitations, revelations, violence, rescue, death, new scriptures, murder, restoration of divine truths, conflict, persecution, and endurance. In less than two centuries, however, Mormonism has achieved the status of being a great American religious success story.

The saga begins with a teenager in New York named Joseph Smith, who announced that he had been visited by God and His son Jesus Christ, that he had been given an ancient record and the power to translate it, and that he had been chosen to restore Christ's New Testament church to earth. This claim brought a swelling outcry from other religions, and people in general. For their part, the new converts interpreted their neighbors' outrage as a sign that they belonged to the true church.

Mormon history officially began April 6, 1830, when Joseph Smith (1805–44) organized the church (officially known today as the Church of Jesus Christ of Latter-day Saints) in Fayette, Seneca County, New York, in accordance with the laws of that state. Only a few weeks earlier, Joseph's translation of the record on the golden plates with the aid of his seer stone, had been published as the Book of Mormon. These golden plates, which he found in a nearby hill, contained the account of ancient people on the American continent. The Smiths, a poor farming family, were already marginal in the community—thought of as "visionaries." Both Joseph and his father, Joseph Smith Sr., had the reputation of using seer stones to hunt buried treasures. Yet according to historian Richard Lyman Bushman, "early church [members] had in common a sympathy for a visionary religion."

Many of the Smiths and their friends had their own religious visionary experiences. One of young Joseph's most publicized acts after the Church's organization was casting evil spirits out of convert Newel Knight. He first asked Knight if he believed: "If you know that I can, it shall be done." Joseph showed this same kind of self-assurance for the rest of his life.

The citizens considered it preposterous that God would visit an unschooled youth; and when Joseph announced that all "churches were corrupt" most of the spiritual leaders and regular citizens found further reason to condemn this young upstart. Despite, or perhaps because of, this persecution, the new church grew fast in western New York and northern Pennsylvania.

Before the end of 1830, a "decree hath gone forth from the Father" that the Saints should gather "against the day when tribulation and desolation are sent forth upon the wicked." In January 1831, Joseph Smith announced that this gathering place would be "the Ohio" where a quartet of missionaries headed to Missouri to preach to the Indians, descendants of Book of Mormon peoples, had made a core of converts. By spring, Kirtland, Ohio, had become Mormon headquarters. Three groups, one led by Lucy Mack Smith, Joseph's mother, had reached the new Zion. A strong branch of the

Church from Colesville, New York, continued on from Ohio to Independence, Missouri, in August 1831.

Although the new church was just one year old, hundreds obeyed the Prophet's call to forsake all for the gospel. Joseph instituted a "law of consecration and stewardship"—a provision to assure economic equality—about this time in Missouri. The Mormons were encouraged to give all of their means to the Church's newly appointed bishop, Edward Partridge. They would receive back enough for their needs and would "receive an inheritance in Zion" for their contributions. It was a bold step, but Joseph saw how eager the people were for the word of the Lord. Much was demanded of these Missouri Mormons, but their reward would be the supernal gift of building the city of Zion, centered on a temple to which Jesus Christ would return to begin his millennial reign.

The old settlers in Missouri greeted this announcement, not only with derision and suspicion but also with downright hostility. The culture clash was, in retrospect, inevitable between the Missourians, largely emigrants from the South, and the Mormons, largely from New England. Differences in education caused a further gap. W. W. Phelps, printer of the Church's new newspaper in Independence, published an article that seemed to hint at a welcome for free blacks, a very unpopular position with the Missourians. Proselytizing among the Indians across the state line in Indian Territory led to swift rumors that the Mormons were trying to meddle with the uneasy peace that existed. Politically, the Mormons voted as a bloc; and their swelling numbers created genuine alarm at their political dominance, which was only a matter of time if this trend continued. Particularly offensive was the Mormon claim that God accepted only their "restored" church and that all other churches were corrupt. In conversations and in print, Mormons claimed that Missouri, their new Zion, would be given to them as their divine right. In July 1833, Jackson County residents armed themselves, destroyed Phelps's print shop, tarred and feathered Bishop Partridge and Charles Allen, another member, and ordered all Mormons out of the county. November 1833 found the Mormons, most of them ill-clad and ill-provisioned, huddled along the banks of the Grand River across the county line in Clay County to the north of Jackson County.

Although Joseph made a number of quick visits to Missouri, he spent most of his time in Kirtland, where a similar pattern of alarming in-migration and religious claims turned the tide of public opinion against the Mormons as well. Joseph and Sidney Rigdon, a convert who had become second in importance to him, were attacked by night in Hiram, Ohio, and tarred and feathered. Others launched a series of legal actions against them. Former friends and new enemies had various complaints against the leaders; some were trivial, some were serious.

In 1834, Smith formed and led a paramilitary unit, known as Zion's Camp, on a 900-mile march to western Missouri to try to restore the Missouri Mormons to their lands in Jackson County. The Mormons were relying on vague assurances from Missouri's governor that he would support their legal claims, but he reneged on what the Saints had envisioned as a promise, probably correctly predicting how unpopular such a move would be. Members of Zion's Camp were unprepared and undisciplined; tempers flared, friction broke out, and the expedition fizzled when an epidemic of cholera, some cases fatal, swept through the camp. The Prophet, who had forbidden the Saints to sell any of their Jackson County holdings—which left them truly without resources—returned to Ohio. However, the expedition proved to be a valuable test of loyalty and gave the Mormons some basic training in moving large numbers of people that helped prepare them for the travels that came later.

Although Clay County residents had originally been hospitable to the refugees when it appeared that their stay would be only temporary, they also became alarmed as the Mormons lingered on. By the summer of 1836, the best solution seemed to be for the Mormons to move northeast into the almost uninhabited upper part of Ray County, where separate counties, Daviess and Caldwell, were created.

Meanwhile, although the Saints in Kirtland had built a magnificent temple at staggering sacrifice, attempts to launch a Mormon bank resulted in spectacular failure and apostasy. Joseph Smith fled from Kirtland by night in January 1838, never to return. By the time he and a handful of devout disciples reached Missouri, he optimistically saw the new Mormon city of Far West as the gathering place, anchored by yet another temple. Some prominent Saints in Missouri, however, were also disturbed by the turmoil and religious developments. Some apostatized, while others were forcibly expelled.

Pursuing a headlong policy of community building and ingathering, Joseph Smith in Missouri continued to alarm the old settlers. Violence flared in the summer of 1838; and by fall, both sides had armed, with lines between official state militia, including Mormon units, blurred by the creation of vigilante groups on both sides. Destruction of property and bloodshed on both sides was terminated when Joseph Smith and other leaders surrendered at Far West in October 1838, and the Saints agreed to leave the state, a brutal midwinter ordeal as they crossed the state eastward to reach Quincy, Illinois.

After spending the winter in jail, Joseph Smith and his companions were allowed to escape. By April 1839, he was rallying his people on the banks of the Mississippi and had made arrangements to buy the beginnings of a town named Commerce, which he renamed Nauvoo. Once again, the gathering was heralded. Illinois welcomed these new taxpayers, and Nauvoo quickly became one of the largest cities in Illinois. It was the Mormon headquarters for seven years, during which time the Church flourished, received the first converts from England, and sent many missionaries throughout the United States and England to preach the "gathering."

Converts streamed into the area. What quality of faith caused them to lay their all upon the altar and make the gathering their most important spiritual and physical objective? Once again, their very success drew the alarm, and then the hostility, of their neighbors. Joseph Smith announced, "I glory in persecution. . . . I would be like a fish out of water, if I were out of persecutions." Certainly, it was a persuasive argument to Saints raised on Bible stories of how the righteous were persecuted. Opposition proved that they were, in fact, God's chosen people. But the same pattern of resistance, hostility, and expulsion, was playing itself out again in Nauvoo. This time, however, it would end in the death of their prophet.

Charlotte Haven, a non-Mormon who was visiting relatives in Nauvoo in 1843, found nothing compelling in Joseph Smith. She described him as "a large, stout man, youthful in his appearance . . . expressing great shrewdness, or I should say cunning. . . . I, who had expected to be overwhelmed by his eloquence, was never more disappointed than when he commenced his discourse. . . . This he did in a loud voice, and his language and manner were the coarsest possible. . . . [He is] an egotist and boaster."

However, to the Saints like Martha Haven, a distant cousin to Charlotte, Joseph was the Lord's prophet. Part of the secret of his success was the ability to instill in them a belief that he spoke for the Lord. He also spoke "to the common feeling . . . [and] universal want." He proclaimed that the divine power of healing and miracles was within their reach; that their faith could help them overcome all things, that everyone could have visions and great religious experiences. Captain Dan Jones, a convert from Wales, thought him "the godliest man on the face of the earth." Convert Curtis Edwin Bolton, on meeting the Prophet in 1844, exclaimed: "I never in this life shall look upon his like again."

Historian Kenneth H. Winn identified the Saints' hero-worship of the Prophet as the source of the Gentiles' greatest fear: "Non-Mormons recoiled from the church members' slavish devotion to their prophet . . . and their economic and political unity. . . . Mormons did subvert and distort the political and social institutions . . . where they settled . . . [which] resulted partially from a defense against gentile attacks."

It was a rare observer who could examine the Mormon phenomenon objectively, but one was the Rev. Samuel A. Prior, a Wesleyan minister, who wrote: "Although I could not agree with them about religious matters, yet I liked their honesty, their knowledge, and their willingness to examine everything deliberately and impartially." Prior stayed to hear the Prophet preach on 1 Peter 1: "I listened with surprise . . . for instead of a heap of inconsistent assertions, [and] disconnected, disordered sentences . . . he made his way with skill and wisdom unexpected by me. . . . [He] convinced me that he was worthy of the character of 'rightly dividing the word of truth' and giving impartially to saint and sinner. . . . I went away compelled to change completely my opinion of him from his head to his toes, and about religion and his character from end to end."

Joseph was a handsome, charismatic man with piercing blue eyes and a mesmerizing presence, but it was his self-assurance in acting as a modern prophet that helped convince those who gathered that they were the "chosen people." He held all the political and religious power in Nauvoo by early 1844 and then declared himself a candidate for president of the United States. Exacerbating the fears of neighbors were doctrinal innovations like secret temple ordinances and the equally secret practice of "celestial marriage" or polygamy. High Masonic and military promotions, bestowed lavishly as rewards to faithful men, also proved alarming outside the city.

In a letter to relatives on December 27, 1843, Martha Haven reported some of the rumors of hostility that welded the Saints into tight unity: "The Missourians are determined not to let us alone. . . . One of our men was kidnaped [sic] last night. . . . I expect [Missouri] will not give them up unless our governor gives up Joseph Smith. I don't think they will ever have the pleasure of taking him. God will ere long come out in vengeance against them. I like Nauvoo, and had rather be here than at the East even if we are driven. . . . I would never advise anyone to come here but true-hearted Mormons."

Sarah Scott, aware of the growing anti-Mormonism, wrote her mother on April 13, 1844, only two months before assassination ended the lives of Joseph Smith and his brother, Hyrum: "I never fully understood the place in holy writ where the Lord says he will have a tried people until I came here with the Church. Sometimes I almost fear that I shall give up but by the help of the Lord I mean to endure to the end."

Matters came to a head in early June 1844 when Joseph Smith ordered the destruction of a new press in Nauvoo under the leadership of former Mormons who could not follow Joseph across the line into polygamy and theocracy. It was interpreted universally as an attack on freedom of the press. Joseph Smith was arrested and jailed. Within days, a mob with blackened faces overcame token resistance by the guards and killed him and his brother, Hyrum, on June 27, 1844.

This martyrdom only stirred the devoted Mormons to greater determination and zeal; and those Gentiles who had found Joseph intolerable found the continued Mormon presence at Nauvoo equally unendurable. Once Brigham Young had gathered the reins of succession into his hands, it was a race between finishing the temple—the most visible emblem of Joseph's new theology—and the hostility, suspicions, and violence of Illinois neighbors. Enmity increased in direct proportion to the Saints' zeal and dedication. It was not safe for a Mormon to walk the streets of neighboring Warsaw. According to Joseph Smith Black, "I went to assist William Wallmark to move to Nauvoo. While I was walking in the streets of Warsaw, boys and old men would hoot and yell at me and some of them threatened to kill me because I was a Mormon."

Brigham Young, senior apostle, led the Saints out of the United States and into what was then Mexico. They would not be defeated. They grasped the iron rod of their faith and pulled themselves over every barrier and cruelty. Asserting the chorus of their new hymn, "All is well," they moved toward their promised land despite freezing winds, cold mud, starvation, rain, deserts, and Native Americans.

Family/Community of Faith

The family is among the few universal institutions of humankind; and migrating was a family affair among the Mormons, differing in nature from the experiences of Oregonians and Californians. Most religiously inspired migrations are family affairs—for example, the Pilgrims, the Puritans, and the Dutch in South Africa. Since Mormons believe that the family unit remains intact in the next world, they have highlighted the importance of family and community among believers probably more than any other people. The Saints moved as villages on wheels—a whole faith, culture, and people.

Moving as families was not only the natural thing to do, but it also minimized the trauma of being uprooted and thrust into a new and often challenging environment and society. Not only did the Mormon family provide security and comfort, but the common bond of religion strengthened the sense of community while crossing the Atlantic in immigrant ships, while traveling by train, boat, or wagon to their various points of departure, and, especially, while crossing the plains to their New Zion. The community of faith became a substitute for the old way of life in their former community.

The obverse of this exemplary unity was that Mormonism could also shatter families. If conversion separated a son, daughter, or spouse from the larger family, Church leaders encouraged him or her to immigrate alone if other family members would not. Death also rearranged and winnowed many family groups en route, but the community of the immigrating company filled the void as best it could.

Although Guy Keysor called the Camp of Israel a "business city," it had strict rules and valued obedience, discipline, labor, music, and recreation.

Immigrants and Origins

An estimated 16,000 Mormons crossed Iowa in 1846; and while many were foreign born, most were typical Americans. The number of immigrants in Utah swelled from 6,000 by the end of 1849 to 20,000 by the end of 1852. The Mormon census of 1856 listed 76,335. By the time the railroad reached Utah in 1869, some 54,700 Saints had come to America. The *Encyclopedia of Mormonism* listed about 51,000, approximately 38,000 British and an additional 13,000 from Europe, especially from Scandinavia. We believe 75,000 Mormons crossed the plains between 1847 and 1868. About 7,000 Mormons died en route. Conway B. Sonne estimates that 54,700 emigrants crossed the oceans as part of their journey of obedience. At least 20,000 more gathered from all parts of the United States during those years. Probably more than 5,000 chose to stay in other parts of the country than Utah or eventually drifted away, totaling about 80,000 who joined the Mormon Church during the first fifty years.

Mormon missionaries first reached England in 1837; and from England, missionaries spread to Ireland, Scotland, and Wales, but also to Denmark, Norway, Sweden, Iceland, France, Italy, and Germany, Holland, South Africa, Polynesia, Australia, New Zealand, even India. From all of these countries, converts gathered to their new Zion. Many of these immigrants were at a disadvantage in not knowing English and in being woefully unaccustomed to life on the American frontier. Mormon immigration officials tried to minimize these disadvantages by organizing the foreign immigrants into companies while they were still in Europe so that they traveled together all the way to their new Zion. Leaders who knew the requisite languages acted as guides and agents. In general, the system worked well. Sometimes companies mixed nationalities, but ethnic or national differences were suppressed in favor of religious unity. Their shared faith created strong cross-cultural bonds. We found little evidence of discrimination or inter-cultural conflict.

General Health/Economic Status

The majority of pioneers were between ages twenty and fifty, for the known and rumored hardships discouraged most older people. According to Merrill Mattes, historian of the Oregon migration, "The great migration required youthful vigor for its fulfillment; over 95 percent of the immigrants were probably ages sixteen to fifty." Occasionally, a traveler commented that women had more endurance than men. Catherine Hahn, a bride during the California '49 flood of migration to the goldfields, wrote: "The men seemed more tired and hungry than were we women." However, the Mormon companies, moving as communities, had a greater portion of older pioneers and babies.

Most overlanders (by which we mean the general American western migrants, not exclusively the Mormons) were middle class, for it was not cheap to go west. A proper "fit-out" cost between $500 and $1,000. According to historian Sandra Myers, "The very rich did not want or need to go and the very poor could not afford the trip." Mormon immigrants were usually poorer than non-Mormons. B. H. Roberts, a British convert who immigrated as a boy, wrote: "This gathering was of the common people . . . of the same class that 'heard Jesus gladly' . . . practically of one class from first to last." There were a few middle-class families among the Mormons, but the rest came from the working classes.

The Trail Experience in Mormon History

Although this study focuses on immigrants who traveled by wagon, we also include some information about ocean voyages and rail immigrants. It is important to remember that, after 1849, there were two trails to the Salt Lake Valley; one was east across the Sierras and one westward across the Rockies. However, most typically, the Mormon Trail began in Liverpool, or Hamburg, or Stockholm. Certainly it commenced in Boston, New York, Philadelphia, or New Orleans. Occasionally the journey began in states like Maine, New York, or Mississippi. During the first dozen years, the Mormon emigrant vessels arrived in New Orleans "because it was cheaper," according to President Brigham Young. Non-Mormon American emigrants, in contrast, came primarily from the Midwest: Missouri, Ohio, Indiana, Illinois, and the border states of Kentucky and Tennessee.

In the early years, St. Louis and especially Independence, Missouri, were the major jumping-off spots for Oregonians and Californians, and provided the emigrants with a good selection of cattle, supplies, and wagons. The Saints most often used the greater Council Bluffs area for their final staging area but might also begin their journey along the Missouri or Mississippi rivers.

The crossing of the plains turned into a great event, not only in the lives of most pioneers, but in the minds of their descendants. It became the final test of faith and obedience. Contemporary Mormons revere their heritage of faithful ancestors and talk with pride of those who "crossed the plains" for the sake of religious freedom. Even modern Mormons who have no pioneer ancestors vicariously share this heritage, and stories about pioneers trailing clouds of glory surround these Saints.

Sources

Trail journals kept by pioneers are often sparse, revealing little of personal and intimate life. Everyday concerns of weather, feed, distance, sickness, accidents, and nature predominate. They recorded loneliness for loved ones left behind, fear of Indians, major landmarks, the scenery, births, emotions, costs of goods, cooking, washing, traveling conditions, traveling companions, cholera, sickness, and death. Many noted the number of graves with morbid regularity as if they were confirming their own existence. The specter of death on the trail filled them with the greatest anxiety. However, while most journals are quite prosaic, some contain highly educated, amusing accounts of the trek west.

Given the difficult conditions under which many such accounts were written (work-stiffened hands, holding a pencil, trembled from cold and hunger), the marvel is that we have so many. Those fortunate enough to have ink occasionally had to let it thaw out. The lack of literary skills of most Mormon diarists is balanced by the number of accounts available. Over 1,200 are known, and new ones are not infrequently discovered or made available. These accounts not only add to our understanding of the Mormon experience but also contribute much to the understanding of the whole westward movement in U.S. history. The Saints left behind what may be the largest single body of written accounts, making it possible to write this social history. Our approach is to focus on the people who traveled the Mormon Trail in their journey of obedience—not the trail.

Oregon Trail expert Merrill Mattes spent years compiling his *Platte River Road Narratives*—a total of 2,082 accounts that include all of the narratives he was able to find. It is excellent for providing varied accounts, although he excerpts brief highlights and riveting snippets, rather than complete accounts. On the Mormon side, Davis Bitton listed more than a thousand trail sources in his *Guide to Mormon Diaries and Autobiographies;* and since its publication in 1977, dozens more have become available. Some of the copies we had were not even mentioned in Bitton's *Guide.*

For about four hundred miles—the distance between Fort Laramie and Fort Bridger—Mormons traveled with those also bound for Oregon and California, at least until cut-offs allowed the other two groups to bypass part of that direction. Salt Lake City became a popular supply station for the gold rush pioneers and even for some going on to Oregon.

Victorian-era women, steeped in modesty, left no intimate passages that shock the sensibilities or intrigue the researcher. Historians have to read between the lines in many cases. Mormon women diarists, however, are often superior to men in their literary quality and range of topics. Until recently, few historians paid attention to the records left by women, since Frederick Jackson Turner's influential paradigm of conquering the frontier privileged the male perspective. Historian Sandra Myers wrote: "We cannot understand the frontier without considering the experiences of the young married women." We should not ignore accounts by unmarried pioneers either.

While we have based our study primarily on a core of about 500 Mormon sources—Stanley spent several summers photocopying journals in Utah—much of what we report here can be considered typical for the 500,000 pioneers of the nineteenth century. The few Oregon/California accounts we include should help the reader get a broader picture of the westward movement that forever changed America's history and destiny. At times these quotations augment the Mormon experience but sometimes reveal differences between the two groups. It is important to remember that Oregon- and California-bound pioneers had to prepare for a longer journey than those en route to Zion. Many of those accounts brim with humorous or sarcastic comments. While the Saints had a more serious purpose in traveling the trail and their accounts often reflect this attitude, many of the other pioneers showed a more carefree attitude—especially the young '49ers.

This is the story of a people, a culture, a religion. We hope by the last page you have discovered what the Saints lived for, died for, and what they believed. You don't have one without the others in the history of the Saints.

Chapter 1

The Flight from Nauvoo

It seemed as though there was something more than human nature which caused them to feel so joyful and happy to leave their comfortable homes and to go out in the dead of winter with so many young children to face the cold and the storms, and not even knowing where they were going. It seemed to me that we must be in possession of some power besides the power of man.—George Whitaker, 1846

Preparation and Panic

A long line of wagons waited at the cold, dreary, muddy Mississippi River at Nauvoo, Illinois, in mid-February of 1846. The ferry was halfway across the river to Iowa with two wagons and four oxen; an empty skiff was pulling in. It was a scene so picturesque and poignant that an artist could have dipped a brush in oil colors and produced a masterpiece. Big log fires warmed cold hands on the Illinois side and across the river in Iowa. A few of the wagons sported bright colors, a sharp contrast to the gray world everywhere else. The men called to their children, neighbors, and dogs; women huddled in heavy coats, woolen shawls, and warm hats as they comforted children who cried. The dogs barked, cows mooed, sheep bleated and spooked, horses gave a nervous snort, and left piles of manure on the ground. Children yelled to each other, and the sounds—some cheerful, some sad—floated back to those Mormons who remained behind in a city in panic and prayer.

It marked the sixth time some of them had had to flee for their lives, and they must have wondered, "Where in all the world will we find a safe haven, a permanent Zion? When will the Red Sea part for us?" Some of them would eventually see the Pacific Ocean and know how it felt to go "from sea to shining sea" for the sake of their belief in the gospel.

Four months earlier, the homes and yards of the Saints in Nauvoo presented an equally busy scene as preparations began for an orderly departure for a new Zion when the weather permitted their journey west in the spring. Grass, water, and game would be plentiful. A company of men was called to head out early, searching out a new home for the Saints. The others would follow. Timber, wire, iron, and copper helped strengthen the old wagons, and a few new ones boasted coats of paint. Bathsheba Smith opened up her parlor in Nauvoo "as a paint-shop in which to paint wagons. All were making preparations to leave." And the Smith home was only part of the bustle: "The fall of 1845 found Nauvoo, as it were, one vast mechanic shop, as nearly every family was engaged in making wagons," she described.

Little hands and big hands held hammers, scissors, hoes, and axes. Women and girls sewed and knitted warm clothing, wagon covers, and tents. They ground corn and wheat, dried breadstuffs into a long-lasting sea biscuit, dried fruit, and sacked up corn meal, rice, and beans. A bit of finery, a piece of embroidery from the past, and a few family heirlooms were tucked into trunks as tears trickled down cheeks, only to be smudged away by resolute hands.

The end of 1845 also found Mormon leaders Brigham Young and Heber C. Kimball performing special temple ordinances in the nearly completed temple. On occasion, they were there all night. Young wrote: "December 31, 1845. Elder Heber C. Kimball and I superintended the operations in the Temple, [and] examined maps with reference to selecting a location for the saints west of the Rocky Mountains, and reading various works written by travelers in those regions." Those who had been called to go early prepared physically and spiritually for that trek to find Zion.

The preparations for leaving the Mormon city on the Mississippi were bustling but controlled when reports began to circulate that mobs were not willing to wait until spring and that the government would interfere to stop the exodus. Mobs had burned the homes of the Saints in Illinois and in Iowa as early as 1843, even before the assassination of Joseph and Hyrum Smith, the Mormon prophet and patriarch. Matthew Caldwell, a non-Mormon who had married a Mormon woman, was living in Hancock County at that time. He wrote sympathetically:

> Most of my neighbors by this time were Mormons, and I found their persecution was rampent [sic] wherever they went, because their belief was so different and so changed from that of the other churches. These persecutions continued and gradually grew until the homes of several of my neighbors were burned. I well remember these burnings. In the year 1843, one morning I counted fourteen Mormon homes burning at the same time. . . . After these burnings, there was not a house left standing within seven miles from my home.

Three years later, the persecution had become even more intense, and this time some of it was from former high officials who, when Joseph was assassinated, had now become enemies of the Mormons. Joseph Fielding wrote on January 29, 1846: "It is generally expected the County is to be put under Martial Law. Affidavits have been made at Washington by Sidney Rigdon [a former counselor in Joseph Smith's first presidency], and William Smith [Joseph Smith's younger brother and an excommunicated apostle] . . . that we intend to go and bring on the Indians against the Government, and the Design is to prevent our going by putting us under Martial Law and to hem us in on all Sides."

A letter from Illinois Governor Thomas Ford contained news that gave the exodus a greater urgency: "I think that it is very likely that the government at Washington will interfere to prevent the Mormons from going west of the Rocky Mountains." This letter was no doubt meant to hasten the departure. Ford wanted the Saints out of Illinois.

It is no wonder this news sent most Saints into a frenzy of activity and pushed many across the river in a panic, unprepared for a winter on the prairies. What had been planned as an orderly departure of about a hundred families turned into chaos. As they waited in the cloudy morning to get across the river to a spot called Sugar

Creek, the staging ground, their anxiety must have increased. The first wagon, that of Andrew Shumway, crossed the swiftly moving, ice-clogged Mississippi River on February 4. Soon a long line of wagons was crossing in skiffs, flatboats, and other makeshift ferries. More smiles than tears appeared as the last good-byes echoed in the cold air. Calls of "git up" drifted from the river; and despite the urgency to flee, a sense of adventure and excitement brought cheer. Those preparing to leave saw it as yet another test, necessary to see if modern Israel was worthy of eternal rewards. Orson Pratt wrote: "We are cheerful and rejoice."

Brigham Young, "the Lion of the Lord" and undisputed leader, called the Camp of Israel to order on February 17. "Acting the part of the father to everybody," he issued strict rules and regulations, imposing order by a quasi-military organization of tens, fifties, and hundreds. "There will be no rule we cannot keep, but there will be order in camp," Young announced from his wagon. The leaders refined the exodus and issued rations of their own to the hundreds of Saints who had appeared, expecting the Lord to send manna from heaven. Heber C. Kimball reached the camp at Sugar Creek with a two-year supply of staples for about twenty-four but shared the food generously among those who had fled across the river unprepared. His supplies were gone within two weeks.

Wagons arrived and departed. Some daring souls like newlyweds Horace Whitney and Helen Mar Kimball Whitney tested the depth of the ice on the suddenly frozen Mississippi by riding their ponies across. Helen was resplendent in a green merino riding dress that contrasted dramatically with her little white pony. Some Saints like Joseph Lee Robinson stayed behind and outfitted wagons for others during the spring of 1846 so they could go west. "Old Brother Thayer begged me to help him," he recalled. Generously, Robinson "furnished a new wagon . . . hitched two yoke of cattle . . . on to it and [he] took them away." Robinson also helped L. T. Johnson and others.

Sarah Studevant Leavitt recalled, "We soon found we had to leave the place if we meant to save our lives, and we got what little we could from our beautiful farm. We had forty thousand bricks that my husband and sons had made for us to build a house, and part of the rock to lay the foundation. For this we got an old bed quilt, and for the farm a yoke of wild steers, and for two high post bedsteads, we got some weaving done."

Heber C. Kimball was among the lucky Saints who was able to trade his new brick two-story home for thirty-five yoke of oxen. Joseph Fielding "sold my House and 20 Acres of Land for 200 Dols in Trade, taking 2 Horses, a Waggon, a Coat Cloth, and a few [dollars] in cash."

Martha Haven lamented to her mother: "We have sold our place for a trifle to a Baptist Minister. All we got was a cow and two pairs of steers, worth about 60 dollars in trade." Some Saints almost boasted about leaving with nothing—"trusting God like Abraham." Martha P. Jones wrote: "In 1846 we started for the mountains without purse or script [sic], wagon or team. We had our two selves and eight children." They were with the "poor company" in September, but many others were at Sugar Creek in February with inadequate rations and animals, expecting help from the leaders.

Mormons were not the only westward-bound pioneers whose planning proved inadequate. Thomas M. Miller's family, en route to Oregon in 1850, "started out with plenty of provisions, but a good many that year ran short, so we shared ours till we were also out of food. From Fort Hall on we lived pretty much on corn bread, sage hens and jack rabbits."

On March 1, 1847, Young climbed on his wagon tongue and announced: "Attention, the camps of Israel. I propose to move forward on our journey." Conditions, however, tested even his iron resolve. The conditions under which Nauvoo was abandoned were so chaotic and premature, the Saints so ill disciplined and inexperienced, that the most difficult part of the whole Mormon hegira was across Iowa in the muddy spring of 1846. Tempers flared. Eighteen-year-old Abner Blackburn

> joined Brigham Youngs company as a guard. They were in great fear of a mob and crossed over the river and established a winter camp on Sugar Creek in the state of Iowa. . . . I trained the cattle round a day or two before we started on our higeria; loaded up with live stock. . . . Well, we started and such a time I had with that team of raw unbroken wild steers. I was in the road part of the time and that was when I was crossing it. My waggon ran against borth Brighams amidships

and tore off the whole stearn end, but arrived in camp after a fassion. The next day [we] had a few more mishaps. . . . [T]he oxen geed off the road and upset the waggon and its load in the mud, the Lord's annointed and all. The boss [BY] come along and began to scold me for carelessness. I handed the whip to him and told him I was working for acomodation and there was no glory in it. "Never mind," says he. "Try and do better." Prophets, Priests, Apostles, and the Lords anointed all eat togeather with the vulgar. There was but a step between the sublime and the rediculous.

Young knew by the end of May that the journey for most of those in the wilderness would have to be postponed until better plans and conditions existed. Most families were already in dire circumstances. In contrast was the orderly, well-prepared departure that Ursulia Hastings Haskell's family made three months later at the end of May 1846:

> We started from Nauvoo the 30th of May. Had as good a waggon as any of them, three yoke of oxen with flour enough to last us a year, ham sausages, dry fish, lard, two cans hundred pounds of sugar, 16 of coffee, 10 of raisins, rice with all the other items we wish to use in cook[ing]. [O]ur wagon is long enough for both our beds made on the flour barrels. Thales [her son] and I sleep at the back and F[rancis] and Irene [Pomeray, her daughter] and husband at the forward end. . . . It is painted red. It has eight bows eighteen inches across, a hen coop on the end with four hens. . . . We put on one thick drilling, then three breadths of stout sheeting over that and then painted it, the heaviest showers and storms do not beat through only a few drops now and then. . . . [The first camp] we chained our oxen to the wagon after baiting, eat some bread and milk and a piece of pie and went to bed in our wagon, never slept better.

Ursulia arrived safely to Council Bluffs and spent a "tolerable" winter in that area of Winter Quarters, where Young and company got permission to stop in Indian Territory that had been assigned to the Omahas and Potawattami. "We have lived in our log cabin through the winter very comfortable," she wrote. "We have a brick chimney and hearth. . . . We have plenty of provisions except vegetables." Ursulia and her family left for the valley in June of 1847, two months after the vanguard company had set out in April, and apparently had few problems with lack of food or clothing the first year because they were so well-prepared.

For those who tried to follow the apostles in February and March, the mud in Iowa was crippling. Patty Sessions wrote in March: "Brigham Young came up with his company driving his team in mud to his knees, as happy as a king." Not everyone rejoiced in the mud. It oozed over shoetops and covered tents, bedding, and wagons. When the wagons got stuck in mud, a near-daily occurrence, boys and men pushed against them in mud sometimes up to their knees and hoped that it wouldn't suck their shoes off.

The Saints were "seeing the elephant." This expression, used in many Oregon Trail accounts to indicate hardships and danger, was rarely mentioned in Mormon journals, but Mormons "saw the elephant" all the time in the spring of 1846 and beyond.

By late June 1846, Captain James Allen of the U.S. Army of the West arrived to enlist five hundred soldiers to help fight the War with Mexico—fulfilling Young's earnest search for resources to help his people move. When recruits were slow to sign up, Brigham begged, bribed, and thundered. Eventually about five hundred came forward to form the Mormon Battalion—reluctant, half sick, half starved, ragged, and worried. They were not the Book of Mormon's two thousand stripling warriors. Some were young and unmarried, keyed in to the adventure. Sixteen-year-old Lot Smith stood on tip-toe to reach the height requirement. More were married and concerned about the welfare of their already struggling families who must be left behind for a year. A few were able to take their wives as "laundresses."

Joseph L. Robinson left Nauvoo with his two wives and children in June. Although there was some mud, sickness, and loss of cattle, the weather was moderate. When Joseph arrived at Mount Pisgah, Brigham Young was there, recruiting "at the request of the United States Government." Young had already calculated the financial rewards of this march and later told participants: "Your going into the army has saved the lives of thousands of men." Young appointed Robinson to take important documents back to Nauvoo and alert those still there about the need to sign up. Joseph pitched a tent for his family and obediently retraced his steps to Nauvoo.

The loss of those men, and a few dozen who were sent off on trading and proselytizing missions, forced the leaders to establish a winter camp. Dozens of men were also sent to guard the cattle in various locations. When the Saints reached Council Bluffs on the Missouri River and after meeting with the Potawattami, most crossed the river into a temporary camp that they named Winter Quarters (present-day Florence, Nebraska). Most felt that having a river between them and their enemies made for greater safety.

Getting to Winter Quarters through the awful conditions in Iowa was a spiritual and physical test that would be the beginning of many tests over the next few years, but it would take a lot more than mud to quench the flame of Young's determination to find Zion. It was one of the worst times in the history of the Church, but Young realized that the Saints were ill prepared—physically, mentally, and emotionally. Some were so insecure that they wanted Young's advice about everything. "Should I sell my watch to buy oxen?" William Clayton wanted to know. Young said yes.

George Whitaker noted the anxiety of the group in the spring of 1846: "They did not seem willing for him to go ahead without them, and he was not willing to go with such a large company, so many women and children, as he knew they were not fitted out for a journey of a thousand miles." During the winter of 1846-47, they built log cabins and shacks. Some insulated their wagons as thoroughly as possible and lived in them until November. A few shoveled dugouts into the banks of gullies. Still others built soddies. One estimate put the dwellings in the Mormon village at about 700 log cabins and 150 sod houses. Louisa Barnes Pratt, whose husband was on a mission, lived in a 10x12-foot sod house for many months with her four daughters before buying a cabin for a "five dollar gold piece." The James Madison Flake family, who had lived on a Mississippi plantation, also took up residence in a dugout.

Death and disease left most families mourning. Nearly everyone suffered or would suffer some form of the ague, unspecified fevers, malnutrition, scurvy, and other diseases. Occasionally Saints straggled in from Nauvoo with disturbing news about Illinois mobs. Many of the people who had planned to remain in Nauvoo fled, believing that the worst was to come. A few hundred were so poverty stricken that they had no choice but stay in Nauvoo. About the same number went downriver to St. Louis to find work.

Despite the hardships of Winter Quarters, this delay for a season gave Brigham Young enough time to make a plan that would push the determined and pull the reluctant to Zion, to check more information, talk to more knowledgeable trail experts, to evaluate, plan, prepare, pray, and plead with the members to "resist evil" and "obey the brethren." Young turned to scolding, threats, and, on occasion, sarcasm to keep his people in line. He was a practical, no-nonsense man, less visionary than Joseph Smith. Although some rejected or avoided Brigham Young's leadership—among them James Emmett, Lyman Wight, and Alpheus Cutler—Young's approach helped rally the distressed, frightened, sick, and weary Saints to plan their journey across the plains for yet "another Zion."

Winter Quarters became Brigham Young's training ground. Disease, deaths, contention, and poverty were so constant that he and the others must have had many hours of doubt and despair. The Saints needed Young; he needed the Saints. They heard this message from him at Winter Quarters: "We are willing to take our full share of trouble, trials, losses and crosses, hardships and fatigues, warning and watching, for the kingdom of heaven's sake; and we feel to say; Come, calm or strife, turmoil or peace, life or death, in the name of Israel's God we mean to conquer or die trying."

It was a message they could relate to. The future of the Church of Jesus Christ of Latter-day Saints might have been much less heroic and successful without that time to prepare financially, mentally, physically, and prayerfully for the trek. The Mormons were safe from mob violence at Winter Quarters, but they still had to confront internal problems and deal with the Indians who rustled their cattle. Nauvoo was a painful memory, and a new Zion seemed like a dream that might disappear like the fog and mist from the Missouri River.

The Mormon Battalion was a financial blessing that enabled Young to hold the Saints together during that dreadful, freezing winter. Despite attempts to sell the Nauvoo Temple, there were no buyers; and the wages and clothing allowance allotted to the battalion, which Young appropriated to benefit the whole community, enabled the Saints to hang on, even though the soldiers' families were even more destitute than the average Saint. Leadership sometimes requires ruthlessness, and Young rose to the challenge. Battalion families complained openly about the lack of money, food, and housing. Young had assured the recruits that their families would be cared for, but he shifted the burden to the already staggering bishops of wards that materialized among the huts of Winter Quarters.

Other problems concerned the open practice of polygamy and the law of adoption, which permitted families to become spiritually adopted or "sealed" into families of the leaders. Both practices generated jealousy, and men argued about who they wanted to be "sealed" to since this doctrine, begun in Nauvoo, would guarantee them a better reward in heaven. Adoption was abandoned before the end of the nineteenth century, and so, as an openly supported practice, was polygamy.

A bright spot at Winter Quarters was the strong bond of friendship, faith, and determination to endure that emerged among the sisters, many of whom had been members of the Nauvoo Relief Society (1842–44). They discovered their own spiritual powers, blessing each other. Helen Mar Kimball Whitney witnessed this spiritual resolve in June of 1847: "The little meetings which the sisters held twice or three times a week, were begun in the month of May, while we had the privilege of Eliza R. Snow, Zina Young and a few others who went with the first company that left Winter Quarters in June . . . and the love of God flowed from heart to heart." She added: "Our experience comes nearest to that of the children of Israel after their departure out of the land of Egypt than any other people of whom we have any record, though I believe we were a more patient people."

Eliza R. Snow wrote on June 1, 1847: "This is truly a glorious time with the mothers & daughters in Zion altho' thrust out from the land of our forefathers & from the endearments of civiliz'd life."

In April 1847, Brigham Young led a vanguard company consisting of 143 men, three women, and two boys in search of a haven for the Saints—somewhere in the Great Basin beyond the Rocky Mountains.

Camp Life and Routine

Lilburn W. Boggs, the infamous governor of Missouri during the Mormon War of 1838 and the expulsion of the Saints during the winter of 1838-39, was one of the thousands traveling overland to Oregon in 1846. At Fort Laramie, Boggs's company constantly badmouthed the Mormons but were themselves so quarrelsome, rude, and loud, that, when the Mormons appeared a year later, the soldiers were curious about these maligned Mormons. The contrast with the Missouri camp was so marked that James Bordeaux, the fort's manager, "remarked to Bro. (A. P.) Rockwood that there never had passed Ft. Laramie such a company as this. . . . They felt a pleasure in seeing us, and showing us thro. . . . When Ex. Gov Boggs passed thro he was all the time railing about the Mormons being bad people. . . . The people at the fort several times expressed their great pleasure at seeing us, expressing themselves that we were the best behaved Company that had passed there."

On July 24, the journey to find Zion ended when the pioneer group reached the Valley of the Great Salt Lake. Two other companies arrived that September. About 100 Mormon Battalion soldiers and families and some Mississippi Saints also arrived in the valley. About two thousand wintered in the valley, even though Young and most of the men with him headed back to Winter Quarters for their families almost immediately. They arrived by the end of October, weary and hungry, but the promise of Zion was now a reality.

"To Your Tents, O Israel"

In June 1848, many well-prepared Saints set out from Winter Quarters for Zion with glad hearts and thankful minds. This time, the weather was good and they were eager, relieved that the journey was underway at last. Brigham Young and Heber C. Kimball both led large companies that year, and neither man would see the Missouri River again. Thomas Bullock recorded: "[There are] 1891 souls, 623 waggons, and 2012 oxen." Those who could not afford a "fit-out" remained in the Council Bluffs area on the east side of the Missouri because their arrangement to camp on Omaha tribal lands had expired.

As soon as they crossed the Missouri River, the pioneers considered themselves "on the trail." Their love/hate relationship with the river manifested itself in nicknames like "Misery Bottoms & Old Muddy Face." Some called it "too big for its breeches." The Platte River came in for its share of insults: "A mile wide, a foot deep, too thick to drink, too thin to plow, but makes a pretty good river if you stand it on its head." The Platte River offered recreation and beauty along with the quicksand and mud. It meandered across middle Nebraska and much of Wyoming. More importantly, it went in the right direction and was the lifeline that got all of the pioneers started on their journey west.

About 75,000 other Mormons followed in the next twenty-five years. Those years brought death, disease, accidents, chaos from weather problems, and other dangers; but these problems would have existed anyway. The pioneers also made new friends, attended festivities, celebrations, baptisms, and worship services. They saw awesome scenery, spectacular sunsets, and night skies that filled poetic souls with awe. There was a little hell and a lot of heroism and beauty. Many pioneers, especially the foreigners, mentioned the landscape's exotic beauty. Jean Rio Griffiths Baker, an English convert, was enthralled with the Iowa prairie and wrote May 19, 1851: "The weather is now fine and the flowers are lifting their heads and looking more beautiful than ever. There are a great variety of flowers growing on the prairie such as are cultivated in our gardens at home. We are constantly stalking over violets, primroses, daisies, bluebells, lily of the valley, and columbines of every shade ... and wild roses ... perfum[e] the air for miles."

Hannah Tapfield King, also an English convert, commented in her trail diary:

> July 6, 1853: The fireflies are beautiful here. They are like diamond dust over every thing at night.
> August 3, 1853: Camped at 1 oc [o'clock] after passing the Bluff ruins—They are very beautiful—They stand out in bold relief with a silent eloquence that speaks trumpet-tonged [sic] to every thinking mind—They are looking eternally silent.

French convert Gustave Henriod penned a witty description of camp routine in 1853:

Life on the plains cannot be very well described with such a pen as mine nor imagined or appreciated by a stoic. . . . [We were] yoking up half wild oxen every morning, staking down the tents every night, picking up buffalo chips to cook the food, loading and unloading boxes and bedding mornings and evenings, in the saddle or on foot guarding the stock every night and driving loose cattle in the day, digging trenches around the tents to keep from being drowned by the torrents, singing the songs of Zion, mending a broken wagon, carrying on your back across some deep stream about 140 lbs. of female avoirdupois without losing your feet on the rocky bottom of a river, washing your clothes—everybody forgot a clothes line.

The basic requirements for a suitable campsite were water, fuel, and grazing for the stock. Sometimes a stop forced by the weather left the pioneers without any of these amenities. Sometimes they chose a rise or hill so the wind, which blew all the time in Nebraska, would blow away insects. A "dark camp" was used when danger from Indians was feared. The camp would stop in daylight, get their supper, travel a few more miles until dark, and spend the night without fires that might give the campsite away. As trail use increased, good campsites became scarce and companies often traveled farther than they intended.

On the treeless plains, the most common fuel was buffalo chips. Elmeda Harmon wrote in 1848: "Often our food cooked over open fires made of buffalo chips would be seasoned with the manure. I would vomit it up and try and try again to enjoy the rough fare."

Despite the sometimes harsh and tragic realities of camp life, Saints left behind many beautiful, inspiring, and humorous vignettes of trail experiences and family life. Abner Blackburn described the trek of the Mormon Battalion soldiers and the Mississippi Saints who had camped at Pueblo, Colorado, over the winter of 1846–47 and were only a few days behind Brigham Young's pioneer company when they reached Devil's Gate in Wyoming:

Sunday, July 18, 1847: Some weare in the shade reading . . . some mending clothes, others shoeing cattle, and a number in a tent playing the violin. By an by a runner come around to notify [us] that our minister was a going to observe the sabbath and preach a sermon. All hands quit work and the fiddle stopt playing [but then some] went into a tent to play cards, & few took their guns and went hunting and a few herd the sermon. Such is life on the plains.

F. W. Blake, a Mormon en route to Utah in 1861, remembered this scene after trail life ended:

> Groups of men and women are seen in all directions at various duties, children playing about in freedom, horses grazing, the grotesque figure of an Indian visitor on horseback or mingling with the people to trade is often seen. The river [Platte] runs coiling around the tree decked soil within twenty yards from us and the constant range of bluffs with their grassy coverings run from east to west in the distance. The sun shines down the bright reflections on the picture and gives a finish which shows out the connection between heaven and earth and how the latter is improving the property of the former.

Amelia Stewart Knight, traveling with her husband and seven children en route to Oregon in 1853 on the north side of the Platte, left some terse comments about her experience:

> May 13, 1853: Sand all around ankle deep; wind blowing; no matter, hurry it over. Them that eat the most breakfast eat the most sand. . . .
>
> May 25, 1853: It was no fool of a job to be mixed up with several hundred head of cattle and only one road to travel in, and the drovers threatening to drive their cattle over you if you attempted to pass them. They even took out their pistols. . . . [The Knights rushed by anyway.] The head teamster done his best by whipping and hollowing to his cattle. . . . We left some swearing men behind us.

"The tents are scattered over the hills," Mary Elizabeth Rollins Lightner noted in 1863: "When the camp fires are lit at night it is a beautiful sight, it makes me think how the Children of Israel camps must have looked in the days of Moses when journeying in the wilderness." The Saints took great comfort in comparing themselves to the ancient children of Israel.

Mary Elizabeth was one of the rare Mormon pioneers to mention the "pint of dust" consumed that so many Oregonians complained about. On August 1, 1863, she wrote: "Among the hills and rocks most of the day, and dust an inch thick. . . . Had breakfast of bacon, fried cakes and coffee, traveled on a good road for miles, then stopped, cooked dinner, wind blowing a gale of sand all over us. I think we will get the proverbial peck of dust before we get through."

She added: "I write by fire light. Danes at prayers, our folks the same while I, poor sinner am baking bread. I don't much like our preacher, he strokes his beard too much and speaks too low."

Pioneers who left reminiscences of the trail dwelled far more frequently on the good times than the monotonous and typical aspects of travel. Daily domestic chores were performed as soon as the wagons stopped. Men (and some women) unhitched their teams and took them for water. Besides cooking, baking, and laundry, mothers crammed in other responsibilities: giving someone a hair cut, pulling a tooth, nursing a new baby, soothing a sick child.

Young girls did their share, mending clothes, milking cows, or fetching water. Children with sacks in hand or aprons, rushed for buffalo chips or twigs, went bathing or fishing, and scampered over wagon tongues and around the wheels playing tag or other games with an ever-present neighbor. Occasionally a baptism occurred, and there were constant administrations for the injured or sick. Men and boys looked for green meadows for their livestock. Sometimes they had to herd the cattle miles out on the prairie to find pasturage.

While many of the pioneers, especially the youngsters, found the travel pleasant, the reality included cold rain, blistering heat, strong winds, stampeding cattle, barking dogs, scared sheep, mooing cattle, and squealing pigs. Wolves howled in the distance, children cried, teenagers yelled back and forth, women wept for comforts left behind, men threatened each other, parents quarreled, and mosquitoes and other insects feasted on the hapless victims. (The real tragedies of the fourth and fifth handcart companies were unrepresentative of the migration as a whole.) Occasionally, someone was disfellowshipped or threatened with punishment.

"None but Saints could be happy under these conditions," Eliza R. Snow had written earlier in Iowa. Rain and lightning were the main culprits in some camps where everything seemed to go awry. Tents blew down, wagons were blown into the river or away from camp, water soaked everything, everyone got drenched, and some grain had to be thrown away. Rainy weather prevented any food from being prepared unless a large tent was available.

Patty Sessions captured another scene when her company was not far from the valley in 1847: "Had a meeting to settle a quarrel.

Cut 3 off from the church. . . . Had a fuss with Sister Hunter and family this morning. . . . Sister Hunter would not come. [W]e took the children along [and she said] Perrigrine [Patty's son] shall be kiled for she has backers. . . . Br Pratt took her [and] had her bound with a cord and put under guard."

In 1855 Isaiah Moses Coombs, who had the grim task of transporting the body of a dead missionary in a lead-lined coffin to Utah, had his spooked oxen run away with the body, but he later recovered it. At one point, some of his starving company "grubbed for willows" in hopes of finding them edible. He also lost a lot of oxen. "Of the four oxen I started with not one lived to reach Salt Lake." After nearly two weeks of starvation, a trapper supplied them with meat. As a special burden, Coombs had left his pregnant wife in Illinois. She refused to gather with the Saints, and never came to Utah. He wrote stoically:

> [Trail life is one] which no earthly consideration would tempt me to lead. The knowledge that this is the only way God designs gathering his people at this time makes me endure it. . . . I was placed in charge of about ten yoke of our worn out cattle that could but just creep along in the rear. Long before night I found myself . . . and cattle ready to lie down in the road with fatigue. . . . I felt far more lonely . . . and tried to grope my way but the road was [so] covered with the drifting sand that I was completely baffled. I let the oxen take their own course and plodded on by their side. . . . At last, I observed a light . . . which proved to be the fires of my friends.

Gender Roles

Nineteenth-century American society was thoroughly divided into masculine and feminine spheres with male patriarchy dominating social life and providing the normative values. This dynamic held true on the immigrant trails and the frontier as well. The heavy Mormon emphasis on family, however, enabled women to gain status as "Mothers in Israel" and as midwives. Although the Female Relief Society of Nauvoo had been in existence only since 1842, it supplied a model for women's solidarity, charitable activities, and community involvement. Eliza R. Snow, its secretary, brought the minute book with her, and it became a visible symbol when the society was revived decades later in Utah. Not the least of Eliza's achievements was to assert that the society had somehow had a continuous existence, despite a quarter century's inactivity. (It was suspended in 1844.) On the trail, women who had worked together in Nauvoo "gathered as friends to support and minister to one another through prayer, testimony, and the exercise of the gifts of the spirit."

Brigham Young outlined his views of women succinctly: "It is their duty to bear all the children they can . . . and when she has reared them up to deliver them to their Fathers instead of meddling with her husband's business." Male and female roles and work were sharply defined, and Young was far less concerned about "the needs of women" than Joseph Smith had been. However, women were the foundation of home and family, agents of civilization, and the keepers of morals and family traditions. Sarah Sutton, en route to Oregon in 1854, took good dishes and tablecloths in complete faith that she would continue her daily routine: "I am going to start with good earthen dishes and if they get broken I have tin ones to take their place. I have 4 nice little table cloths so am going to live just like I was at home."

The transition from farm life to trail life was not as great as it might seem. At best medical care was poor even in the States, sanitation little understood, and child-bearing risky. The routine of family life, cooking, washing, and child-care was arduous and continual, even before they began their journey. However, the realities of trail travel demanded variations in "separate spheres" thinking. Many women and girls drove oxen and did other typical male work, so gender distinctions were often ignored. Spunky Louisa Barnes Pratt, one of few women to ride horseback, helped organize a meeting en route to Council Bluffs in 1846 to protest how men called them to prayers: "If the men wish to hold control over women let them be on the alert. We believe in equal rights." It was a daring statement in 1846, two years before the first women's equal rights meeting in Seneca, New York. Louisa also left a charming description of "riding horse back. By that means I could render some assistance in driving the stock. Ephraim Hanks . . . [who] had charge of the loose cattle, was a dashing rider, [and] gave [me] some lessons in that art till I became very expert. He assumed the name or title of Captain, and gave to me that of Commodore. I was quite proud of my title; arose early in the morning, [and] mounted my horse to help gather up the stock."

Furthermore, if men had to do women's work, they could. Most of the cooks in the pioneer company of 1847 were men and most had to do their own laundry, even though they complained about "sore knuckles." Twiss Bermingham, a Swiss convert, washed, cooked, mended clothes, tended children, and cared for his wife, who was in fragile health, on their journey to Zion in 1856 by handcart.

Typically trail life was harder on the women than on the men. One Oregon immigrant noted that she "kept a brave effort to be cheerful and patient" but sometimes left camp and gave way to "sobs and tears." The lack of privacy for bathing, elimination, and sleeping was especially difficult. Some pioneers kept chamber pots or chamber chairs in the wagon. The trail rule for "rest" stops was: "Gents to the right, ladies to the left." The women used their wide skirts to shield from view women who had no chamber pot. Women were expected at all times to be ladylike, and we have found no records to explain what happened to those imprisoned in tents and wagons all night with mixed sexes.

A modern, visual interpretation of this mid-nineteenth-century ideal, despite a marked lack of realism, is the "Madonna of the Trail" statues. In 1928 the Daughters of the American Revolution erected thirteen of these impressive monuments featuring a pioneer mother with children on what was then the "Ocean to Ocean Highway." (Among other places they may be seen today at Garden Grove, Kansas; Lexington, Missouri; Lamar, Colorado; and Albuquerque, New Mexico.) Mormon women on the trail, like other American women, were expected to preserve the pre-emigration values, norms, and traditions of civilization, and maintain a home-like atmosphere despite monumental odds.

Latter-day Saint camps included many single Mormon women immigrants in contrast to the Oregon Trail where, according to Lillian Schlissel, they were rare. There were at least eighty-four widows and single women in the ill-fated Martin Handcart Company of 1856, for example. Single men, widows, widowers, and orphans were fitted into Mormon traveling communities. Single men were hired as teamsters, drivers, cattle tenders, and handy men. Single women assisted with children, cooking, and elderly family members. Both sexes thus acquired a sort of temporary family on the trail.

Trail Communications

Travelers had a normal desire to keep in touch with loved ones on and off the trail. On May 4, 1847, Charles Beaumont, a returning trapper on the Oregon Trail, crossed the Platte River to meet the pioneers. In exchange for a little bread and salt, he agreed to take some letters to Winter Quarters if they could be written within fifteen minutes. In six and a half minutes, fifty letters were ready. Thereafter letters went back and forth via Saints traveling in both directions. Regular mail service began in 1850 as the federal government established mail stations. It was not uncommon for westbound immigrants to find letters waiting for them at such stations. Letters could even be sent to England from some mail stations such as those at Kanesville (Council Bluffs) and Fort Laramie.

Less conventionally, letters were placed in a slotted stick, between two pieces of wood, or in a moccasin hung from a tree. Some messages were written on bleached bones, for their whiteness made them conspicuous. Buffalo skulls (even human skulls) and shoulder blades and elk skulls—called bone mail, bone letters, or "bulletins of the plains"—served as paper. The pioneers enjoyed reading these messages although there was an urge to exaggerate Indian massacres and distances to various spots on the trail.

Sometimes there were messages under messages. One intrepid Oregon pioneer left so many messages, that others reading them added a word or two about his "stupidity" and "jackass" status. Thomas McIntyre, who returned from a mission to England in 1859 in the Rowley Handcart Company wrote: "I saw some anti-Brigham Young comments [on the trail]."

William Wood, a Mormon from England, commented in 1862: "Upon these bones much writing was left regarding the trains, and information given as to the health and success and often times a few words from some loved one would be written on the rib of an ox stuck in the ground along side of the trail telling the oncoming friends of the incidents of travel and much interesting matter."

Wood, who had been separated from his fiancée because of space limitations and a cranky captain, was particularly concerned that he would read: "Miss E. Gentry has made love to someone or married someone or is to be married to someone." Bone mail died out in 1862 when most old bones (and a few new ones) were collected and transported to the East where they were made into phosphate.

After the Western Union Telegraph line was completed in 1861 (in three months and twenty days), immigrating Mormons also sent and received telegraphs along the trails. Companies and some individuals were anxious to keep Salt Lake City advised about their condition, position, company rosters, number of wagons, and stock so that proper preparations could be made to receive the company. These lists, published in the *Deseret News*, are valuable today in reconstructing the great exodus.

Clothing

Pioneer men dressed in heavy boots, strong trousers, shirts, jackets, and coats. Broad-brimmed hats protected the heads and particularly their eyes. Women, however, were severely disadvantaged by female fashions and conventions of modesty. Nothing could have been more awkward and dangerous than the long skirts of that era as they struggled to climb in and out of wagons, stoop over campfires, or move quickly in case of emergency. Mormon and Oregon Trail accounts are replete with stories of long skirts that became entangled in ox-chains, wagon wheels, brakes, and other parts of wagons. Many females were dragged under oxen and wagons by such totally inappropriate attire because they dared not don trousers. These skirts also got dirty, soaked up water (particularly from the dew), and took a long time to dry. Artist Frederick Piercy, who reached the Salt Lake Valley in 1853, recommended that future women travelers should "not wear their dresses quite so long, and that if possible they provide themselves with India rubber galoshes and very large sun-bonnets."

Thomas Kane, public friend to the Mormons who visited the camp near Council Bluffs in 1846, left a kind but idealized version of women and their clothing. As a sign of their gentility, despite their poverty, he describes: "Although their ears were pierced and bore the loop-marks of rejected pendants, [they] were without ear-rings, finger-rings, chains, or brooches. Except such ornament, they lacked nothing most becoming the attire of decorous maidens. The neatly darned white stockings, and clean, bright petticoat, the ar-tistically clear-starched collar and chemisette, the something faded . . . lawn or gingham gown, that fitted modishly to the waist of the pretty wearer. . . ."

Buttons, bows, ribbons, aprons, petticoats, and bonnets became assertions of femininity and domesticity, distinguishing women from men and Indian women. In 1852, Amelia Bloomer innovated "bloomers," a mid-length skirt over pantelettes that reached shoe tops. Bloomers were a safe, sane, and modest costume, but Mormon women shunned them. They considered bloomers a dress for "liber-ated" women that would send radical sexual and political messages. Lucy R. Cooke, who spent the winter of 1852–53 in Salt Lake City before traveling on to California, wore a version of the bloomer cos-tume; and Hosea Stout, a Salt Lake resident, made a derogatory note in his diary: "Today the first 'bloomer' appeared in the city, puz-zling the casual observer to determine sex."

Nineteenth-century dresses were made from gingham, calico, linsey-woolsey, satin, pongee (silk), alpaca, brocade, and flannel. Even though the length was impractical, probably the more durable fabrics requiring the least amount of care were the most popular for travel dresses. The all-purpose sunbonnet came in styles varying from the practical to the stylish, with and without back "curtains" to protect the back of the neck. In 1857 one handcart sister lost hers and was compelled to continue bareheaded in the sun for a thousand miles. Another handcarter left her shoes on the bank of a river and had to continue on barefooted.

Victorian women, and especially Mormon women, were nearly silent regarding underclothing. According to Oregon Trail expert Jeanne Watson, women usually wore under their petticoats "a che-mise or under-drawers made with a split crotch, which must have made personal hygiene a bit easier." Some women actually found hoops helpful in keeping their skirts off the ground. However, if a stiff breeze swayed the hoops until legs showed, they were consid-ered immodest. Some women tried to solve that problem by weighting their hems with rocks but abandoned this device when the hems blew bruisingly against their shins.

Wading across streams caused a dilemma: lift your skirt and show some leg or drag it through the water and then walk for miles with the wet skirt flapping against your legs? In 1861, for example, F. W. Blake, who failed to keep his eyes on the far horizon, observed that some "girls pulled their dresses up to the knees (some above) and they paddled away in fine fun through two streams" in Nebraska. Near Fort Laramie some soldiers considered it "quite a sight" to "see the women wade across the river, with it being two or three feet deep." Other sisters pulled up their petticoats crossing mud holes.

As another problem, plants and bushes caught and ripped the fabric of dresses to shreds. In Mary Ann Rich's account of reaching Emigration Canyon in early October 1847, she noted: "The longest place on my dress was just a little below the knee. I had walked over the brush, driving my team to keep them in the road, and could not stop to untangle my dress when it got fastened in the brush, but had to walk on, leaving parts of my dress behind."

Some Scandinavian women blessed their wooden shoes, which held up longer than leather shoes. Some English immigrants wore "clogs," shoes with wooden soles reinforced by iron strips and leather tops. When shoes wore out, too often rags wrapped around their feet were the only replacements.

The long hours of daily sameness were reinforced by the slow plodding of oxen, dull routine, and the monochromatic nature of the Great Plains. After hundreds of miles of sky meeting land at an unbroken, undifferentiated horizon, the hot sun, and the wind, monotony could lull weary travelers into a dangerous urge to sleep. Most physical and emotional energy centered on getting to the next campground. This stultification and confined life contributed to carelessness, resulting in accidents and even death. Indians became a welcome diversion, as were trail "curiosities."

Food

Since travelers had to carry almost all of their provisions with them—they could count only rarely on finding berries or being able to fish or to kill game—the staples also were almost the same: flour, corn meal, bacon, sugar, tea, coffee, beans, parched corn, rice, dried fruits, and other commodities that would not deteriorate—for example "sea biscuits" and dried fish. Some brought bottled goods such as pickles, dried meats, vinegar, cheese, pickles, oatmeal, molasses, and bran meal. One company even mentioned gourmet items like canned oysters! However, many bottled goods were discarded, consumed quickly, or given away because they took up so much space and weighed so much. Amelia Knight, bound for Oregon, spent the evening of May 1, 1853, at Council Bluffs "packing things away for an early start in the morning. Threw away several jars, some wooden buckets, and all our pickles. Too unhandy to carry."

The Saints were given instructions on what to bring, and wagons were carefully inspected at Winter Quarters. Young had sent instructions back east as early as January 1845 listing items to pack for heading west.

Those who traveled with chickens and cows could count on eggs, butter, and milk at least some of the time. Many also herded pigs and sheep along the trail. Cacti, when peeled and sprinkled with sugar, became a good substitute for fruit. When possible the travelers also gathered walnuts, hazel nuts, hickory nuts, butternuts, and more than a dozen kinds of wild fruit.

Natural saleratus found around lakes was a workable substitute for baking soda. Robert Sweeten ate his first orange without removing the peel and was not well pleased with the flavor. John Jaques tasted ice cream for the first time in 1856 in St. Louis; it cost ten cents. On occasion, immigrants bought provisions from the Indians and settlers at places like Fort Laramie. By 1850, a number of trailside establishments and supply stations existed at places like Mount Pisgah and Garden Grove, Iowa, and Genoa, Nebraska. Corn, peas, cucumbers, beans, buckwheat, potatoes, pumpkins, and squash could be obtained at reasonable prices. Water was about 25 cents a keg at these stations.

Under duress pioneers could, and did, eat old shoes, leather, saddles, worn-out draft animals, deer antlers, even carrion and boiled bones, flour mixed with melted snow water, or a "soup" made of boiled willow leaves. One way to prepare an animal hide to eat was to scrape the hair off, soak the hide, boil it, and eat everything, including the glue. A better way, however, was first to scorch the hide, which not only made it easier to remove the hair, but also removed the bad taste it acquired during scalding. Boiling the hide for one hour in plenty of water would extract the glue, and the water could then be thrown away. The final step was to wash and scrape the hide again, then boil it to a jelly. Once cooled, it could be eaten with a little sugar.

At times, self-rising flour was available. Mixed with water, it could be fried in a pan. Mormon Battalion soldiers mixed flour and water until it was thick, and wound it around a stick or string, held it over the fire until brown, and served it with a pinch of sugar or salt.

The Word of Wisdom did not fare well on the trail. Although the prohibition on tea, coffee, alcohol, and tobacco is currently strictly required for Mormons in good standing, it was considered just good advice before Heber J. Grant became Church president in 1918. Tea and coffee were all-purpose drinks, and boiling water for their preparation saved many lives, the germ theory being unknown. Tea and coffee also made potable some of the brackish, muddy, and alkaline water they had to use or go without. A few had lemonade powder with which they disguised ill-tasting water. According to Helen Mar Whitney, Joseph Smith urged the Saints in Nauvoo to drink tea and coffee to ward off disease from drinking bad water and sometimes served tea to the sick himself.

The folk wisdom of the day recommended adding a cup of vinegar to a barrel of water to make it safe to drink. Some tried to settle muddy river water with eggs or cornmeal. The resulting drinks were dubbed "Platte River Cocktails." Some mules en route to California refused to drink the water but would drink coffee-flavored water.

Although the Word of Wisdom also proscribed alcoholic drinks, the Saints not only used them for medicine but also for mild celebrations. On February 4, 1847, Patty Sessions celebrated her fifty-second birthday at Winter Quarters in grand style: "We had brandy and drank a toast to each other." Although women seldom drank, some men over-indulged, especially at military installations, trading posts, and other gathering places on the trail. According to Hosea Stout, Chief of Police at Winter Quarters, rewards and fines often included whiskey: "My horse threw me off one day when I was trying to catch one that had got loose and I was allowed a pint for my good intentions and endeavors to catch the horse and fined a quart for having the bad luck of being thrown off while doing it. This was our custom."

On February 3, 1848, at Winter Quarters, a group called "The Defenders of Nauvoo" had a party to dance off the memories of the Battle of Nauvoo, during which the last Mormons were expelled from the city in September of 1846. "They had a high time, some being very high," wrote Hosea Stout.

Trail's End

The Saints exulted when they finished their trek and first saw their new Zion, their future home. Some cheered, shouted "Hallelujah," and tossed their hats in the air or waved handkerchiefs. Some considered it a "pretty town," a "glorious sight," a "grand sight," "paradise," and "enchanting to the eye." In 1847, one of the first pioneers wrote: "I could not help shouting, hurra, hurra, hurra, there's my home at last!" In September 1847, Patty Sessions almost uttered a prayer. "It is a beautiful place. My heart flows with gratitude to God that we have got home all safe, lost nothing, have been blessed in life and health. I rejoice all the time."

Not all were so delighted. There was no city to greet the three women who came with the pioneer company of 1847 or the six women from the Mormon Battalion who joined them at Fort Laramie. At least two of them saw only a wilderness, a reptile's paradise. "I have come 1,200 miles to reach this valley and walked much of the way," said Clara Decker, one of Brigham Young's wives, "but I am willing to walk 1,000 miles farther rather than remain here." Her mother, Harriet, agreed: "We have traveled fifteen hundred miles over prairies, deserts, and mountains, but, feeble as I am, I would rather go a thousand miles farther than stay in such a place as this."

Brigham Young paid no attention to such comments. At a meeting of the second large group of Zion-bound Saints in 1847, he announced firmly that he knew of no one "who was not pleased with the location." Even after settlements were established, some immigrants found it "barren," "discouraging," "disappointing," "lifeless" and "tasteless," a "patch of sagebrush," "a rather dreary place, and "Oh, have we come all this way for that?" The feelings of disappointment eased as the years passed.

The critics who thought Mormonism would be a short-lived religion have been silenced. The city blossomed under the work of many hands with irrigation water from the mountains. In a few years, relative peace and prosperity replaced hunger and poverty, but the tensions with "the outside world"—primarily the fight over polygamy and theocracy—lasted until the end of the century.

The Saints ended their search for a Zion in the mountain valleys and eventually in the savage desert in southern Utah, and other western states such as California, Nevada, and Arizona. The more desolate the spot, the more strenuously Brigham Young urged settlement. Very few said no to Brigham, and most of the places proved adequate, if not ideal.

The Saints persevered despite frozen wastelands, burning deserts, mud, floods, long marches, starvation, and desert isolation, and drought. Louisa Barnes Pratt caught the spirit of the Saints when she wrote in June 1846, in Iowa: "Yesterday we traveled over the most intolerable roads. . . . I was led to exclaim, what is there in all the world the Mormons will not attempt to do?"

Chapter 2

Religious Life

Notwithstanding the snow storms and inclemency of the weather, our camp resounded with songs of joy and praise to God–all were cheerful and happy in anticipation of finding a resting place from persecution . . . and rejoice that we have the privilege of passing through tribulations for the truth's sake. —Orson Pratt, 1846

By the end of 1846, Apostle Orson Pratt knew what "the privilege of passing through tribulations" really was. God was the reason they were sick, and the reason they were well. After the flight from Nauvoo, whatever the affliction suffered was deemed another test. Brigham Young announced at Winter Quarters: "All of this pain, sorrow, death and affliction is for a wise purpose in God . . . and glory in the Eternal world." Some who heard that comment might have wondered what God's wise purpose was in sending scurvy instead of fresh vegetables. However, the Saints, ever mindful of the scourges suffered by the original children of Israel, bore most of the tribulations in meekness and prayer.

Not everyone rejoiced, however. There was a lot of grumbling in Iowa and in Winter Quarters. Eliza R. Snow, who witnessed some unseemly polygamy problems at Mount Pisgah in June 1846, wrote: "It is a growling, grumbling, devilish, sickly time with us now."

A more structured religious life began at Winter Quarters in 1846, but there wasn't much difference between the religious activities and the regular activities in Mormon camps. Winter Quarters was just a long camping experience, but a real village atmosphere soon emerged. As Orson Pratt mentioned, some felt it a privilege to suffer, and suffer they did. This was not normal human affliction. It was divine suffering, designed to refine God's chosen people.

Most leaders tried to keep life on the trail as normal as possible, including religious activities; and they succeeded fairly well in the beginning. In the semi-permanent camps, such as at Garden Grove, Mount Pisgah, Kanesville (formerly Council Bluffs and named for Thomas Kane), and Winter Quarters, religious life was more regulated than it had been in Nauvoo. Twenty-two branches, wards, and districts, each with its own bishop, began at Winter Quarters. Most meetings were in the Council House, with others in the Log Tabernacle at Council Bluffs. Such congregations had not become well established in Nauvoo where there never was a proper meeting-house or chapel. Tithing became more systemized, and fast offerings became an important part of caring for the poor—which in Winter Quarters included nearly everyone. The requirement was to fast once a month for two meals and give what was saved as the fast offering.

The Word and Will of the Lord

Brigham Young knew that before the Saints continued the journey to the Great Basin, they needed to understand and accept rules that would override individual preferences or the inevitable friction of the trail. This was not an individualized journey from one place to another; it was a religious pilgrimage—part of the divine plan of gathering. Young announced his revelation giving the "word and will of the Lord" in January 1847, establishing the order of travel and the governing authority of the company. It also reiterated that the Lord's people "must be tried in all things" and admonished the Saints to remain faithful "in keeping all my words." It dealt with the most urgent need at hand: getting to Zion and maintaining order while en route. It was the only revelation Young ever wrote down.

"The Word and Will of the Lord concerning the Camp of Israel in the journeying to the West" stated that the Saints should be organized into companies, subdivided under captains of hundreds, fifties, and tens with a president and two counselors at the head of each company, all under the direction of the Twelve Apostles. All Saints were placed under a strict covenant to "walk in all the ordinances of the Lord." This revelation reads very much like the instructions given the original children of Israel as recounted in Exodus 18:21–27.

The sense of urgency is strong in Young's speeches during this time. The Saints' flight into the wilderness would be to their final promised land, their Zion. It would be the first time the Saints would be alone in their own little piece of the world, and Young reminded them over and over what was expected—no—demanded: "Remember when you leave the Gentiles you will have yourself to imagine evil. . . . Don't come into my company unless you can obey the Word and Will of the Lord . . . or the Priesthood [will] be taken away."

These were dire threats—even scare tactics—but Young's determination to accomplish this massive organizational procedure foresaw the linking of the spiritual and the temporal, hand in hand. The reiterated theme was obedience. Heber C. Kimball echoed this message, threatening that the Twelve would abandon the disobedient. "I want to have the Holy Ghost in our midst . . . and not have the Twelve drove from our midst for if they were it would be the greatest curse [to] befall us."

New converts like Martha P. Jones Thomas, en route from Kentucky to Missouri in 1837, reveal the dilemma some of them faced who had led independent lives before joining the Church and gathering to Missouri in 1837:

> It was something very new to us to be led by anyone and obey him in all things. In this we did not fill the bill very well. It did not take our [unnamed] leader long to tell us sharply that if we did not harken to his counsel better, the wind storms would overtake us. [Some] said they would lead themselves. Our leader called them "Judas Company." Old father Hendricks [said] "I don't see why we can't travel without a leader as the Judas Company do. They get along as well as we do." You should have seen our leader roll out from under that wagon and call the attention of the company. [He] said if we did not do better and acknowledge him as our leader, the judgements of God would come down upon us. . . . We did not know how to be led, though we might lead part of the time.

Howard Egan, one of Kimball's "adopted" sons and a member of the 1847 vanguard company, left this account of a typical sermon on obedience from Heber C. Kimball in 1847: "The principal part of the time was occupied in exhorting the brethren to faithfulness and to obey the council of those whom God had placed in the church to lead and direct the affairs of His Kingdom. [Kimball] said that if we were faithful the angel of the Lord would be before us and be around about us to ward off the harm of the destroyer."

The handcart Saints of 1856 heard sermons that also stressed: "Do your duty, obey the brethren, believe in the church, and believe in the gospel." According to John Chislett, member of the James A. Willie Company, obedience was the theme of most sermons: "Meetings were held nearly every evening for preaching, counsel, and prayer; the chief feature of the preaching being, 'obey your leaders in all things.'"

Those camps without apostles or other well-known leaders present displayed more independence; and even after Brigham's fiery sermon to the pioneers on May 29, 1847, conflicts surfaced. For example, Thomas Bullock, traveling with the vanguard company in the summer of 1847, was plagued by George Brown, his wagon mate:

> June 12: After closing up my journal, I went to pack away the goods in my wagon . . . when George Brown said, "the Captain's orders were to see about the cattle." I told him I would as quick as I could. . . . I then started after the cattle and met G. Brown & told him I had seen them all. He asked why I had not gone when he told me, "instead of idling & fooling away your time." I replied "O Good God, what a lie, if you say I have been idling. . . ." He then struck me with his Whip saying, "I am ready for a fight. . . ." George Brown has lied to and about the Lord's anointed [and] I have been abused & reviled.

Missionary Work and Baptisms

Continuing to preach the gospel on any occasion when non-members were present and willing to listen was an expectation of all Mormon elders. They often gave just a single sermon expressing essential gospel principles, then asked candidates for baptism to come forward.

Men have been sent on missions since the Church was organized. This method brought in major important converts such as Sidney Rigdon, Heber C. Kimball, Orson Pratt, and Amasa Lyman. Heber C. Kimball was sent to England as a missionary in 1837 from

Kirtland, Ohio, and he had great success in the Preston area. He baptized the first Jewish convert, Alexander Neibaur. He met and baptized William Clayton in the River Ribble. Clayton migrated to Nauvoo in 1840, became Joseph Smith's personal secretary, and kept journals for many years about Church doctrine, their journey west, and important events. His diary is considered to be among the best in Church history.

The first black Mormon, Elijah Abel, ordained a seventy by Joseph Smith in Nauvoo, was eager to share his faith. He went on a mission to Canada and New York in 1838. Joseph Smith sent him with John E. Page, Heber C. Kimball, Lorenzo Snow, and Orson Pratt to Cincinnati, Ohio, on another mission in 1843 only to meet internal resistance. "They respected him but the brethren felt wisdom forbids that we should introduce [him] before the public." Brother Abel visited with black citizens, but there is no evidence that he made any converts.

Franklin D. Richards and his family left Nauvoo in May of 1846, following the exodus of the other Saints. At that point, he was called on a mission and obediently departed, leaving behind two sick wives, one with a small daughter and the other in the last stages of pregnancy. Jane Snyder Richards wrote her memoirs. "We reached sugar creek twelve miles distant the first night and there my husband left us to go on a mission to England. It was a great trial to us all. . . . I felt as though it was doubtful if I [would be] living on his return [and] I only lived because I could not die." She barely made it to Winter Quarters. Here she visited Mary Haskin Parker Richards, wife of Samuel Richards, also on a mission. Franklin Richards found Jane the only member of his family alive on his return in the summer of 1847.

One of the most important mission calls was received by Orson Spencer, who was sent in the fall of 1846 to England to edit the *Millennial Star.* Spencer's wife had died soon after they fled from Nauvoo in February, leaving her five motherless children in a little cabin at Winter Quarters. The oldest was then fourteen, the youngest about two. Brigham Young saw that all five children were brought to the Valley before Spencer's return, late in 1848. John Taylor, Orson Hyde, and Parley P. Pratt were sent to England at this time, also in

1846, to check on some financial business. Pratt left behind eight wives and many children.

Fifteen-year-old Barnard White had barely gotten off the ship from London in 1855 at New York City when Church leaders there told him: "The Lord wants you to be a missionary." He served six months in that area while waiting for the rest of his family to arrive from England, and the family then traveled on to Utah.

Even though about 500 men were in the Mormon Battalion and dozens were already serving missions, without any explanation in his journal, Young called twenty-seven additional missionaries in late October 1847, soon after he returned to Winter Quarters on the backtrail from reaching the Salt Lake Valley in July 1847. On November 23, he called seventeen more, but these were all no doubt assigned to trade and barter with farmers in the communities of Iowa and Missouri for needed commodities. Even short assignments were called "missions" during that period.

On the trail, despite the press of other duties, some nonmembers applied for baptism. For example, Heber C. Kimball baptized six into the Church in 1848: On July 2, "After meeting was dismissed there was 2 candidates for baptism, some that come from Illinois that never belonged to the Ch. Jasper Twitchell and Sarah. (His wife)." A month later on August 6, "I went forward this morning and baptized 4 young men that did not belong to the Ch; their names is William Mathews, Geo Clawson, John Hopper & James Steel."

On Saturday, July 8 1848, Kimball recorded: "John Pack baptized a man and his wife that started from McDonough County, Illinois for the Bay of San Francisco." Wilford Woodruff also noted in his diary on July 10, 1850, when he was traveling from the Winter Quarters area to the Salt Lake Valley: "Drove 20 miles on the Platt. . . . Camped on the bank of the River. I baptized 14 persons for the remission of sins & confirmed them & 2 for Health."

Occasionally someone bound for Oregon would travel with a Mormon camp for protection. When they joined the Church, the Platte River became their baptismal font. Jean Rio Baker witnessed several baptisms in 1851. Her group helped some immigrants bound for Oregon who asked to join the company after cattle were stolen. One of them was impressed enough to listen to the nightly sermons.

Jean wrote on July 19: "Mr. Pierce was baptized this evening." They were still on the trail September 15, when she recorded: "Meeting in the afternoon. Sermon from Captain Brown on the kingdom of Heaven. . . . John Tout, who had been baptized during the week, was then publicly received into the Church."

However, preaching directed to Gentiles was usually not well received. Jonah Myers, a non-Mormon en route to Utah as a teamster hauling merchandise in 1865, left an account about "two Mormon Elders with us who were just returning from Europe. . . . One of them used to like to preach, mostly at night when we could not get away from him, and he had become a regular nuisance, so I started in apposition to him on the other side of the corral and I soon had the biggest crowd. He said we were a gang of ungodly reachees, [wretches?] and we would burn for it in the next world, but we took chances on that."

William Howell and other brethren baptized what may be a record number for an ocean crossing—fifty-two—in a large barrel of ocean water as they crossed the Atlantic in 1851 aboard the *Olympus*. There were incessant, dangerous weather problems, and Howell impressed the crew and other travelers with his prayers and faith. (See also Chapter 14.) In other cases, some leaders of emigrating companies built a platform out over the ship's side and baptized directly in the mighty Atlantic.

An interesting early practice of the Saints was baptism for the restoration of health, which began in Nauvoo and continued in the Salt Lake Valley. For example, thirteen-year-old Helen Mar Kimball was taken to the Nauvoo Temple in 1842 by her father, Heber C. Kimball. "I was not sick in bed, but looked like a walking ghost," she later recalled, "and it took but a few steps to exhaust [me]. Early one morning . . . my father had William [her brother] hitch up his horse and buggy and take me up to the Temple . . . . He took me to the Font under the Temple [where] water had been pumped the day before and there baptized me for my health, which I regained more rapidly from that time." In the Edmund Ellsworth's handcart company, the first to cross the plains in 1856, rebaptism for health was part of the experience. James Starley was baptized four times for his health between 1854, when he joined the Church in England,

and 1857 in Utah—an average of one baptism per year—possibly as a precaution.

Rebaptism also served as a symbol of recommitment. After arrival in the Salt Lake Valley in July 1847, Brigham Young, even in a weakened state as a result of what is commonly called "Rocky Mountain fever," felt it necessary to set the proper example on this important symbolic new beginning. Wilford Woodruff noted August 6:

> Br. Kimball called upon me & informed me that the Twelve were going soon to the water to be Baptized for the remission of their sins to set an example to the Church. . . . We considered this A duty & privilege as we come into a glorious valley to locate & build a temple & build up Zion we felt like renewing our Covenant before the Lord and each other. We soon repaired to the water & President Brigham Young went down into the water & Baptized all his Brethren the Twelve that were with him . . . & sealed upon us our apostleship & all the keys, powers & Blessings belonging to that office.

William Clayton wrote August 7, 1847: "In the evening many of the brethren went and were baptized on the dam by Elder Kimball for the remission of sins. Elders Pratt, Woodruff, and Smith attending to confirmation. I went and was baptized amongst the rest. It has been recommended for all the camp to be baptized and this even they have commenced it."

During 1855–56 when Brigham Young's counselor, Jedediah M. Grant, spearheaded an internal revival called the Mormon Reformation in 1855, nearly everyone was rebaptized as a sign of recommitment.

Sermons and Admonitions on the Trail

Because of starvation, financial problems, disease, and death, there was much contention in Winter Quarters. Brigham Young sounded the call to "cease to do evil" a few months after the Saints had spent too many days and nights in circumstances such as Orson Pratt described in his journal on April 16, 1846: "During the night, the mud froze hard. To any but Saints, our circumst[ances] would have been very discouraging, for it seemed to be with the greatest difficulty that we could preserve our animals. . . . Many [people] . . . were nearly destitute of food."

Brigham Young and Heber C. Kimball issued many warnings and threats, particularly that the Twelve would abandon their faithless followers, leaving them on their own. During the fall of 1846, Heber C. Kimball "counseled the bishops to teach the people to cease their complaining and seek diligently after the Holy Ghost, that the Twelve might not be driven from their midst." It was a doomsday warning. Brigham Young's manuscript history laments: "They did not relent."

Kimball redoubled his efforts: "I instructed the Bishops to hold meetings where the Saints might assemble, confess their sins, pray with and for each other; humble themselves before the Lord and commence a reformation that all might exercise themselves in the principles of righteousness." He painted a bleak picture of the possible consequences: "If those who had received the Holy Priesthood did not abide their covenants . . . before the Lord . . . those who did would be taken away from their midst, and the wicked would be smitten with famine, pestilence and the sword . . . and [I] warned those who lied and stole and followed Israel that they would have their heads cut off, for that was the law of God and it should be executed."

Mary Parker Richards, the young wife of Samuel Richards, recorded another Winter Quarters address of a similar severity: "Bro Woodruff . . . said if there was any under the sound of his voice who felt as if the journey was too great . . . or the trials too hard . . . to endure, his advice to such would be to go into their Waggons & shut themselves up . . . & pray to the Lord to take away their lives & grant them a burial with the Saints of God as their death would prove a blessing to their posterity who would ever believe that their fathers died in full belief of the Gospel of Christ."

Accompanying this "stick" of threats was the "carrot" of promises: "I told the brethren if the people would do as I said they would be saved." In a more reflective mood, Brigham Young wrote a genuinely pastoral letter to Jesse Little in February of 1847: "I feel like a father with a great family of children around me in a winter storm, and I am looking with calmness, confidence and patience for the clouds to break and the sun to shine so that I can run out and plant and sow and gather in the corn and wheat and say, Children, come home, winter is approaching again. . . . I am ready to kill the fatted calf and make a joyful feast to all who will come and partake."

The month before, it seemed that the harsh admonitions were at last bearing fruit. On January 4, 1847, Willard Richards wrote from Winter Quarters to Charles Coulson Rich, who was the leader in Mount Pisgah, in Iowa: "We have had quite a reformation at this place of late, which has caused good feelings to prevail in the breasts of the Saints. The health of the Saints is much improved lately. The Bishops are diligent in watching over their wards; preaching and prayer meetings are multiplied."

Brigham Young and the other leaders must have felt a surge of relief and thankfulness as they prepared to depart in April of 1847. On April 2, Young "informed Bishop [George] Miller . . . that when we moved hence it would be to the Great Basin, where the Saints would soon form a nucleus of strength and power sufficient to cope with mobs." Young, though focused optimistically on the Saints' future home, did not underestimate the difficulties of transporting the Saints. A new wagon ran between $65 and $100 in St. Louis, a price beyond the resources of many Saints.

Young took drastic measures on the trail on May 29, 1847, tongue-lashing the lively young men in the vanguard company who played cards and checkers, swore, and danced. Much sobered, the camp spent the next day, a Sunday, in fasting and prayer. According to Albert P. Rockwood, "This morning . . . all is still and quiet about the camp save the tinkling of cow bells and now and then the Neigh of a horse. The Meek & Quiet spirit of the Lord broods over us. Fasting and prayer is the order of the day. . . . At 20 min before 12 o clock the sacrnt meeting commenced. At this time the twelve and ten others of which I was one, took our priestly apperral and retired to the bluffs and saught a retired place for prayer."

Brigham Young was too weak from the fever to say much when they finally arrived in the valley on July 24 but, according to Woodruff, "informed the brethren they must not work on Sunday that they would loose five times as much as they would gain by it. . . . And there should not any man dwell among us who would not observe these rules."

His second message, delivered four days later when he was feeling stronger, unleashed fire and brimstone rhetoric against their enemies. According to Woodruff, on July 28, 1847, Brigham "spoke of the saints being driven from place to Place, And said the only way Boggs, Clark, Lucas, Benton & all the leaders of the mob [from Missouri] could have been saved in the day of the Lord Jesus would have been to have [them] come forward voluntarily & let their heads be cut off & let the blood run upon the ground." This statement seems to be the earliest expression of what became the controversial doctrine of blood atonement.

Shall We Begin . . .

The main exodus from Winter Quarters began in early June of 1848. Helen Mar Kimball Whitney, Heber C. Kimball's daughter, who had married Horace Whitney, was traveling in her father's company and contrasted the order of the Mormon companies favorably with the wildly independent non-Mormons, including both temporal and spiritual aspects: "The Mormon companies were all orderly, and were truly models by the side of those who followed in their trail who were not governed by the same strict rules and religious motives and principles. . . . Our salvation, both temporal and spiritual, depended upon this course, and our history is a wonder and a marvel to those who have . . . review[ed] it in all its ups and downs. . . . God . . . has brought us deliverance every time; and it is our wish and purpose to trust Him still."

Just to make sure they remained orderly, Heber C. Kimball spoke to his company on June 8, 1848, at the beginning of his second (and final) journey to Zion: "Shall we begin from this night to have a reformation, to cease from swearing, profane language, murmuring, angry feelings to our cattle and each other, and begin to attend to family prayers, etc?" His company unanimously voted to do so.

Brigham Young, who had started to the Salt Lake Valley earlier in the summer of 1848, delivered a sermon, recorded by John D. Lee on July 16, assuring the Saints that "ceasing to do evil" will get them "into the Kingdom of god."

> Brethren, with regard to preaching while on this Journey I have but little to Say to this People. If they have & cease to do evil I will warrant every individual safe into the Kingdom of god, the unbeliever not accepted, [excepted?] for there is no man but what has more or less of the light of christ, for he is the light that lighteth every man that

cometh into the world & this is the [word] according to the revelation of Jesus christ in me. Now, brethern, my council to you is to cease to do Evil and do good, for every man will be Judged by his works. It is not the good, righteous feelings that I have that will present me or any other man blameless & acceptable before the Lord, but it is the good that we do to one another. . . . Here, Lord am I & my works, do with me as it seemeth thee good.

Young could now develop more nuanced interpretations of scripture since Zion was a reality at this point. He would continue to chastise his people for thirty years, but this message showed an early concern with the power of Christ's atonement. He continued:

Let every person act on the principles of right according to the light he possesses for Jesus is the light of every man that cometh into the world. . . . This people knows a great deal; they know the principles of the Gospel and it far exceeds the knowledge of the Christian world. . . . I feel as willing today to do my duty as ever I did. I am now as willing to go to the ends of the earth & preach the Gospel if it was my calling as ever I was. I have traveled & preached till the blood has squashed in my boots.

Once on the trail, any elder could be called on to preach. Zebulon Jacobs had this privilege Sunday, August 2, 1868: "Drove 12 miles to a small spring creek and nooned. . . . In the evening a meeting was called. I was called on to speak. Gave a few every day remarks about traveling, how to get along and have patience for the longest journey comes to an end sometime."

Sabbath Observance

Both at Winter Quarters and in the early stages of travel, the Saints held regular Sunday services supplemented by morning and evening prayers. Young spoke often about the need to keep the Sabbath holy. Except for obedience and his call to cease to do evil, this was one of his main themes. In the Iowa camps of 1846, George Whitaker, a young teamster for Parley P. Pratt, wrote: "We never traveled on Sunday. We always rested on that day. We would put on our Sunday clothes and have a meeting. We always tried to camp by a grove of trees on Saturday night so that we could meet in the shade on Sunday. We enjoyed our meeting just as well as though we were in a fine meeting house."

Converts from England were reluctant to give up traditional Sabbath observance. Jean Rio Griffiths Baker wrote May 2, 1851: "Sunday. We started this morning, much to my regret, for I do not like Sunday traveling, but our captain gave us a reason to do so, the fear of not being in time to meet the company at the bluffs." This emergency measure was effective and the united companies traveled on together from the meeting place at Council Bluffs.

However, the rigors and realities of trail life, the weather, accidents, fears, and other problems eroded daily religious activities and traditional Sabbath observance. Lost travel time had to be made up on Sundays. In the summer of 1848, Young announced one week that his company would travel on the Sabbath because it was too far to water. Religious services were often held "according to the dictates of geography, not the Old Testament." Weekdays substituted for Sundays, as Martha Spence Heywood noted in 1851: "The principle also is to stop one day in seven as a Sabbath, but not arbitrarily on Sunday. Circumstances have to guide whether it be Saturday, Sunday, or Monday."

Most overlanders faced the same dilemma but quickly adapted to trail requirements. The Oregon Missionary Company of 1838 left Westport, Missouri, a day later than the American Fur Company, so they could avoid traveling on the Sabbath. Mary Richardson Walker, one of the three women, rode sidesaddle most of the time. The next day, rushing to catch up with the American Fur Company, the group rode twenty-one miles without resting. Mary, who was six weeks pregnant, was reduced to tears. (Historian George R. Stewart claimed that, on the trail, "women held up better than the men." Mary Walker, despite her pregnancy, acknowledged that she dealt with trail conditions better than her husband, Elkanah Walker.)

Catherine Haun, en route to the California goldfields, wrote in 1849: "If we had devotional service the minister—protem—stood in the center of the corral while we all kept on with our work. There was no disrespect intended but there was little time for leisure or that the weary pilgrim could call his own. . . . The men seemed more tired and hungry than were the women."

Prayers

In addition to camp prayers, individuals were encouraged to engage in secret prayer. Heber C. Kimball, on the trail in 1848, recorded a humorous incident: "One evening I went out to pray; another of the brethren came out after me for the same purpose. I was on my knees praying; he came along & his eyesight not being good, he thought I was a stump or something else; he kicked me in the face; this was the only time I got kicked for praying."

Ten-year-old Amelia Eliza Slade (Bennion), traveling with her mother and five siblings in 1864, suffered through the deaths of two siblings. When her mother also fell ill and Amelia heard her beg for someone to take care of her children, she seized her sister "by the hand" and the two little girls "ran off . . . into the sagebrush and kneeling down we prayed in all our childish anguish, 'Please, Heavenly Father, don't let Mother die. Please make her better, in the name of Jesus, Amen.'" Her mother recovered.

Formal prayer circles, associated in Nauvoo with the Quorum of the Anointed and temple services, are known to have taken place near Mount Pisgah, Winter Quarters, along the Platte River, atop Independence Rock, and at the Needles on the present Wyoming-Utah state line. Rockwood's mention of "priestly apperral" suggests such a prayer circle. Wilford Woodruff climbed Independence Rock with a group of elders on June 21, 1847: "I . . . went to the north end, which is the highest part. Here is an opening or cavern which would hold 30 or 40 persons, and a rock stands on the highest peak of about three tons weight. We got upon this rock and offered up our prayers according to the order of the priesthood." Later at the Needles, near the Utah border, Woodruff wrote: "We prayed earnestly for the blessing of God to rest upon President Young & his brethren the Twelve & all of the Pioneers Camp & the whole Camp of Israel & and House of Israel, our wives & children, & relatives of the Mormon Battalion."

Administrations

When illness struck, the laying on of hands, or administration, was common, nearly always preceding more complicated rites like baptism for health. The Mormons drew this practice from the New Testament. Generally, two elders participate, one anointing with consecrated olive oil, and the other "sealing" the blessing. Patty Sessions, a midwife in Nauvoo and Utah, fell ill and was sick so long in the summer of 1846, that her burial clothes were prepared. According to her journal, the camp doctor said she was almost gone, and many announced that she was dead. However, Brigham Young and Heber C. Kimball administered to her, and she recovered.

Aboard the *Swanton* in 1843, Lorenzo Snow was among a group of emigrating Saints from England when a young German sailor was suddenly taken sick. The captain and everyone despaired of his recovery. Some Mormons urged the captain to allow Apostle Snow to administer to the young man; and eventually, the captain reluctantly consented. Snow "laid his hands on the head of the young man, prayed and in the name of Jesus Christ rebuked the disease and commanded him to be made whole. Soon after, to the joy and astonishment of all he was seen walking the deck, praising and glorifying God for his restoration." Several baptisms resulted from this miraculous healing. (See Chapter 14.)

Ephraim Hanks, who is remembered for his humanitarian aid to the Martin Handcart Company at Devil's Gate, is less well known for miraculously healing a dying man when nineteen others died that day. Hanks heard a weeping woman pass him in the darkness:

> She went straight to Daniel Tyler's wagon [and] . . . told the story of her husband being at the point of death. . . . Elder Tyler remarked, "I can not administer to a dead man." Brother Tyler requested me to stay and lay out the supposed dead brother [but] we went to work and built a fire . . . warmed some water, and washed the dying man. . . . I then anointed him with consecrated oil over his whole body and we laid hands on him and commanded him in the name of Jesus Christ to breathe and live. The effect was instantaneous. The man . . . sat up . . . and commenced to sing a hymn. His wife . . . ran through the camp exclaiming; "My husband was dead . . . The man who brought the buffalo meat has healed him."

Isaiah Coombs, who was ill in 1855 at Mormon Grove, was asked to ride twelve miles to deliver a message. He begged off saying he was racked with pain. The company leader, Daniel Spencer, said, "Oh, no, you shall not die, you will have a pleasant canter over the prairie and I promise you in the name of the Lord that you shall return feeling much better and that you shall be sick no more." According to the record, it came to pass.

Beginning in Nauvoo and extending through the first few years of the twentieth century, Mormon women also anointed and blessed each other for healing, especially before giving birth.

Women blessed several babies who fell ill in Winter Quarters; and one baby, given up for dead, recovered after Presendia Huntington B. Kimball, a plural wife of Heber C. Kimball, administered to the infant. On February 23, 1847, Patty Sessions and her husband, David, "laid hands on the widow Holman's step daughter. She was healed."

On the trail in the Mount Pisgah area in 1846, Sarah Pea Rich healed young George Patten who had been "put in our care" but who fell ill and, despite their nursing,

> got worse. [One night] Mr Rich [Charles] came to my bed, wanted to know if I could watch... [He] thought the boy could not possibl[y] live ... so I took my seat and began to reason with myself [and] I could not give up. I neald down ... and plead with the Lord to spare his life [and] when I got up I was lead by my feelings to put a teasponsfull of ... oil in his mouth. . . . I did not see that he swallowed the oil so I anointed his face and head with oil asking the Lord to bless the same [and] to my great joy I noticed that George had swallowed the oil. I then took couriage, got some viniger, swabbed it with a soft swab I rubed his tounge and mouth. . . . I then gave him a little branda and watter; he swallowed that. I then made some tea ... and he swallowed that. . . . [Soon] George opened his eyes. So I told my husband what I had done and how humble I felt while praying to the Lord to spare the boys life.

Helen Mar Kimball Whitney wrote that her mother, Vilate Murray Kimball, became an angel of healing in 1847 in Winter Quarters:

> At the time when numbers were laying sick with the terrible scourge that was carrying off so many of the Saints, being made easy prey for disease and death in consequence of the weakened condition to which they were reduced by long privations and exposure, and death seemed determined to lay them low, my mother would go from door to door ministering food and consolation to the sick, and pouring out blessings upon them. . . . She seemed to grow stronger in body . . . and

in blessing she was blessed [and] with fasting and prayer the sick were healed and made to rejoice.

Other Miracles

It is not surprising that a people so closely focused on their religious beliefs felt the Lord strengthening them during their trials and intervening with providential mercies and miracles. Assigning great value to these experiences, they gratefully recorded them in their personal writings. The experiences run from not being afraid of Indians or wolves, finding scarce game, and locating lost stragglers, to events that were unusual by any measure.

For example, when some of the poorest Saints were driven from Nauvoo into Iowa by anti-Mormon factions in September 1846, they huddled on the riverbank, without the means to go either forward or back. Teenager Mary Field Garner later remembered, "The food of the entire camp was gone so there was extreme suffering and we were all so cold and hungry. . . . There was no light except a candle which flickered out in the wind and rain as it was carried from one place to another to care for the sick and comfort the dying. It was under these conditions that God sent a countless flock of quail to feed us. They were so tame we could catch them with our hands. Some of the men made wire traps so they could catch several at a time."

The marveling Saints killed about fifty quail and caught fifty more alive. Some were cooked immediately for breakfast. Quail, like turkeys, chickens, grouse, and pheasants, are classified as Galliformes and built for quick takeoffs and fast, short flights. Crossing a mile-wide river was unusual; and this particular flock, totally exhausted by the strenuous flight, fluttered to the ground within the Saints' reach. They served as manna from heaven regardless of how they arrived.

Parley P. Pratt had a young son fall under the wheels on the journey to Zion in 1847. It was in a sandy spot, and the youngster received no injury. It was considered a miracle. Even more miraculous was the healing of Nancy Maria Love who fell under the tongue of her wagon, which was heavily loaded with freight. Eliza R. Snow noted: "She looked crushed, but after administering by some of the elders she revived." A few days later, she was milking her cow again.

One miracle involved a trail fire. Seventeen-year-old Johanna Kirsten Larsen Winters from Denmark was in the Leonard G. Rice Company, which included Brigham Young Jr. in 1867, two years before trail travel ended. En route they found themselves in the direct path of a terrible prairie fire; but as it bore down on them, Brigham Jr. "stepped upon the highest part of the wagon, raised his hand and said, 'Brethren and Sisters, stand still, we are not here to be destroyed, there is our deliverance.'" They saw a small cloud form quickly, then rain fell in torrents. "We thanked the Lord for our deliverance, and went on our way rejoicing," Johanna said. They arrived in Salt Lake City without further incident.

Another body of miracle stories reports rewards for generously sharing food. A poor woman whose husband was with the Mormon Battalion, came to Charles C. Rich at Mount Pisgah asking for food. All he had was twenty pounds of flour for his own family. Rich instructed his wife, Sarah, to give the woman the whole amount for "the Lord will provide." According to Sarah,

> That evening a wagon driver came up to the door, stepped out, and said: "The spirit tells me you are out of money and tells me to help." He then handed Brother Rich $50.00. He was a Quaker he used the word thee. Brother Silwell also bought some flower [sic] and left with us to give to the poor of that place; he also let us have some grociryes. [sic] He was a wealthy bachelor, traveled on to Winter Quarters and assisted others to start to the mountains.

Soon afterwards, while at Winter Quarters, James Madison Flake and several others helped the Rich family who had arrived in that area. Accompanied by a hired man, Sarah Rich went out in the camp looking for food: "We met brother Ezra T. Clark with a sack of flower [sic] and a bushel of potatoes . . . enquiring where I lived. . . . We got a little shugar, a little coffee and tea [and] started home, passed brother Flakes whom I had never seen. He was just finishing dressing a calf [and] he said: "Sister Rich send that man here and git a quarter of this calf." I did so and reached home with plenty to eat."

Speaking in Tongues

Glossolalia—speaking in tongues—began as early as the 1831 in Kirtland, and this spiritual gift was doubtless a great source of spiritual strength as the Saints faced the trek westward. On December 29, 1846, at Winter Quarters, Brigham Young recorded: "I felt to thank the Lord for the privilege of praising Him in the song and dance. I spoke in tongues and conversed with Elder Kimball in an unknown tongue."

The sisters also spoke in tongues frequently. Also in Winter Quarters on Sunday, February 14, 1847, Patty Sessions recorded: "Went to a meeting and prayed and sang in tongues that a sister might deliver [her baby] safely." A few months later on the trail, Patty recorded two cases of children speaking in tongues, one of them her eleven-year-old granddaughter Martha Ann: "We had a little meeting in our wagon. . . . My granddaughter, Martha Ann, had the gift of tongues, but through fear did not speak. After the sisters had gone she asked me to let her and Martha Van Cott have a little meeting. . . . We went into our wagon and she spoke in tongues and prayed. I gave the interpretation." This tradition continued on the trail, but glossolalia is no longer a part of the Mormon experience.

Evil Spirits

Rare but memorable spiritual experiences were encounters on the trail with evil spirits. Hosea Stout was both baffled and saddened by the strange actions of his young son Hosea on the trail in Iowa. He recorded on June 27, 1846:

> My child seemed strangely affected to night after laying hands on him we found him to [be] troubled with evil spirits who I knew now were determined on his destruction. He would show all signs of wrath to wards me & his mother. . . . His looks were demoniac accopanied [sic] by the most frightful gesture I ever saw in a child. At times I felt almost to cowl [cower] at his fierce ghastly and horrid look and even felt to withdraw from the painful scene for trulty the powers of darkness now prevailed here. . . . Thus alone my wife & me over our only and dearest son struggled in sorrow and affliction . . . . He gradually and slowly declined [and] its spirit took its leave of its body without any apparent pain but seemed to go to sleep.

One entire camp was affected by evil spirits in 1846, according to Joseph Lee Robinson, on the trail before reaching Winter Quarters:

It was with difficulty that I could get my breath. Behold, suddenly there was a general outcry in the camp. In every wagon there was a disturbance. Some children were crying and some panting for breath. We inquired what the matter was, but no one knew . . . except they felt bad. . . . It was plainly manifested to me that it was evil spirits. They were trying to smother us to death. . . . I called upon the Lord [and] rebuked the evil spirits. . . . They left . . . [and] the noise stopped and everyone felt easy and quiet and could go back to sleep.

Wilson G. Nowers, a returning missionary, witnessed another frightening scene aboard the *Olympus* in 1851: "A lad by the name of Mackensie, twelve years old, . . . in the dead of the night came leaping from his bunk, shouting at the top of his voice. . . . He was possessed of an evil spirit, which was so enraged that for hours the brethren labored to exorcise him; but this proved effectual only for a short time, as the evil one returned bringing others. . . . There were seven of them [evil spirits and] they followed in the wake of the Saints."

Oscar Stoddard, captain of a handcart company in 1860, recorded how a woman named Elizabeth Taylor, who was camped with a handcart company at Council Bluffs in 1860, "was seized with severe jerking and twitching till it seemed as though she was going to die. . . . I laid my hands upon her head and . . . rebuked [the spirit]. During her convalescence she informed [us] that while at Council Bluffs spiritualism was quite common and that in a family where she resided they often had sittings or circles headed by the circuit preacher. She began to . . . . fear their influence and resolved to break away from them."

So, the trail Saints had experienced all manner of religious and evil situations on their journey to Zion. The wonder is there was so much success after so many obstacles. It was indeed "a marvelous work and a wonder."

Reaching Zion

Brigham Young summed up Mormonism in 1862, fifteen years after the Saints entered the Salt Lake Valley: "Our Work, our everyday labor, our whole lives are within the scope of our religion."

Whether the Saints had driven a wagon, pushed and pulled a handcart, herded the cattle, or walked the entire route on blistered feet, the promise of better days and freedom to worship in peace awaited in the Valley of the Great Salt Lake. The Saints, some of whom had wandered along the banks of the Missouri and Mississippi rivers, and the flatlands of Illinois, Missouri, and Iowa for nearly fifteen years, found a haven at last near a huge salt-water lake and towering mountains.

Many of the pioneers waxed poetic when they recalled seeing the valley. They had surmounted tragedy, starvation, and struggle. Their faith and determination—and Brigham's exhortations and threats—had brought them home. It must have looked like heaven after the experience at Winter Quarters. It must have also felt like heaven. Wilford Woodruff wrote on July 24, 1847, thoughts that were no doubt shared by many who had traveled in that vanguard company:

> Our hearts were surely made glad after A Hard Journey from winter Quarters of 1,200 miles through flats of Platt River, steeps of the Black Hills & the Rocky mountains And burning sands of the eternal Sage . . . to gaze upon a valley of such vast extent entirely Surrounded with a perfect chain of everlasting hills & mountains Covered with eternal snow with there [sic] inumerable peaks . . . towards Heaven presenting at one view the grandest & most sublime seenery Probably that could be obtained on the globe. Thoughts of Pleasing meditation ran in rapid succession through our minds while we contemplated that not many years that the House of God would stand upon the top of the Mountains while the valleys would be converted into orchard, vineyard, gardings [sic] & field by the inhabitants of zion & the Standard be unfurled for the nations to gather.

Martha P. Jones Thomas, who left Nauvoo in the fall of 1846, with nothing but her eight children, "trusting God like Abraham," earned the money for a "fit-out" to Zion, by weaving in Council Bluffs. She summed up her experience with this comment: "Who could not acknowledge the hand of God in our deliverance."

Chapter 3

Trades and Chores

There was nothing left to barter for food. A nephew of Brigham Young's came to see me and . . . I told him what I needed, but I had nothing left but my Husbands violin and nobody wanted that. He replied he would take that but all he had was about a gallon of wine that had been given him in exchange for goods. . . . That I eagerly took and Elizabeth [a sister wife] lived on it for some time. —Jane Snyder Richards, fall 1846

Work for Goods or Cash

On February 25, 1846, hundreds of men looking sleep deprived stood huddled close to a campfire at Sugar Creek, Iowa, or walked around to check on their cattle. Roosters crowed and cows mooed to be milked. One of the men announced that it was 12 degrees below zero. A few children chased each other across the camp, while dogs barked and growled, and slipped down in the snow. Teenagers, staggering outside to tend to chores, yelled greetings to friends. Women, layered in heavy coats, stirred corn meal mush near an open fire in front of their tent, or held their hands toward the blaze to warm them for sewing or knitting. It was the coldest day since the first wagon crossed the Mississippi River three weeks earlier.

Colonel Hosea Stout and his hundred policemen armed with rifles guarded the camp. Another hundred men, under John Scott, guarded the three artillery wagons. The flag was raised, and the bugle gave a resounding blast as Brigham Young, obviously afflicted with rheumatism, came from his tent, climbed stiffly on his wagon, and called the camp together. Everyone except the animals gathered to listen: "Attention the Camps of Israel. [There are] jobs of chopping cord wood and splitting rails [which can] be obtained to advantage . . . on the Demoines river above Farmington. . . . Shall we go where we can get work?"

Of course, the brethren responded in the affirmative. The camp waited for some latecomers, and it was March 1 before they finally were ready to move toward the town of Farmington, a few miles away.

The good news that work was available was one of the first bright incidents since the hurried exodus from Nauvoo. One of the first duties the men performed while still encamped at Sugar Creek, was to build a log house for someone named James Wallace in exchange for the wood that the camp used from his claim.

On March 1, Heber C. Kimball announced a message to the whole camp from Brigham Young, who was sick in his tent: "[It is] my wish to move to another location that as long as we are so near Nauvoo, [the] men are continually going back and neglecting their teams and family, and running to me for counsel about a little property they have here or there or somewhere."

A few wagons pulled out immediately. Young waited in camp for his carriage, which arrived about sunset.

After they left Sugar Creek, the men had great success in securing contracts from local farmers for husking corn, splitting rails and fencing fields, grading stretches of roads, constructing bridges over troublesome streams, removing fallen dirt from coal beds, digging wells, building houses, clearing farms, and whatever other honorable employment allowed them to earn money and supplies. B. H. Roberts, a later Mormon historian, described the Mormon migrations of 1846–47 as "the march of an Industrial Column."

George Whitaker, age twenty-five and a convert from England, described the spirit of the workers on the trail in 1846: "Every man was put in his proper place to work. Some worked at cutting house logs, some at building houses, some at cutting timber for rails, some at splitting rails, some at plowing, some at planting corn and vegetables, while others commenced to put up the fence, and a certain number were sent out to herd and take care of the stock. Every man went to work with a will. There were no idlers amongst us. We were all full of life and spirit."

The highest known wage in 1846 was earned by sixteen-year-old George Washington Bean who said he received fifty cents per hour to unload barges at Montrose, Iowa. He said he could carry a "pig" of ore in each hand. (Each one weighs about 100 pounds.) Other men earned half that for doing the same chore.

Music Helps Feed the Pioneers

The first town they came to was Farmington. William Pitts's Brass Band played its first concert and was warmly applauded. Most of the time everyone worked in exchange for feed for animals and themselves. Occasionally they got a little money plus dinner. The settlements in Iowa nearer to the Missouri River offered the best opportunity for trading. Communities like Farmington and Bonaparte on the Des Moines River offered a bit of everything. Sometimes immigrants went south into the Missouri settlements to work and once raised a log house in exchange for oxen, cows, and provisions.

Those with musical talent discovered that they were in great demand everywhere. John M. Kay, a noted soloist with Pitts's Brass Band, sang for money, food, and drinks. (One night they made $25.70.) William Clayton, who played the violin, reported with considerable umbrage that a farmer "promised to give us [the band] some honey if we would play for him. . . . We learned afterward that [J. F.] Hutchinson had a pail under his cloak and got it full of honey . . . and kept it to himself, very slyly."

Later, at Council Bluffs Indian agent [Major Robert B.] Mitchell issued a welcome invitation to the band to perform for him and dine with him. Clayton noted on June 20, 1846: "Went with the band to hold a concert at the village. Many went from the camp. The Indians and half breeds collected 10 dollars and 10 cents and gave it to us and the agent Mr. Mitchel gave a dinner."

Leonora Taylor, who also attended this event, left a great description: "About seventy persons dined at Major Marshals [Mitchell's] they had quite a dance. There was a number of half breed Squaws danssed very well indeed, we went to the store and got some things we needed and had some songs from Br. [John M.] Kay and had a deal of musick upon the whole we spent a very pleasant day."

As Whitaker noted, the men each had a chore, but the women did most of their chores without much compensation. Leonora Taylor wrote June 21. "I knit & sewd in the tent all day took a long walk in the evening. . . . [We] sewed & knit, I could not dry the cloths. . . . [Two days later]. Pouring down rain . . . cut a pair of trousers for Father & began them. . . . Very hard storm came up." On July 15 in the Mount Pisgah area, Eliza R. Snow wrote in her diary: "commence[d] to braid. . . . I have braided for one hat pr. day since I return'd."

A spirit of good will and self-sufficiency emerged among most of the Saints who were able to stay healthy, a difficult task in itself. Once the main camp was selected and named Winter Quarters, some women without menfolk worked on constructing their own cabins, including applying mud to chinking. Eliza Maria Partridge Smith Lyman, a plural wife of Joseph Smith, then of Amasa M. Lyman, began to plan for better quarters in late October 1847:

> My sister Caroline and I have been trying to build a log house for ourselves as we do not feel quite comfortable where we are. . . . We first got possession of an old house which we pulled down and had the logs moved to a spot when we wanted it put up again. As we could not get any one to lay it up for us, we went at it ourselves then some brethren came and laid it up the rest of the way and put a dirt roof on it. Then I built a fireplace till it was about as high as my head, and some brother topped it off for me. We have one window and three panes of glass.

Caroline, Eliza's younger sister, was also a plural wife of Amasa Lyman.

Like these two sisters, women whose husbands were with the Mormon Battalion or on missions bore much of the responsibility of meeting their own needs, with moments of helpfulness like the men who helped the women finish their cabins. Brigham Young had promised to look after the battalion families and appointed eighty-eight bishops "to take care of the families of the soldiers." Robert Gardner Jr. was among these bishops: "Maney a evening I have visited the familes of men . . . in the Batalyon [Battalion] . . . and found them in open log houses without any chinken [caulking, or mud] and it snowed as fast inside as it did out side. . . . I would go and cut them some dry wood, help all I could, but it seemed hard times but there was no one there to blame for men was so scarce, and so maney sick and dying that I have had to go and help the sexson [sic] to biry the dead."

Joseph Lee Robinson, who settled in Winter Quarters, was asked to care for the wife of John Roylance, compassionately putting her needs first. He recalled: "We kept Sister Roylance with us. As she had no tent and some of her children were sick, I deemed it wisdom to first build her a house. So . . . we went to with our mights, cut and halved logs and put her up a little house, built a fireplace and moved her in."

Mormon converts from Europe who paused in big cities after arriving in America found work in places like New Orleans or St. Louis. In 1847, William K. Barton, a convert from England with his family "landed in New Orleans with six pence. I spent the winter there and then went up to St Louis the middle of April and obtained work at Peoples Garden. I got nine dollars per week painting. Kept me and my family."

John Davidson Burt, a young convert from Scotland, also found work in the mines near St. Louis in 1848: "While conversing with [a] driver, I learned that I could get employment at the mines if I were a miner. I told him that I was [and] rode out to Gravois, found employment, and in two days commenced working, earning from two to three dollars each day. I continued to labor in the mine and saved a little money and sent one hundred dollars to Scotland for the passage of my parents and brother to St. Louis, where they arrived in the fall of 1849." (This practice was soon discouraged because so many stayed permanently in those cities to work).

George Whitaker from England revealed the wage scale at Winter Quarters where Brigham Young tried to build a grist mill. He recalled that, in the spring of 1847, "I had been working on the mill dam and helping to dig the mill race for five or six weeks and was making a dollar and a quarter a day. I had taken the money home and it was a great help in supporting [my family.]" As a contrast, the sexton in Winter Quarters, Elijah Abel, received $1.50 per grave.

This project gave a lot of men the chance to earn the first money they had received in many months. It helped revive the spirits of the people and brought better food into the community. The sick season had eased and the weather was milder. Whitaker said it was the "most severe winter . . . I had . . . experienced before, or since." He also wrote that the ice was three feet thick on the Missouri River. "Teams traveled back and forth across the river for three months."

Pausing to Farm

Joseph Fish, who was age seven in 1847, recalled: "My father built a log house, fenced some land and put in some corn, doing what he could to provide for his family, and get means to continue the journey west. When after wood he would get out hickory timber and during the winter evenings shave out axe handles which he took to Trading Point and sold for 10 cents each."

Children as young as ten had to take major responsibility on the trail. David C. Hess inherited heavy burdens when his father died in June 1846, leaving him the oldest of four children at home. His brother John C. Hess was with the Mormon Battalion. David helped build a house of "bark elm, and put in a farm of buckwheat and corn" to support his mother and three siblings.

During planting season, some women followed the plows, dropping corn, potatoes, and other seeds. It was not uncommon to see a woman handle heavier farm chores. They also helped gather in the bounty in the fall. Eliza Maria Lyman, in addition to the expected female tasks of quilting, washing, and baking, "went and dug potatoes all day" on October 21, 1847. Two days later, she proudly recorded: "We dug 23 bushels today making 57 bushels of potatoes that we have put in the cellar. We live mostly on vegetables, but with very little corn."

Many of the leaders in Winter Quarters had farms and raised some vegetables that fall, but they were not too successful. George Whitaker, among many others, mentioned not seeing any vegetables for two years. Some of the women lost teeth and hair from scurvy. Eliza Maria Lyman wrote October 25, 1846: "My hair has nearly all come out, what little is left I have had to cut off. My head is so bare I am compelled to wear a cap." Louisa Barnes Pratt lost all of her teeth during those two years of sub-standard existence in the Winter Quarters area.

Trading and Barter

Skill at trade and barter was essential to survival in the cash-strapped frontier of the mid-1840s and '50s. In temporary camps like Mount Pisgah and Council Bluffs, Mormon craftsmen made baskets, chairs, wash boards, tables, shoes, cloth, clothing, goggles, and hats. Samuel Gifford made 400 chairs and sold them for $6.25 each. Some even cobbled together wagons and rifles from scrap iron.

William Huntington had barely settled at Garden Grove, Iowa, when he began to send back trade items to Missouri. On April 30, 1846, he received cheerful news: "I will say to my joy and that of the camp that a little before sundown my son John Arived in camp after an absence of ten days [of trading]... [and he] disposed of most of the Property they took with them. John sold our bed and got me a cow."

On July 2, 1846, Lorenzo Dow Young got his wagons across the river at night by a part-trade, part-cash arrangement: "Started and came to the river and crossed one waggon and three cow," he journaled. "... However after dark I learned the ferry boat was going over again to carry over Bro. Brigham. I went down and told them if they would take on my other two waggons I would treat to a half gallon [of wine?] and give fifty cents in cash. They agreed they would. I went over and got back about half after ten, tired almost to death." Young made another interesting trade earlier on Sunday, May 21, 1846: "This morning I went and traded my overcoat for a yoke of steers, got them home and yoked them up." He also sold his brother Brigham a cow for ten dollars.

Few financial avenues were open by which women could earn money during the 1840s and '50s except for sewing, baking, and teaching school. Martha Jones Thomas wove and dyed two hundred yards of plaid and striped material for dresses as well as forty yards for wagon covers while waiting in Kanesville (later Council Bluffs) to continue her journey to Zion. Some women spun yarn for fifty cents a week, while others worked in a boarding house for a dollar a week.

On November 6, 1846, Eliza Maria Lyman wrote: "Washed for Sister Hakes for which I got a bushel of corn to feed mother's cows."

Harriet Decker Young, in the summer of 1846, laid in a good supply of candles: "I took some wicks and set down after three o'clock in the afternoon and put on 26 dozen of wicks and dipped candles before I went to bed."

At Winter Quarters in 1847, Louisa Barnes Pratt and her four daughters were at the point of starvation just like everyone else. (Her husband was on a mission.) "On a time when I was out of food I went to Col. Rockwood with a request he would buy a feather bed of me, which I offered for 12 dollars. He was preparing to go to the mountains . . . and had not the means to spare. . . . I had nothing in my house to eat . . . and I [believed] deliverance will come in some unexpected way. I called at Brother Busby's. . . . He began inquiring about an old fashioned crane [a fireplace tool]. . . . 'If you will sell it, I will give you two bushels of corn meal and take one to your place this evening.'" Louisa agreed, and Busby delivered the corn meal as promised. The main cereal of that time, corn was often eaten, with slight variations, for all three meals.

Jane Snyder Richards made two important trades in the fall of 1846. One was swapping her husband's violin for wine but the other was a "bolt of cotton cloth" which she "was obliged to dispose of in exchange for the necessaries of life or to pay for services rendered me. [It] was intended as extra covering to the wagon." So many people had departed from Nauvoo without weather-tight covering for their wagons that Young complained: "I was forced to hand out cloth and tent ties" before they left Sugar Creek.

In the spring of 1847, George Whitaker, trying to prepare for the journey to Zion, received supplies and even a wagon from relatives, so he went to Iowa and Missouri to trade those items for

> our provisions and some cows and what we needed for the journey. . . . We would trade as we went along, if we saw anything we wanted. Sometimes we would go out of our way to farm houses to see if they had any wheat or corn for sale. So many of the brethren had been down . . . the country had been cleaned out for grain. Brother [in-law] Joseph Cain offered a saddle for sale. They said it was the very thing they wanted. Brother Cain wanted $10.00, they told him they would give him 60 bushels of corn for it. He soon closed the bargain and

we got our corn, bought our two cows, did our other trading . . . and started back for Winter Quarters.

Teaching School

The going rate for schoolteachers in 1847 in parts of the Midwest was one dollar per week, plus board. The wages were meager and, often as not, the teacher had to collect the tuition from his or her pupils in commodities. The board was often the bare necessities needed for survival. Records show that more than a dozen small schools sprang up at Winter Quarters. Emmeline B. Whitney, a plural wife of Newel K. Whitney, taught school for the Heber C. Kimball family in Winter Quarters in 1846–47. Louisa Barnes Pratt said her oldest daughter, age fourteen, also taught school for a while.

Lucy Meserve Smith, a plural wife of George A. Smith, had a gift for teaching Native American children that made her much sought after by Protestant missionaries and Indian agents. She taught at "the Pawnee mission school" near Council Bluffs for six months and proudly reported: "They, the Missionaries, offered me double wages if I would stay longer as I had such good control over the old folks as well as the children. . . . I was proud to earn money to purchase my necessaries to prepare for the valley. . . . [The children] wrote me a kind little token saying 'I love you well as my own people.' The Indian agent, Mr. Miller, [Mitchell?] and the interpreter, Mr. Saunsisee used to visit my school often. They took delight in hearing the children sing . . . . These men brought other agents in to see the progress of the children." Unfortunately, Lucy does not specify the amount of her wages.

When Martha Spence (later Heywood), a middle-aged schoolteacher who had joined the Church in Ireland, reached Council Bluffs on May 16, 1849, she began to look for work while awaiting the opportunity to continue her journey to the valley. She had traveled alone and felt displaced at first but soon found Mormon friends. She earned money by teaching and agreed with Brother Joseph Johnson for room and board, paid for with part of her earnings plus sewing. She mentioned in her journal that her "earnings turned out to be very meager."

Things had improved a year later. In 1850 Martha taught school for two dollars per week, with room and board provided: "I was anxious to get employment to earn my own living . . . . I spent a few days with Mrs. Joseph Young [in Council Bluffs] and while there the chance of a school opened itself which I accepted and in a few days located myself in Springville [probably Iowa] and found myself presiding over an interesting group of juveniles of all ages. . . . I have [now] located myself here in Joseph E. Johnson's family for the purpose of making 'Caps' but was disappointed in not getting materials."

Food and Wine

The Saints welcomed spring's wild fruit found in several spots along the Iowa route. Brigham Young twice mentions personally picking wild strawberries near Council Bluffs—on June 18 and June 19, 1846. Wild grapes ripened that fall. On October 7, 1846, Lorenzo Young and his wife, Harriet, "went up the River 12 miles to gather grapes. . . . Towards night we went to fix a place to camp." The next morning, they "rose early. . . . After picking about 3 hours, we had filled our vessles." That same month, Wilford Woodruff made about twenty gallons of wine from the wild grapes he picked. One unnamed sister made eighty gallons of elderberry wine and sold it "to get a fit out for going west from Council Bluffs." Patty Sessions and others also made what they called grape wine, while Leonora Taylor made beer on several occasions.

In the fall of 1846, Priddy Meeks was delighted to discover in upper Missouri that "here was chickasaw plums and . . . elderberres [sic] in right order for making wine, and we turned in and made eighty gallons of wine. We put a hundred and fifty pounds of sugar in it, which made it splendid. And it proved the means of my making a fitout in the spring." (That was nearly two pounds of sugar per gallon.) A folk, but effective, doctor, Meeks also earned some of his supplies by providing herbal medical assistance during the years in Iowa.

Once on the trail, the tasks of meal preparation broke the day into distinct periods. Women cooked a hot breakfast. Dinner at noon often consisted of cold left-overs, so that they could be on the trail again quickly. Supper was the biggest meal of the day, cooked once they had camped for the night. Some immigrants used small stoves, but most cooking was done over campfires. Cast-iron Dutch ovens were a versatile resource for either boiling or baking, since they could be set on the flames and have coals piled on the lid. Patty Sessions baked peach pies on a kettle of coals she had in her wagon.

John Jaques, traveling with the Martin Handcart Company, reported a heartbreaking cooking disaster for the already starving pioneers close to Devil's Gate. A number of the travelers combined their meager flour allotment to make a big loaf of bread and waited patiently for it to bake:

> When done, the bread was the whitest and lightest [we] had ever seen. When [we] came to eat it, the flavor was extraordinary We had never tasted anything like it before, and this is the way it happened. Somehow or another, about half a pound of soap had fallen unnoticed ... into the camp kettle and had frozen there. At night when the kettle was rinsed out, the soap remained fast at the bottom, still unnoticed in the dark. The kettle with water it in and the soap also was set on the fire to get hot. With ... the soapy water the bread was made and very soapy was the taste thereof, but the family could not afford to do without a day's rations, so some of them tried to eat it. Others refused.

Jaques's sister-in-law, Sarah Loader, commented that "it was the one time that John Jaques got all the bread he could eat for the other members did not relish it very well." A few days later the rescuers arrived and those starving Saints got some nourishing food and warm clothing.

Thirteen-year-old Mary Powell, traveling with the Ellsworth Handcart Company in 1856, was the oldest daughter in a family of eight. While waiting in camp to begin the journey, she recalled: "Each day I took pains to watch the women bake bread in their bake-kettles. I knew that I should have to do the baking when our own kettle came ... [so] I took the kettle and went off ... took dough and made twenty four beautiful brown biscuits. ... I took the biscuits and surprised Mother."

The Mormon women seldom had tables or chairs, meaning that they had to perch on wagon tongues with their plates in their laps to eat and from which they fed their youngsters. If they were not lucky enough to have a small stove in their wagon (which required constant climbing in and out), they had to cook over an open fire.

Smoke and dangling hair got in their eyes. Their backs ached from the constant stooping. Their clothing could blow into the flames if they were not constantly alert. Cooking in a rain or windstorm redoubled the difficulty. Sometimes women held an umbrella over themselves and tended the fire and food with the other hand.

Frederick Piercy, an English artist traveling with Mormons in 1853, praised American stoves and washboards: "The stoves with which they cook are a credit to the ingenious and economising spirit of America. [Some] English women told me that they really would not be able to manage with English stoves as with an ordinary American stove they could cook three times as much with a great deal less trouble. They also praised the American washing-board which have lately been improved upon by substitution of zinc. Wood, by repeated friction in water, becomes rough. . . . These washing machines certainly save labor."

Water for cooking often had to be scooped from muddy streams and contained animaculae big enough to be seen. At higher altitudes, a particular problem was the fact that water boiled at a lower temperature. This meant, for example, that beans could cook all day and never get tender.

When baking soda ran out, natural alkali, or saleratus, served as a substitute. It could usually be found on the shores of small lakes near Independence Rock. Many women said it was just as good as baking soda.

Churning turned out to be no chore at all on the trail. Cows were milked in the morning, the cream poured into the churn, the dasher added, and a clean towel tied around the top of the churn to exclude dust and dirt. Then the churn was fastened to the back or side of the wagon. The jolting during the day's travel churned the butter.

Harriet Decker Young, one of the three women in the vanguard company, noted on Sunday June 6, 1847, that she reverted to the old-fashioned way. "Remained in camp. . . . Held 2 meetings then started on and traveled 7 miles and camped . . . in the most beautiful place we have found. . . . I churned and picked a mess of greens, eat supper and went to bed."

Interestingly, the competent Harriet noted in her diary on May 26: "We set a hen, and think of trying our luck in raising chickens while traveling." They must have had plenty of chickens with them because it takes about a dozen eggs to "set a hen." Unfortunately, she does not comment on whether this experiment succeeded. It probably did not.

Fuel was seldom plentiful once the pioneers started up the Platte, and they became resourceful about picking up odd pieces of wood during the day, dried sunflower stalks, sagebrush, and "flood wood," that is, driftwood on the banks of the Platte or larger creeks. It was a rare treat to use surface coal near present Glenrock, Wyoming.

By far the most universal trail fuel was dung from the innumerable buffalo that had not yet been massacred to near-extinction in the 1840s and 1850s. This fuel went by a variety of names: buffalo chips, *bois de vache* ("wood of the cow"), meadow muffins, prairie coal, or cow pies. It is not surprising that dried dung burned; it was mainly grass. However, it burned quickly, as much as two or three bushels being required for the typical meal. It also had to be very dry, could not be used in stoves, and left many ashes. It burned without visible flames, like charcoal, and was also odorless, although a common joke was that a steak cooked over such fuel required no pepper. Hosea Stout reported that the women were displeased with the smell when chips became wet.

Howard Egan, who did the cooking and laundry for Heber C. Kimball in the 1847 vanguard company, reported on May 15, 1847: "The feed is good, but wood is very scarce and the buffalo chips are not a very good substitute for wood when they are wet. This morning I baked some bread and fried some antelope meat, made some coffee and had a very good breakfast, all cooked with wet buffalo chips."

Youngsters, especially the girls, were usually assigned the collection task. According to Edwin Pettit, an eleven-year-old orphan traveling with his sister in 1847, they started to see buffalo in western Nebraska and had plenty of chips for a while. "Some of the daintier sex, instead of picking them up with their hands, used tongs to gather them. Before we had gone very far, they got very bravely over this, and would almost fight over a dry one." James Linforth, a convert from England, commented in 1853: "Young ladies who in the commencement of the journey would hardly look at a chip, were now seen coming into the camp with as many as they could carry."

Buffalo chips even made their way into a folksong, author unknown:

> There's a pretty little girl in the outfit ahead.
> Whoa Haw Buck and Jerry Boy.
> I wish she were by my side instead.
> Whoa Haw Buck and Jerry Boy.
> Look at her now with a pout on her lips,
> As daintily with her fingertips
> She picks for the fire some buffalo chips,
> Whoa Haw Buck and Jerry Boy.

Brigham Young, noting the glee of the pioneers to hunt, issued a warning that there would be no "sport" killing of buffalo by Mormons. The pioneers began to see wood again near Fort Laramie. Archer Walters noted in his diary August 25, 1856: "Plenty of wood. Quite a treat after burning so many Buffalo Chips." Most fires were ignited with "lucifer matches," cherished for their immediacy; but flint and steel could also be used. A rather dangerous substitute was saturating a rag with damp gunpowder, sprinkling dry powder over it, and snapping a cap from a pistol near the rag. The exploding cap would ignite the gunpowder which would, in turn, ignite the cloth.

Primitive Dental Work

Some Saints tried their hand at "doctoring," and cleaned and pulled teeth. The going rate appears to have been $3.00 for cleaning teeth and doctoring, but few Saints had that much cash.

Luke Johnson, traveling with the vanguard company in 1847, pulled teeth. William Clayton wrote on April 20, soon after they got on the trail: "After Brother Luke Johnson had got through distributing fish, I . . . asked him to draw my tooth. He willingly agreed. And getting his instruments, I set down in a chair, he lanced the gum, and took his nippers and jerked it out. The whole operation did not take more than one minute. He only got half the original tooth, the balance being left in the jaw. After this my head and face pained me much more than before." It was two days of severe pain before Clayton could stand to eat much. Apparently the rest of the tooth stayed in his mouth.

On October 31, 1846, Lorenzo Dow Young took matters into his own hands. He wrote. "Was sick all day with distress in my head caused by an ulcer tooth." Four days later, still "in dreadful distress," that evening "I got a pair of nippers and drew it, which soon reli[e]ved my distress. Better this morning but was obliged to stay in the house."

There is little said in journals about oral hygiene, but Martha Haven asked her mother to send a toothbrush to Winter Quarters because "there are none here" even though the store stocked such homey items as dress patterns.

Council Bluffs and the Overlanders

Although the Mormons began their migration to Utah in 1847, the Latter-day Saint population at Council Bluffs continued to be replenished by new converts as well as by those unable to continue their journey immediately. It was a popular jumping-off place for the California '49ers when news of the goldfields reached the East. The Saints made great money by providing needed goods and services including grinding wheat, shoeing horses, and repairing wagons.

The women baked bread, sold lemon powder, made flour sacks, spun, knitted, made leggings and other items from deer hides, sewed linen shirts, baked pies, bread, and cakes, and boarded the California-bound travelers. Men traveling to California without their families often found poor victuals at the taverns and were willing to pay well for home-cooked meals. According to Mary Ann Stearns, she and her mother, Mary Ann Frost Stearns Pratt, who started west in 1852, did many of these same things: "Early in the spring as the California emigrants came along we baked bread for them, sliced it, and dried it in the oven, so they could have something to eat when it was not convenient for them to cook." This method made a hard, dry type of cracker or sea bread. "We also made cotton floursacks for the emigrants to put their provisions in at 75 cent each hundred, but sewing by hand was rather slow work."

Sarah Studevant Leavitt, a widow with twelve children, six of them still at home in 1849, found the California-bound travelers a godsend:

> My whole mind was engaged in preparing for our journey to the valley. I did everything in my power to accomplish this great work. I

made eleven fine linen shirts for the merchant; I baked pies and bread and cakes for the grocery the boys [her sons?] kept, as there were lots of gold diggers on the way to California. . . . We had a market for everything. There was lots of big men boarding at the tavern. Some of them came to us for victuals, as their fare at the tavern was very poor. . . . It was a great undertaking, as I had but two boys, the oldest fourteen years old, and three girls, two of them young children.

In 1852 William Barton, who had stayed in St. Louis to earn money, moved upriver to Council Bluffs and energetically began working and planning as usual. He doesn't give much credit to anyone else, but I'm sure Sister Barton did her share of the work:

> I . . . built a boarding house for the emigrants . . . charged fifty cents a meal, and also commenced baking light bread. . . . Then I thought I could make lemonade powder, which thing I accomplished, and hired a man to mind my store while I attended to make the powder up. I sold it for fifty cents per pound. I also had a good many goggle glasses to cut, which brought me a cent a glass. In five weeks . . . I had made my fitout which consisted of a span of horses, one yoke of oxen, two yokes of cows, and a good wagon. I paid my debts, sold my cabin . . . and started [to Zion] with five cents in cash, but I had plenty of coffee, sugar, tea, and soap.

According to '49er Margaret Haun, a young bride, they had already been on the road for a month by the time they reached Council Bluffs, where prices were cheap compared to what they would have to pay in California: "Eggs were 2 1/2 cents a dozen—at our journey's end we paid $1 a piece. . . . Chickens were worth eight and ten cents a piece. When we reached Sacramento $10 was the ruling price and few to be had at that. . . . It took us four days to organize [and] bring our wagons and animals to the highest possible standard . . . and say good bye to civilization at Council Bluffs. Owing to the cheapness of eggs and chickens we reveled in their luxuries, carrying a big supply, ready cooked with us."

Trade on the Trail

Lorenzo Dow Young, traveling east in late May 1849 with wife Harriet and her young son, Perry Decker, and about a dozen other Saints on a mission to bring supplies back to the Salt Lake

Valley, mentioned a spectacular trade he made while camped at Fort Laramie. This example shows the eagerness of the California-bound travelers to get to the gold fields: "A man from Ohio showed [us] a valuable horse . . . reduced in flesh, a new wagon, a valuable set of carpenter and joiner tools, everything pertaining to a good camp outfit and a good stock of provision for four men . . . worth between three and four hundred dollars. He traded this property . . . for a California pony worth . . . about forty dollars."

Lorenzo also had orders to escort Dr. John M. Bernhisel to the Missouri River to act as the Church agent to the federal government in Washington, D.C. Young was also sent back east to bring fruit trees, groceries, clothing, and a flock of sheep. Lorenzo got so very sick before returning to Utah in the spring of 1850 that he ordered a "zinc coffin" in case of his death. Although they bought 200 tree seedlings and hired an extra wagon and driver to drive them to the valley, only three trees matured. He also bought 500 sheep and 80 head of cattle, but 127 of the sheep were lost to a miserable night of rain, mud, sleepy night guards, and hungry wolves. They also had a lot of trouble with Indians both coming and going back, and two California teamsters deserted them midway on the trail for an easier trip to the gold mines. One might call it the trip through hell, but Lorenzo regarded the expedition stoically.

Fort Laramie: An Oasis on the Trail

On the trail itself, opportunities for trading were limited to within one's own company, except at Fort Laramie and Fort Bridger. Archer Walters, a member of the Willie Handcart Company in 1856, wrote: "Camped 3 miles from Fort Laramie. Trucked away [traded] a dagger for a piece of bacon and salt and sold one for One dollar and one-fourth. Bought bacon and meal and Henry [his son] and me began to eat it raw we were so hungry." John Jaques, who was traveling in the Martin Handcart Company the same year, recorded in his diary on October 8, at Fort Laramie: "I took a cup of tea at Brother Haven's and another at Sister Dove's. Got a little salaratus from Brother Haven and a little salt from another brother." The next day, he and several men in the company went to Fort Laramie "to buy provisions, etc. I went and sold my watch for thirteen dollars. I bought from the fort commissariat 20 pounds of biscuit at 15 cents, twelve pounds of bacon at 15 cents and 3 pounds of rice at 17 cents and so on."

West of the Missouri River, Mormon blacksmiths found their services in heavy demand, especially to reset wagon tires and shoe animals. In 1847 at Fort Laramie, for example, Appleton Harmon stayed for the winter of 1847–48, earned $300 as a blacksmith, and went back to Winter Quarters to get his wife.

Some said no to instant cash. Thomas D. Evans, an ironworker from Wales, "was offered $10 per day to remain in Iowa City, but money was no inducement to me then, as I had looked forward so long to the time when I would be released to emigrate to Zion. Many of those who stayed behind to better their circumstanced died of cholera, and many apostatized."

Saints also established ferries on the Elkhorn, Loup, Platte, and Green rivers and did some contract bridging of the Green River and parts of Echo Canyon (in present Utah).

An example of particular resourcefulness was that of Thomas Waters Cropper, who had traveled to Zion in 1856 as a boy. As a young man in 1864, he served as a "down-and-back" teamster—taking wagons from the Valley to meet Mormon immigrants at whatever point the railroad:

> One of the teamsters bantered me into a trade—his buckskin pants for my cotton ones. His [pants] had been wet and had shrunk. His were way too short [and] I could not wear them but the trade had been made. I had a cow hide in my wagon [and] while riding I cut the pants and the cow hide into strips and braided nice ox whips. I put a sign on the wagon, "Whips for Sale". We were meeting many immigrants and the whips sold readily at $1.00 each. I obtained $20.00 from the sales. This, together with the money I earned while waiting for the immigrants, I spent for clothing and equipment. A trunk cost me $5.00; a suit of clothes was $12.00; a pair of shoes, $2.00. I came home a well dressed young man.

Wagons

The Saints used all kinds of wagons, buggies, and carriages as they set out westward. Most were ordinary reinforced farm wagons, about ten to twelve feet long and about four feet wide; generally made of hardwoods such as ash, elm, maple, hickory, and oak with hoops over which twilled cotton cloth or waterproof canvas was spread. These coverings could be closed at each end. The huge, lumbering Conestoga wagons, beloved of Hollywood, were seldom seen on the trail.

Because the trail required fording so many streams, the wagon bottoms were usually caulked or covered with canvas so they would float. The pioneers of 1847 had great luck with a homemade boat made of leather covering a wooden frame. They called it the "Revenue Cutter." Oregon-bound pioneers used animal hides as early as 1843 to cover canoes.

In the main Mormon exodus of 1848, the wagons were marked with the initials of their leaders or numbered according to whatever group they belonged to in an attempt to keep better order in the daily line of march. These numbers also sometimes indicated who was first in line to cross the river. Mormons seldom named their wagon tops, but other pioneers painted on names and mottos like "Badgers," "Hoosiers," "Rough and Ready," or "Ho! for California" in bold letters.

Not all wagons were headed west. Some turned back east, having "seen the elephant" one time too many. Amelia Stewart Knight, en route to Oregon, caught the pathos of one family on Sunday, May 6, 1853: "Here we passed a train of wagons on their way back, the head man had been drowned a few days before in the river called Elkhorn . . . and his wife lying in the wagon quite sick, and the children were mourning for the father. With sadness and pity I passed those who perhaps a few days before had been well and happy as ourselves."

Other Domestic Chores

With few labor-saving devices, the burden of other domestic multiplied. Washing clothes was always an arduous task for women, and laundry on the trail was particularly difficult. Thomas L. Kane, who visited the Mormon camps in 1846 at Winter Quarters, found Mormon laundresses a colorful note: "Along the little creek I had to cross were women in greater force than blanchisseuses upon the Seine, washing and rinsing all manner of white muslins, red flannel, and parti colored calicoes, and hanging them to bleach upon a greater area of grass and bushes than we can display in all our Washington Square."

In 1848 Emily Dow Partridge Young, one of Brigham's plural wives, left a charming and highly romanticized account of "wash day" on the trail:

> Once a week we stopped for a general wash day. Fires would be kindled here and there, children sent for wood to keep them up; tubs, washboards, and other things used in washing would be dragged forth from their places in the wagons; posts fixed in the ground and where there were not bushes enough, the lines stretched from one [post] to the other; and everyone doing something, if it was only singing a lively song or whistling a merry tune to keep the workers in good humor. In the morning the train of wagons would be off again, clean and neat as such conditions could make them.

This delightful picture probably eroded into a much more sporadic schedule under the rigors of trail life. More often, women seized opportunities such as a wagon break-down en route if they were near enough water. Some, either without washtubs or the time to unpack them planted clothing in a stream and stamped vigorously with bare feet. William Clayton and Wilford Woodruff, traveling with the vanguard company in the summer of 1847, complained that washing clothes rubbed the skin off their fingers. Washboards of the period were whittled of solid wood, not the lighter zinc that soon replaced it. The men had obviously been contented to leave the laundry to their wives.

Strong lye soap was the detergent of choice; but when it gave out along the trail, women had no time or materials (lye, animal fat, and ashes were required) to make new soap. They quickly learned to use cactus agave, which looked something like a pineapple and, when pounded, frothed up into good suds. Men sometimes helped to the extent of making and feeding the fires under the kettles in which the clothes were boiled, and hauling the endless buckets of water. Getting clothes really clean was a constant problem, and most women took the philosophical position that their newly washed clothes, though not quite white, were quite clean for "brown."

Howard Egan accepted the duty of also doing Heber C. Kimball's laundry while traveling with the 1847 vanguard company. However, he also relinquished it at the first opportunity. En route back from the Valley to Winter Quarters in September 1847, his company encountered a company of Valley-bound Saints and camped together: "Took supper with Brother Samuel Moore this evening. Sister Moore washed some clothes for me. The evening was pleasant."

Mormon women's sphere encompassed the duties of making and maintaining clothing—in fact, virtually anything to do with fabric except in exceptional circumstances where no women were available. Patty Sessions records in her diary of knitting a mitten on February 12, 1846, while crossing the Mississippi River from Nauvoo. The next day, she "made me two red night caps out of flannel." On March 17, 1846, while she was camped in Iowa, Patty ironed.

Eliza R. Snow, who was traveling with the Markham family recorded on February 14, 1846, that she and Sister Markham "did some needlework tho the melting snow dripped thro our [wagon] cover." Eliza Maria Partridge Lyman stayed in the home of Sidney Tanner, the brother-in-law of her husband, Amasa Lyman, in Iowa on February 10, 1846. During her stay, "I cut and made a dress for Mother Tanner." A week later, "Mother Tanner gave br [Amasa] Lyman twelve yards of factory [material] to line his waggon cover, which I made in the morning. About two o'clock we started for the camp [Sugar Creek Camp] where we arrived about sundown."

Camped in tents in the fall of 1846, the women sewed even before their huts were constructed. Virginian Barbara Ann Evans, who had joined the Church in 1836 at age eighteen, "did considerable spinning in the tent [near Council Bluffs], also quilted several quilts. One great blessing, we were generally well. . . . The men cut hay and put up log huts. My husband [David] made a sideloom, and I did considerable weaving that winter."

Ten years later, John Powell, while waiting for repairs on a handcart, "secured work." According to his daughter, Mary Powell Sabin, "He laid the foundation, also dressed the corner-stone for the first court-house in Omaha. He received eight dollars per day. He needed this money for said he. 'I cannot let my children go bare-footed across the plains.' Father brought me a pair of shoes, the ugliest I've ever seen in my life. It was the best he could get . . . . This man offered father eighty acres of land if he would settle in Nebraska. He also was willing to help erect a house for us." Powell refused.

A few Mormons, especially in the handcart groups, did stay in Iowa and Florence, Nebraska. That decision might have saved their lives. While many of the Saints died before they reached their promised land, others no doubt shared the sentiment of Jane Snyder Richards, who said, while giving birth while starving and bereaved: "I lived because I could not die." A violin for a gallon of wine, and a leather saddle for sixty bushels of grain tells a story of survival—a picture of giving and receiving worthy of a poet or an artist.

Chapter 4

Recreation and Social Activities

[The Twelve led] off the dancing in a great double cotillion, [which] was the signal [that] bade the festivity commence [and] they did dance. French fours, Copenhagen jigs, Virginia reels and the like forgotten figures executed with the spirit of people too happy to be slow, or bashful, or constrained. Light hearts, lithe figures, and light feet . . . —Thomas L. Kane, July 1846

Dancing

In February 1847, Brigham Young urged those who were well enough at Winter Quarters to "dance all night. . . . I want you to sing and dance and forget your troubles. . . . Let's have some music and all of you dance . . . dance all night if you desire to, for there is no harm in it." The dance chased away the blues where Mormons camped in the fall of 1846 and the winter of 1846–47. Dancing was probably the number one diversion during that time. Latter-day Saints have always loved this activity and eagerly adopted Psalm 150 for its inspiration: "Praise ye the Lord . . . praise him with the timbrel and dance." Saints danced in the Nauvoo Temple's unfinished second story during the winter of 1845–46. Orson Hyde left one charming story about Parley P. Pratt who apparently was not among those with "light feet." "When dancing was first introduced in Nauvoo among the Saints, I observed Brother Parley standing in the figure and he was making no motion particularly, only up and down. Says I, 'Brother Parley, why don't you move forward?' Says he, 'When I think which way I am going, I forget the step and when I think of the step I forget which way to go.'"

The weather did not interfere with dancing at Sugar Creek. The Mormons danced because they were happy and danced because they were sad. They danced in the snow and danced in the mud. They danced because entertainment, socializing, singing, concerts, dancing, and other activities helped lighten the burden of the exodus.

Helen Mar Kimball Whitney said the only way they could get warm in the camp at Sugar Creek (and later) was to dance: "The band played every evening . . . there being quite a number of young people in my father's family we could form a cotillion or French four by the big log fire, and often we did so at evening, and danced to amuse ourselves as well as to keep our blood in proper circulation. I there took my first lesson in the Danish waltz. The weather was so cold it was impossible to keep warm without exercise."

This Danish waltz was not as "risque" as the standard waltz, made popular in Europe in the early nineteenth century. Young forbade anyone from participating in that more scandalous dance in his presence. Leaders suppressed protests by asking, "Under what other circumstances could you catch a man holding your wife or daughter like that and not get very suspicious?"

Dancing was a universal pastime, one requiring no special talent or props. In the absence of musical instruments, hand clapping or singing would serve. Thomas Evans Jeremy, returning from a mission to Wales in 1864, wrote on the Sweetwater: "The French, English, and Welsh each tr[ied] to excell each other in dancing." Square and line dances, such as reels, quadrilles, or French fours were popular. Albert Perry Rockwood wrote on April 30, 1847, two weeks into the pioneer journey: "While I am yet wrighti[ng], the violen is going and the brothery are dansing and make merry." Later he wrote down part of a square dance call: "Dosi doe, swing your partner, sachee all, four fins forward and back."

Louisa Barnes Pratt recorded: "When we camped near a level spot of earth . . . the young men would propose a dance. The older ones feeling the absolute need of diversion would accede, as it would cost nothing and would most likely cheer and enliven us on our wearisome journey."

Emmeline B. Whitney (then Newel K. Whitney's plural wife and later Daniel H. Wells's plural wife) mentioned flourishing camp activities in March 1846. About nine days after they left Sugar Creek, her company "pitched ... [our] tents on the side hill ... in rows like a city; it is really a houseless village. Just at dusk the band commenced playing and some of the young people collected and amused themselves by dancing." One of those was Helen Mar Kimball Whitney, the young wife of Newel's son Horace: "The first evening after the warm sun had dried the earth, the young people were out dancing by moonlight determined upon being happy, or at least to snatch all the pleasant moments and enjoy them as they came along."

Thomas Kane viewed the farewell ball held for the Mormon Battalion the evening before the new soldiers departed for Fort Leavenworth in July 1846, and he describes it as a lively affair: "None of your minuets or other mortuary processions ... in etiquette, tight shoes, and pinching gloves, but the spirited and scientific displays of our venerated and merry grandparents, who were not above following the fiddle to the Foxchase Inn or Gardens of Gray's Ferry."

Dancing schools were organized at Winter Quarters in the winter of 1846–47 to give more people a chance to learn those cotillions and Virginia reels. Richard Ballantyne, a young convert from Scotland, described a school conducted across the river at Council Bluffs:

> To keep up the desponding spirits of the Saints, and to prevent as many as possible from being discouraged, President Young gave encouragement to dancing. As many did not know how, dancing schools were established. The cheering music and social pleasure found in this exhilarating exercise did much to comfort the Saints and to dispel their gloom. This I believe, was the beginning of that dancing, which ever since, has been one of the favorite past times in the Church. At first these dances were opened with praise and prayer and interspersed with short and appropriate speeches and songs, and were meetings at which much of the spirit of God was present. And it was the aim and purpose of the authorities to so mix up devotional exercises with pleasure that no excesses ... should be indulged in.... Our house was opened for a dancing school and social parties. Here was where the polygamy dance was first originated.

The polygamy dance—one male partner dancing with a woman on each arm—was still popular in 1860, though the name might have been changed to the "Scottish Reel." At this early stage, even if polygamy were not a factor, the young women would not have had many partners to dance with because so many were away in the Mormon Battalion, trading, or serving proselytizing missions. Among the students were Wilford Woodruff and other members of the Twelve who also met "to learn the proper Steps in dancing."

The young people made way for the 'Silver Greys' in February 1847 at Winter Quarters: "Patriarch John Smith . . . exhorted the brethren and sister to dance, sing, and enjoy themselves. . . . The center of the floor was then cleared for the dance [and] the 'Silver Greys' and spectacled dames enjoyed themselves; it was indeed an interesting and novel sight, to behold the old men and women, some nearly an hundred years old, dancing like ancient Israel."

About two weeks later, a Police Ball was held. Chief of Police Hosea Stout wrote on March 2, 1847: "We had the Police, Twelve & Band present and enjoyed ourselves uncommonly well by dancing, talking, eating sweet cakes & and some little preaching and about had the old Police dance called 'President Marks' return to mormonism, which I may describe some time. . . . [T]he party [lasted] until three o'clock A.M. . . . It is almost unnecessary to say that the Twelve seemed to enjoy themselves well."

Near Independence Rock, Martin Luther Ensign's company "had a dance on the rock." Much "fiddling and dancing" occurred on the rock, but Martin's 1847 company was probably first to dance a cotillion there. Sophia Goodridge in 1850 also danced at Independence Rock. "This evening we had a dance on the banks of the Sweetwater. The whole company participated." Sophia no doubt played her melodeon, an instrument similar to today's accordion. (Several travelers on the Oregon Trail noted that girls played guitars and accordions, but such an accomplishment was comparatively rare among the Saints).

Some emigrants en route to Oregon thought dancing was a great sin, especially Southern Baptists. Sallie Hester of Illinois traveled to California in 1849 with a "Missionary Train" who observed a rigorous Sabbath and maintained limitations on other activities.

Such companies were the exception, however. Dancing was so popular that, in some Oregon- and California-bound companies lacking enough women, men often took the part of women. Lucy Rutledge Cooke, in a letter to her sister Polly, described three men, including her husband William, who dressed like women for a dance at Devil's Gate in 1852. "The Bull Heads [teamsters] all amused themselves with dancing after supper in which Wm joined as hearty as any, the cook of the company we had camped with . . . had found . . . a bundle of woman's clothing which he had put on [and] there was such a demand for this lady for a partner that Wm came for my saque dress & sun bonnet to wear. Oh what guys!" Louisa Barnes Pratt wrote about Ephraim Hanks's escapades. He dressed like a woman, danced, and amused the Saints in 1846 by flirting outrageously. It was thought he "was a female from another company, and provided a lot of amusement to those in on the secret," she commented.

Heber Robert McBride, a "down and back" driver in 1865, "found a company of Danish saints under captin atwood and they were very glad to see us we held meeting [and] had a dance they had music but we could not dance, for we could not dance their way and they could not dance our way." McBride was one of a group of young men who were annually "called" to render this service and drive their own wagon to the staging place, usually in eastern Nebraska. Brigham Young and Heber C. Kimball usually sent a squad of their own personal wagons and drivers.

Music and Singing

Those who loved to sing had many opportunities in the Winter Quarters area. Many evenings were devoted to this activity. Even those with little energy for dancing could still sing. Most trail companies had at least a fiddler, a mouth organist, or an accordion player. Some could muster two or three instruments such as a violin, a fife, and a drummer. A few even had entire bands. Eliza R. Snow commented near Garden Grove, Iowa in 1846, "The morning was ushered in with the music of the band, which was delightfully sublime."

Snow also wrote a number of "Songs of the Exodus." She composed "Song No. 2" (below) as they left Sugar Creek, and her fellow travelers probably repeated it frequently to cheer up the camp. Significantly, she used the term "All is well" six weeks before William Clayton employed it as the refrain for his famous "Come, Come, Ye Saints," whose original title was called: "All is Well."

Song for the Pioneers No 2
The Camp of Israel
By Eliza R. Snow

All at once is life in motion
Trunks and beds & baggage fly;
Oxen yok'd & horses harness'd
Tents roll'd up, are passing by.
Soon the carriage wheels are rolling
Onward to a woodland dell,
Where at sunset all are quarter'd
Camp of Israel! All is well.

Thomas L. Kane praised a young singer at the farewell ball for the Mormon Battalion in 1846: "A well cultivated mezzo soprano voice, belonging to a young lady with fair face and dark eyes gave with quartette accompaniment a little song, the notes of which I have been unsuccessful in repeated efforts to obtain: 'By the rivers of Babylon we sat down and wept. We wept when we remembered Zion.' There was danger of some expression of feeling when the song was over, for it had begun to draw tears but breaking the quiet with his hard voice, an Elder asked the blessing of heaven on all." This young mezzo-soprano was Susan Divine, and the song was "The Maid of Judah," sung to the tune of "Down by the River's Verdant Side."

Kane also admired Pitts's Brass Band: "I knew the peculiar fondness of the Mormons for music, their orchestra in service on this occasion [Battalion farewell ball] astonished me by its numbers and fire drill. The story was, that an eloquent Mormon missionary had converted its members in a body at an English town, a stronghold of the sect, and that they took up their trumpets, trombones, drums, and hautboys together, and followed him to America."

A subgroup in Pitts's Brass Band, the Quadrille Band, played for the popular square and line dances. The first handcart company of 1856 included the Birmingham Band, and in 1863 the emigrant ship *Alesto* had a full brass band of converts from South Wales.

All companies sang popular songs and hymns. Orson Pratt wrote in 1846: "During the evening, as usual, the animating sounds of music, in different parts of the camp, seemed to break gently in upon the surrounding solitudes of these uninhabited regions." Mormons favored hymns such as "The Morning Breaks," "Redeemer of Israel," "How Firm a Foundation," "The Spirit of God," "O My Father," "Hail to the Prophet," and "Come All Ye Sons of Zion,"—hymns still sung today. The most famous Mormon hymn of them all, the Mormon "Marseilles," was the poignant "Come, Come, Ye Saints."

A livelier trail song was the anticipatory "On the Way to California":

> Now in the spring we'll leave Nauvoo,
> And our journey we'll pursue.
> Bid the robbers all farewell,
> And let them go to Heav'n or Hell.
> Down on Nauvoo's green grassy plains,
> They burn'd our houses and our grain,
> When they thot we were hell bent,
> They asked for aid from the Government.
>
> Chorus:
>
> On the way to California,
> In the spring we'll take our journey,
> Pass between the Rocky Mountains,
> For beyond the Arkansas fountains. . . .

Perhaps the second most famous pioneering song was the stirring "The Handcart Song" by John Daniel Thomas McAllister. Some of the immigrants participating in the "divine plan" grew so tired of that song before the journey ended, that they refused to sing it. The second verse reads:

> Ye Saints that dwell on Europe's shores,
> Prepare yourselves with many more
> To leave behind your native land
> For sure God's Judgments are at hand.
> Prepare to cross the stormy main
> Before you do the valley gain
> And with the faithful make a start
> To cross the plains with your hand cart.

Chorus:

For some must push and some must pull
As we go marching up the hill,
As merrily on the way we go
Until we reach the valley, oh.

In the spring of 1857, Brigham Young sent a hand-picked group
of healthy young missionaries east to Florence with handcarts, a
public relations gesture to erase the disastrous ending to the previous season's handcart experience that had trapped the Willie and
Martin companies in Wyoming. Phillip Margetts, a London-born
actor in the group, wrote a jaunty marching song to the tune of "Oh,
Susannah":

No purse, no scrip they bear with them,
But cheerfully they start
And across the plains a thousand miles
And draw with them a cart.
Ye nations, list the men of God
From Zion now they come,
Clothed with the Priesthood and the power
To gather Israel home!
Then cheer up ye Elders
You to the world will show,
That Israel must be gathered soon,
And oxen are too slow.

After reaching Florence, these travelers rested seven days, left
their handcarts behind, and departed for their respective missions.

Parties and Entertainment

The leaders were aware of the importance of social diversions
during trying times, and the trek across Iowa in the spring of 1846
was one of the worst they would endure, followed by a staggering toll
of illness that summer. Mount Pisgah buried about eighty people in
1846-47; but in the fall of 1846, they tried to push gloom aside and
celebrate a bit. Eliza R. Snow wrote about the party given by her
brother, Apostle Lorenzo Snow, and his four wives. Straw substituted for a real floor, its dust sprinkled down with water: "[They]
draped the long walls with the sheet-casing of featherbeds that had

long since been traded for food, and lighted the single room with tallow dips stuck in hollowed-out turnips and made lanterns. They made their own music, toasts, riddles and ended the night with a dish of succotash and prayer." It was a party on the prairie that most of them never forgot.

Quilting parties were so common that they were seldom noted, but many women mentioned making quilts or helping someone make one.

When Charles C. Rich and his family left Mount Pisgah for Winter Quarters in the spring of 1847, Sister Sarah Pea Rich wrote: "Before we left Pisgah the brethren and sisters got up a party for our benefit. . . . There were about one hundred people there. . . . We had a good time and good feelings prevail[ed]; all was sorry to part with us."

Paying calls and having friends for tea parties were popular ways of promoting domesticity and preserving the social amenities of their former lives. Lorenzo and Harriet Young frequently mentioned that visitors "stopped by for tea" in the fall of 1846.

When Brigham Young's vanguard company, returning from the Salt Lake Valley to Winter Quarters, encountered two other Mormon companies on the Sweetwater on September 7, Thomas Bullock recorded impressive festivities, possibly the largest Mormon feast on the trail. Despite a "cold boisterous wind," sleet, hail, and snow, the Taylor and Horne units prepared a banquet for about 130. Thomas Bullock recorded the menu in loving detail: "Roast & boiled Beef, Veal (they had killed the fatted Calf to make merry), Pies, Cakes, Biscuits, Butter, Peaches, with coffee, Tea, Sugar, Cream & a variety of the good things of life." The tables were set with Taylor's white linen and good silverware. B. H. Roberts, who later compiled an account for his *Comprehensive History of the Church*, described: "Several improvised tables of uncommon length covered with snow white linen, and fast being burdened with glittering tableware, gave evidence that a surprise was in store for the weary Pioneers. Supper over and cleared away, preparation were made for dancing, and soon was added to the sweet confusion of laughter and cheerful conversation, the merry strains of the violin. . . . Dancing was interspersed with songs and recitation." Bullock added a bit more about the dancing: "Afterward the brethren & sisters tript 'the light fantastic toe' in the dance, making a large fire in the Willow Patches, which they kept up until about 10 or 11 o'clock."

The merriment came just in time. The next night they camped with Jedediah M. Grant's company, apparently posted no guards, and awakened the next morning to find that Indians had stolen fifty-two horses. Only five were recovered. Thirty belonged to the pioneers, and it was a loss they felt for the rest of their journey.

An example of a Union Supper, held by California-bound emigrants on May 23, 1852, was recorded by Amanda M. Matthews:

> Today lay by resting teams, very pleasant and warm, some of the company killed two deer and an antelope in the afternoon we made a union supper of which each one provided a share, the contents of the table were of four different kinds of meat. A roasted goose, antelope, deer, and pork ham. Light bread with biscuits, Potatoes and beans, onions and pickles, butter and cheese, molasses and honey, apple and peach sauce, pies and cakes. Coffee, tea, and milk with white and brown sugar. Our table consisted of boards taken from our waggons and placed yokes through the center of the barrel and covered with tin dishes, thirty or upwards of us seated on the ground around it. . . . as happy as if seated in a city dining room amid all the splendor earth could afford.

Entrepreneurs along the westward trail offered several forms of entertainment for which even the poverty-stricken Mormons dug up admission. One was panoramas, a travelogue featuring a long pictorial canvas rolled between two slowly revolving cylinders. Kanesville, Winter Quarters, and military posts could frequently mount theater productions or display trained bears. Perhaps the most unusual entertainment was provided by David Moore, a Mormon who crossed Iowa in 1849 with a "learned pig and a magic lantern."

In other cases, pioneers made their own entertainment with mock trials and elections. In the 1847 pioneer company, James Davenport was accused of "blocking the highway and turning ladies out of the way," and "Father" Chamberlain was voted the "most even-tempered man in camp—always cross and quarrelsome." On occasion a "scolding master" was appointed. Sometimes a "camp grumbler" was designated, the only one in camp permitted to find fault. Anyone who had complaining to do had to first call on the camp grumbler—a harmless bit of nonsense which might have defused a few tense moments.

Educational Activities

Educational opportunities such as star-gazing, choir practice, recitation contests, and other mental activities were encouraged. Joseph Fish remembered excelling at Council Point: "During the winter of 1847-48 my brother-in-law, John C. L. Smith taught school. . . . The following winter I attended school . . . which was taught by Brother [John?] Brown, who later became a prominent teacher in Ogden. . . . Our school went up to Kanesville to compete with the school there and came off with the honors. Every one of our schools had a banner with the words 'Go Ahead.' My sister Jane and I gave several dialogues and recitations at the contest."

Orson Pratt brought his telescope on the trail in the summer of 1847. On April 24, he and fellow travelers marveled at the magnified moons of Jupiter. The vast expanse of the plains and clear skies free of modern haze and artificial light presented stunning night skies. Robert Stoney recorded seeing "the aurora borealis, or northern lights, . . . very clear." Perhaps the brethren debated which of all the visible stars might be Kolob, which, according to Mormon belief is one of the great governing stars, closest to the throne of God, so important that its revolutions determine "the reckoning of the Lord's time" at the traditional ratio of 1,000 years of earth time to one day with the Lord. With a little experience one could use the Big Dipper and the North Star as a night-time clock. (They probably did not know that the pot of the Big Dipper has 600 galaxies and each galaxy has 10 billion stars.) Since Ursa Major rotates around Polaris once every twenty-four hours, a quarter turn registered a night guard of six hours.

References to reading on the trail are sparse, almost certainly a natural consequence of the need to give priority to food and tools. The recently wed Helen Mar Kimball Whitney and Horace Whitney, traveling in 1846, had their own wagon where "I could knit or read, and Horace could read or play his flute." Orson Pratt urged the men in the pioneer camp of 1847 to read instead of playing games, but there is no evidence that anyone took him up on it.

Handcart pioneer John Jaques recorded his distress in 1856 when he had to leave behind important books that had cost "hundreds of dollars" to buy and bring over. "It was very grievous," he wrote.

An exception was Jean Rio Baker, who cherished a beautiful bound copy of Shakespeare's complete plays, three inches thick and ten inches wide. Books were frequently abandoned beside the trail, and those with a keen eye, the interest, and room in their wagons could find treasures, providing it had not rained. Richard Owen Hackman, bound for California in 1852, saw "books of every sort and size, from Fanny Hill to the Bible."

In 1859 F. W. Blake studied Davidson's *Grammar*, Chambers's *Pictures of War* which was "certainly very graphic in its exposure of the horrors of war," and Lardner's *Museum of Science* on latitude and longitude. Tripp Bartlett in 1861 mentioned: "I have been reading most of the day I am pursuing . . . Chemistry and reading a novelette entitled *Fred Arden* or *The Jesuits Revenge*, plot laid in Europe and shows up the intrigues . . . of the Romans . . . at the time of the French Revolution."

Holidays

Both Mormons and American travelers commemorated July 4th with elaborate patriotic observances. They generally started at daybreak with gun and cannon salutes, and continued with cheers, speeches, toasts, feasts, parades, dancing, and drinking whatever spirits were available. Music was provided by whatever instruments were available—or even improvised. A fife and drum corps could be made out of box elder branches by forcing out the pith and boring holes into the stem. Cooking pans became makeshift drums.

One Mormon group in 1850, while camped on the Bear River on July 4, fired a thirteen-gun salute for the original thirteen states and gave thirty-one cheers for the number of states. Sarah Marie Mousley described her Fourth of July in 1857: "Rested from traveling, washed, ironed, & baked, attended two meetings and a musical entertainment consisting of dancing, singing etc . . . retired to rest at 11." The celebration included their animals, who were watered and pastured on especially good feed.

Zebulon Jacobs and his friends went the extra mile at a July 4th celebration at Florence in 1861: "Oh, being the glorious day of which every true American is proud, we tried to be as jolly and happy as possible. In the forenoon we had an Indian war dance in costume; in the afternoon sham battles between Indians and whites which was well done. Towards evening we had a grand circus which pleased the people very much. Our Indian exercises frightened some of the new comers very much until they were made acquainted with the program."

Gentile Catherine Haun, who was at Laramie River in 1849, wrote: "After dinner that night it was proposed we celebrate the day and we all heartily joined in. . . . We sang patriotic songs, repeated what little we could of the Declaration of Independence. . . . The young folks decorated themselves in all manner of fanciful and gro- tesque costumes [and] we danced until midnight."

One Oregon-bound company enjoyed thirteen dishes: cakes, preserves, pies, butter, cheese, sauce, rice, beans, sausages, ham, bis- cuits, tea, and coffee. Most companies tried to be at Independence Rock by this day, which had been named by a group of early explor- ers camping there one July 4th.

After 1847, the Saints also celebrated July 24, the date that offi- cially commemorates the pioneers' entry into the Valley of the Great Salt Lake. Richard Ballantyne left a record of a spectacular trail cel- ebration on July 24, 1855:

> [This] was a day of joyful celebrations. . . . As the wagons moved out of camp with flags flying from staffs, the women ran alongside of the column bedecking the heads of oxen with garlands of prairie flow- ers and throwing wreaths around the necks of the men. That night the spirit was still festive. The ladies were busily employed in making con- fectionery cooking, rice pudding, apple tarts, tea, coffee, etc. The breth- ren painted a flag on a canvas 14 by 6 feet. On an upper corner was a star representing Deseret. On top were the wide spread eagle with the ribbon motto, "Oh God, save Israel." Under the eagle was a large bee with the ribbon motto "We never give up the ship." On the opposite side of the canvas were the Star of Deseret with a large beehive having the ribbon motto, "Glory to God and Brigham Young."

Two companies celebrated the 24th elaborately in 1861. Homer Duncan, who was on the Oregon Trail on the south side of the Platte River, wrote: "[We] rolled out at 5:45 a.m. and camped at 10:00 at Ash Hollow in order to celebrate the anniversary of the entrance of the Pioneers into the Valley. The day was spent in rejoicing, singing, music, dancing, and various sports. The weather was fine and the amusements were continued until the late hours." In 1861, Zebulon Jacobs celebrated the 24th on the North Platte:

> At daylight we called out the National Guard, fired a volley of muskets and any other kind of guns that were handy.... [That night] A make shift table set up some 60 or 70 yards [and was] covered with white table cloths. William Pitt of the Nauvoo Brass Band was there too with his violin. The ladies dressed very smart. The feast was venison, boiled and roasted buffalo, puddings, tarts, tea, coffee, etc. The day concluded with speeches, and an oration, someone told some comic anecdotes and there was dancing to the flute and dulcimer until late at night.

Most celebrations ended with a dance, weather permitting.

In contrast, they seem to have observed Christmas only casually. Mary Parker Richards spent her Christmas in Winter Quarters in 1846 doing chores: "A beautiful day. In the morn went home and gathered a large washing of clothes and returned to Jane's [Richards] to spend Christmas over the washtubs. Was washing with all might to dark." That same day Wilford Woodruff spent Christmas at Winter Quarters attending meetings in the council house.

Painting, Drawing, Writing, and Photography

A few pioneers did some painting. At Winter Quarters in 1848, Philo Dibble, for example, did a series illustrating such significant episodes as "The Martyrdom of Joseph and Hyrum" and "Joseph Smith's Last Address to the Nauvoo Legion." Wilford Woodruff declared it to be "the best art in the world." Frederick H. Piercy, an Englishman especially brought over to make some drawings of Church leaders and trail drawings in 1853, illustrated a popular trail book, *Route from Liverpool to Salt Lake City*.

Some time later, Danish convert C.C.A. Christensen painted his now-famous Mormon Panorama of twenty-three paintings, each measuring six by ten feet. It shows not only famous pre-Utah scenes but also several trail depictions: "Crossing the Mississippi on Ice, Leaving Nauvoo," "Wagons Preparing to Leave Winter Quarters in 1847," and "Handcart Pioneers."

Peter O. Hansen, who traveled in the vanguard company, sketched Mount Pisgah, Cutler's Park, mountain men, Indians, U.S.

soldiers, and Council Bluffs. (They are reprinted in Stanley Kimball's biography of Heber C. Kimball.) Some Mormon journals were decorated with fancy endpapers and title pages. Most journal art, however, consists of fast sketches of landmarks like Chimney Rock or Fort Laramie.

Although no photographs that Mormons took along the trail have been found, the LDS Church History Library and the Union Pacific Railroad Archives houses many taken by others. Although photography as we understand it today was not developed until 1887 when the ubiquitous Eastman "Kodak" appeared, period forms include the daguerreotype of 1839 through the subsequent talbotype, calotype, ambrotype, and ferrotype.

Jesse N. Smith wrote on October 26, 1860: "At breakfast a daguerrean artist took a picture of our camp." Henry Hobbs, a convert from England in the 1859 Rowley Handcart Company, left a puzzling comment near Fort Laramie: "They, the Sioux, wanted 2 or 3 of the sisters for wives and one of them took a sister's portrait and [in?] a tin cup it was taken in the same stile as the hirroglpyics [sic] in the Pearl of Great Price." In 1862, some artists took photographs of Mormon camps. In Omaha in 1864, photographers sought out the companies heading west. Mrs. James Rousseau, en route to California wrote: "The girls had their likenesses taken in their bloomer costumes."

Emmeline B. Whitney (later Wells) was one of a few diarists who actually wrote about writing on Tuesday, March 3, 1846: "[I] took a walk in the woods . . . found stems of strawberry leaves green and fresh I intend to keep them as a memorial. . . . Ann [Elizabeth Ann Smith Whitney, Newel K. Whitney's first wife] and I came up on the hill which was very long . . . seated ourselves on a prostrate log and here I am at the present time scribbling."

Eliza R. Snow continued her role as Zion's poetess on the trail. Sadly, her talents were often drawn on to comfort the bereaved: "Mourn not for him, he's gone to rest."

Exploring

Almost all Mormon immigrants originated east of the Mississippi River or in Europe, so the West was a dramatic change, beginning about halfway across Nebraska when the trail entered the broken lands of the Upper Missouri Basin. In western Nebraska, Courthouse Rock, Chimney Rock, and Scotts Bluff guarded the Oregon Trail on the southern side of the Platte River while Indian Look Out Point and Ancient Ruins Bluffs sentineled the Mormon Trail on the other side of the Platte. Wyoming and Utah offered such scenic wonders as Mexican Hill, Register Cliff, Warm Springs Canyon, Laramie Peak, Red Buttes, Avenue of Rocks, Independence Rock, Devil's Gate, Split Rock, the Ice Slough, Rocky Ridge, South Pass, Pacific Springs, Church Butte, the Needles, Echo Canyon, and Cache Cave. Detailed descriptions were rarer than such generalizations as "beyond description," "sublime," "inspiring," "among the everlasting hills," and "the beautifulest scenery my eyes ever rested upon."

James Armistead considered the scenery "wild and romantic in the extreme, in fact a real wilderness." Louisa Barnes Pratt recorded some "romantic" observations along the Platte River in 1848: "Our hearts, at the same time, glowed with wonder and admiration at the beauty and sublimity of the scenery, alone in a great wilderness from the haunts of civilization."

In 1851 Jean Rio Baker, passing west of Fort Bridger, wrote: "The country for the last three days has been beyond description for wildness and beauty. We are, indeed, among the everlasting hills." Like many foreign immigrants, she was enchanted with her first experience with fireflies, "the most beautiful natural phenomenon I have ever beheld." Near the dramatic Scotts Bluffs, teenager Angelina Farley noted in 1850: "The scenery around us is singularly wild and grotesque, the bluffs representing ranges of ruined castles, places, and temples."

Some were reminded of Ireland, of the glorious hills of Scotland, and of Wales. Caroline Barnes Crosby walked all over the Ancient Bluff Ruins and considered them the "greatest natural curiosity I ever saw." Sometimes imaginative Mormons thought they saw the work of Book of Mormon peoples. Several noted that Chimney Rock was "supposed to be some of the work of the Nephites." Mormon Battalion journalists in New Mexico frequently linked petroglyphs to the Nephites.

Like many travelers past and present, Mormon immigrants liked marking scenic wonders with graffiti. A few even crossed over to Chimney Rock on the Oregon Trail to leave their names. In 1854, Hans Hoth wrote that he scratched his name on Chimney Rock "30 ells high." Other favorite spots for such nineteenth-century self-advertisements were Independence Rock, Avenue of Rocks, Register Cliff, and Devil's Gate, in Wyoming and Cache Cave in Utah. Sixtus Johnson enjoyed the "very romantic rocks embellished with the names of individuals who had passed this way."

Climbing promontories was also a pastime for many going west. Chimney Rock was very dangerous, and few are known to have scaled it to the top. In 1858 a dragoon en route to Utah during the Utah War claimed to have reached the promontory. Mormon companies traveling on the north side of the Platte River would have had to cross the river to reach it, but some companies of Saints also went up the south side of the Platte.

In contrast, Independence Rock, huge and turtle shaped, was very easy to climb and thousands did. Devil's Gate was a 1,500-feet long, 370-foot-high gap in a rocky spur, with a spring running at the bottom. Its name perpetuates the notion that the formation bears the profiles of twin petrified genii. It is not especially hard or dangerous to climb, but some died meeting the challenge of leaning out far enough over the edge to see the bottom of the gorge, which usually required forming a human chain. Louisa Barnes Pratt enjoyed the dramatic view at Independence Rock and the delicious cold water hidden from casual view. "[We] left our names with the rest, and as we descended in the crevice of the rock, I saw water. We crowded [around] with much exertions and got to the spring, and drank our fill of the sweetest, coldest water I had [ever] tasted."

In 1848 Lorenzo Brown witnessed dare-devil kids at Devil's Gate: "Some boys have ascended to the top of a rugged path and were seen from below with their feet hanging over the giddy precipice, careless of danger and dropping stones into the abyss below, counting the seconds which each took to fall. This was fool hardy, but boys will be boys." Some pioneers shot off guns to hear the remarkable reverberations. The view is indeed spectacular—well worth the climb.

Many emigrants also climbed The Needles, located very close to today's Utah state line. One traveler thought they reached up "like the pyramids of Egypt," although it is doubtful that any of these travelers had seen Egypt.

Hunting, Fishing, and Riding

Hunting, fishing, and riding were high adventure, particularly to the young men. Hunting was not only fun but could also yield welcome meat for the pot. Almost anything that moved could be a target: deer, antelope, buffalo, bear, turkey, and ducks. Mormons were advised to kill only what they needed and not to waste the meat, a marked difference from some of the trigger-happy American trains.

Fishing was another popular sport. William Clayton and Wilford Woodruff were uncommonly good at fly-fishing. They caught shad near Winter Quarters, and trout and catfish in the Green River and in Black's Fork. Sometimes they used live crickets for bait. The Platte River, so muddy and shallow, offered very poor angling.

According to Henry Stokes in 1862, an unnamed boy caught a fish at Elkhorn River that weighed eighteen pounds. He couldn't even pull it out of the water, so a man shot it for him and helped haul it out.

Horseback riding was popular and sometimes Mormons raced Indians as well as each other. Nathan Tanner, age twenty-eight, was proud when he raced an Indian and beat him at Fort Laramie in 1848.

Other recreational activities included games with balls, mumble peg, stick pulling, pitching quoits and horseshoes, foot races, marbles, jacks, and swimming.

Trailside Flora and Fauna

The trail provided the rare opportunity to pick up snow with one hand and flowers with another. The young people enjoyed the snow and used the occasion to frolic. They also explored the many scenic wonders such as Scotts Bluff. Thomas Bullock recorded in June 1847: "The boys and girls [were] snowballing each other." (The two children in Brigham Young's vanguard company had been joined by five from the Mormon Battalion camp from Pueblo.) In a picturesque "hand of friendship" concerning snowballs, Bullock describes Porter Rockwell looking at and accepting a snowball from a Missouri pioneer camped nearby.

Some of the Saints recorded the increasingly strange and exotic flora and fauna they encountered while westering. Some found huge mammoth bones near the trail. William Clayton dutifully noted these curiosities plus many shrubs, plants, and flowers. Thomas Bullock's curiosity turned out to be dangerous. On May 13, 1847, he recorded: "In picking up Buffalo Dung this morning, I discovered a very pretty green snake, which I played with, on the end of a thin Stick. I was afterwards told that it was one of the most poisonous of Snakes." A day later, he saw wild sage, prickly pear, and "mud Turtle shells."

When they could find a post office, some women mailed dried flowers to friends back home. Emigrants also noted such plants as wild onions, buffalo grass, willows, roses, violets, gooseberries, strawberries, clover, bunch grass, "Spanish soap weed," vines, elderberries, thistles, cacti, garlic, currants, mint, sage, rushes, and such trees as cedar, ash, cherry, oak, maple, apple, alder, birch, poplar, cottonwood, and pine.

Scores of Mormon trail records mention animals: squirrels, ducks, snapping turtles, various kinds of fish, goose, lizards, skunks, prairie dogs, rattlesnakes, antelope, hares, wolves, buffalo, badgers, deer, crickets, spiders, scorpions, toads, ants, mosquitoes, horse flies, mice, eagles, hawks, cranes, martins, pheasants, and magpies. William Clayton wrote May 23, 1847: "A while ago I went out a little distance to view an adder which Geo Billings had discovered. It was a dark brown color about 18 inches long and ¾ inch thick through the body. They are represented as very poisonous."

Bullock and others mentioned a strange huge plant. "[With] stem four feet long, six inches wide, one quarter inch thick, ornamented by prickles top to bottom, top is kind of a crown formed by prickly leaves ten inches long and five inches broad."

Humor/Horseplay

Despite the arduous labor of travel, some diarists recorded incidents of horseplay and practical jokes—not particularly funny by our standards. When Thomas Judd got tired of hearing a little girl ask questions in 1849, he finally told her that if she did not quit, he would push over Chimney Rock and she would not be able to see that famous landmark.

Greenhorns were special targets. Teaching them to "catch rabbits yankee style" was an immigrant version of "snipe hunting." The victim was told to build a small fire, lie down by its side, and hold a sack open for the rabbits to run into. His friends then left to drive the rabbits his way. What they really did was go off, then race back, yelling and pretending to be attacking Indians. Terrifying their victim was their reward.

Mormon immigrants from Europe often misunderstood rough trail ways and were particularly shocked at the language. A Welsh Saint, Albert Lyman, wrote disapprovingly in 1867: "If such language had been used in Wales, they would have been required to ask the pardon of other members."

Lewis Barney, an 1847 member of the vanguard company, engaged in a bit of foolhardy bravado by making fun of Porter Rockwell, a famed dead shot and frontiersman extraordinaire who had a string of bad luck while Barney kept on bringing in meat. The embarrassed Rockwell claimed, "Oh, he kills does and all." Port said he could kill twenty does a day but only went after fat bucks. The next day Porter came in with a dressed antelope saying, "See here what a nice buck I got. I could have killed a dozen does too." Barney came to investigate, thought the kill rather small, found the skin, and discovered it to be that of a nursing doe. Throwing caution to the wind, he shouted, "See here boys, what nice tits Port's buck has!" "Port scratched around for a while in a terrible rage" but apparently was fair-minded enough to realize that he had been well caught and did not hold a grudge against Barney.

Tall tales were a part of trail life, and Jim Bridger was famous for them. No Mormon chronicler has recorded tall tales as part of his meeting the pioneers of 1847, but he regaled others with talk of "a glass mountain, whose sides were strewn with the corpses of animals and birds who had been killed when they ran or flew into it." Another tale concerned "petrified birds singing in a petrified forest."

On June 10, 1848, John D. Lee mentioned what could have been either horseplay or flirtation "between Some Boys, & 2 or 3 young Women who were on the bank fishing. The Boys, as they considered it, had insulted them by throwing Sand on them or in the water so as to make it splash on them & continuing to do so when they were requested to stop." The outcome apparently ended with no major consequences to anyone.

Conclusion

The trail brought arduous labor, much inconvenience, even tragedy; but it also brought moments of light-hearted fun and exposure to some of nature's most memorable beauties. The following two accounts reveal the magic of the trail when all was well. Eighteen-year-old Sara Alexander captured the scene in 1859: "After the suppers were over and everything was cleared away . . . the camp fires [gave] light, [then] singing with accompaniments of guitars, violins, cornets and such musical instruments [began.] Those evenings recall memories of the most spiritual and soul-inspiring religious sentiment I ever experienced . . . all so overwhelming in its beauty and greatness that a heathen must have been impressed with the presence of a God."

When travel allowed energy for observation and appreciation, the memories it offered were superb. Appleton Harmon caught the power of place and spirit of locale along the trail in 1848: "The sun went behind one of the grey granite ranges of the Sweetwater Mountains and soon its gliding rays . . . disappeared and the red sky of the west turned gray like other parts of the horizon and the little stars grew bright, and twinkled in the distance. The moon, cold and pale, was watched as it began to sink behind those rugged peaks that a short time previous had concealed the king of day from our view."

Chapter 5

Camp Rules, Obedience, and Discipline

Brother James M. Pierce was brought before the camp, charged with profane swearing and abusing his team, which charges were sustained, and he failing to make suitable acknowledgment, was disfellowshipped. —Elijah Mayhew, September 9, 1853

The journal of Hosea Stout reads like a prologue to one of Shakepeare's tragedies. Even the brave and obedient, like Stout, were drained by the weary march across Iowa in 1846. He wrote on Sunday, June 28, 1846: "I awoke very early this morning and immediately discovered my child to be dying." It rained and rained. Stout was too sick to do much for his family and had to beg others for food. "Hunger began to grin hard around us . . . and [I] knew not where the next meal would come from." One son had already died; his cows were lost, and his wagon was broken. Time after time he commented on the heartless men around him. The beds were soaked from rain, and his surviving son lay "troubled by evil spirits." This child, "my only son," also died. "Gone too in the midst of affliction sorrow & disappointment In the wild solitary wilderness. Surrounded by every discouraging circumstances . . . to make man unhappy and disconsolate."

Strong policemen like Hosea Stout and others cried apart and together. Stout wondered why God had permitted them to be dashed against the rocks and waves for so many years. In September 1846, his wife Miranda died in childbirth. So did the baby. Stout wrote on September 26, 1846: "Today was another unfortunate day to me. [Miranda] died about two o'clock p.m. . . . There is now only four of us left and whose turn will be next God only knows. . . . When shall my trials and tribulations end?" Stout asked that same question in his diary seven years later.

Constitutions

Structure is essential to social life under the best circumstances. A predictable pattern of interaction among groups, within families, and in meeting strangers must be established. People must feel that they "belong" and share a set of beliefs, behavior, values, and practices. Religion, a preeminently social activity, often provides the security to attempt a herculean task, secures the dominance of group goals over individual desires, and stresses values. Religion supported the Mormons in uncertainty, comforted them in sorrow and disappointment, and guaranteed them eternal salvation if they were obedient.

The Saints' goal of creating a viable social structure on the Mormon Trail was successful—and accomplished despite a wide variety of backgrounds, economic status, social class, educational attainment, and professional and life skills. This remarkable coming together of Latter-day Saints in an economic and spiritual connection proved that religious activities bind people of all classes together and reaffirms their group solidarity. The Saints' constitutions favored a centralized organization, differing from the rather loose structure of most other westering peoples. To this end they formulated constitutions, codes, and rules.

The move west was not the first Mormon experience in traveling in organized companies. One of the earliest formal constitutions was drafted by the Kirtland Camp, who moved a few hundred people from Kirtland, Ohio, to Far West, Missouri. This compact consisted of seven points:

1. All resources would be pooled for the good of the whole company.
2. The camp would be led by one leader with counselors. The members would obey them in all things.
3. Each man was responsible for his family..
4. All camp members were to do the best they could for the good of all.

5. Any pooled money and property left at the end would be redistributed among camp members.
6. The disobedient would be disfellowshipped and left by the wayside.
7. Changes in the rules would be by mutual consent.

The camp was organized into three divisions, and men appointed to the various offices. En route, they added new rules: A horn would signal the times to arise, have meals, join in evening prayer, and retire. The head of each division would appoint a night guard. Everyone would share in the milk whether they owned a cow or not. Travel should be restricted to fifteen miles a day. On August 3, 1838, the camp approved the appointment of three "judges" to settle interpersonal difficulties. In general, this compact worked well, and the Kirtland Camp made the march of some 900 miles safely despite a ragged and contentious beginning.

When the exodus from Nauvoo began in February and March of 1846, Brigham Young announced a military order of tens, fifties, hundreds, and promised: "There will be no rules we can't obey." All Saints were placed under a strict covenant to "walk in all the ordinances of the Lord." Later, in Winter Quarters, Brigham Young announced a revelation as "the Word and Will of the Lord," that reads very much like the instructions to the original children of Israel (Exod. 18:21-27). (See Chapter 2.)

Leaving Winter Quarters in April 1847, just west of the Missouri River, Young announced a system of military titles. He became lieutenant general, Stephen Markham, colonel, and John Pack and Shadrack Roundy, majors. Although details of organization differed during the years of the exodus, it was usually quasi-military and resembled this 1848 model:

1. Leaders were to be appointed or elected.
2. Other camp officers would be added as needed, such as wagon masters.
3. Cattle were to be staked outside the corral, horses inside.
4. No weapons could be fired inside the camp.
5. Sabbath meetings were to be held when convenient.
6. No guns were to be kept in wagons.
7. Animals must be treated with the utmost kindness.
8. Every able-bodied man from sixteen to sixty was eligible to stand guard. (In some camps, boys as young as ten were also drafted as guards on occasion.)

A typical traveling group was ten family units with a captain. One such captain in 1848 was Norton Jacob, who listed his responsibilities meticulously: thirteen men, nine women, thirty-seven children, sixteen wagons, thirty-six yoke of oxen, twenty-nine mules, ten horses, and "supplies and misc."

Obedience

The entire exodus was a long and hazardous journey of obedience. Even for those leaving from Nauvoo, it was a three-month ordeal. Repeatedly, the Saints' leaders warned that disobedience would result in hardships. Even before they left Sugar Creek, Heber C. Kimball warned them that disobedience would bring disaster and reminded them that "a plague came upon Zion's Camp for disobedience ... men fell victims, [thirteen died of cholera] and it will be again under like circumstances."

From the beginning, Latter-day Saints were very particular about obedience, values, norms of behavior, rules, regulations, discipline, camp councils, and written constitutions for at least two reasons.

First, they were modern children of God, an "ensign to the nations." As the "chosen people," they must conduct themselves appropriately or face discipline, even excommunication. Furthermore, for obvious pragmatic reasons, such rules and discipline would contribute to the safety and success of their immigration.

Second, some system of trail justice was necessary to prevent a breakdown of civilization beyond the frontier. Although some Saints chafed under their rules (and probably most Saints chafed at least some of the time), they could see in the Gentile wagon trains on a parallel course the speed with which disorder and violence could erupt from disharmony and disobedience. William Clayton, with a certain amount of self-congratulation, wrote on June 18, 1847: "I found a great difference between the Missouri emigrant companies & our own. For while the men, women & children were all Cursing, swearing, quarrelling, scolding, finding fault with each other & other Companies, there was nothing of the kind allowed or practiced in our own camp." Latter-day Saints were not unique in having constitutions and rules, but it seems that they heeded them better than most trail companies.

About five weeks into the exodus from Nauvoo in 1846, the first real breach occurred when George Miller and Parley P. Pratt went ahead of the others against counsel. Miller, a bishop, was openly upset with Young's heavy-handed control, while Pratt, an apostle, confessed and said he did not intend to be disobedient. Young wrote on March 22, 1846: "I said I wanted a new leaf turned over, and if there was not, a scourge would come upon the Camp. . . . When we get to Miller's encampment, seven miles ahead, we will organize, and if Bishop Miller moves again before our arrival he will be disfellow-shipped from Camp, unless he repents."

Eliza R. Snow's entry for March 27 noted the problem: "Bsp Miller and the Pratts who are encamped some miles ahead, are re-called to attend a court and answer to the charge of disregarding counsel, etc." When the men returned, Young was unrelenting in his criticism and would not even listen to Pratt's explanation. According to Pratt's autobiography: "His letter censured us on account of some of our moves, and as heavy rains had swollen the small streams which intervened between the two encampments . . . and myself being sick . . . we did not immediately attend the council, as requested. . . . He said there was . . . a spirit . . . of insubordination . . . in our move-ments." Pratt took the criticism meekly, humbly apologized, and was not disfellowshipped. Miller would not, later left the Church, and moved to Texas.

Young, with about 2,000 people to worry about, knew how quickly the social fabric could unravel. He was desperate with worry and stress as he acted as father-leader to all of the Saints, includ-ing those abroad, scattered in cities throughout the eastern states, and those struggling on the trail behind him. The obvious disor-ganization and lack of discipline were a source of constant stress. The incident with Pratt and Miller galvanized him into action. On March 27, he recorded: "Up to this period the organization of this Camp was very imperfect [because] so many have been returning to Nauvoo who came on to assist the Camp [and] the different di-visions have been so far separated from each other by storms, bad roads and other circumstances, that it has hitherto been impossible to affect anything like a perfect organization which was the object of the present Council." He wanted to maintain unity and cooperation because he was uncertain, at this point, how far they would travel, followed by hundreds of wagons behind them. It was almost April.

Many of the Saints discovered that following all the rules did not mean finding special favor with God—nor with Brigham either. They knew what the scriptures said. "My people must be tried in all things, that they may be prepared to receive the glory that I have for them; . . . He that will not bear chastisement is not worthy of my kingdom."

Frustrations needed outlets, and there were many moments of disruptive behavior. Those who could not let off steam physically or complain out loud would often turn to their diaries. Hosea Stout, William Clayton, Eliza R. Snow, and others recorded many comments about hardships, injustice, and the irritations of daily life in the spring of 1846. Snow's comments sometimes captured a dark mood: "About noon we came to where a settlement was commenc'd on a considerable prairie stream—I cannot describe the feelings which occupied me while passing this place; it seem'd like a desolation & the washing of the house of Israel; yet I almost doubted if any real Israelite would stop in such a place."

Asking God for Divine Guidance

About a month later, Young discovered that the Saints had short memories. Mount Pisgah, named by Parley Pratt because it reminded him of the location described in the Bible, was meant as a winter camp to help those coming later from Nauvoo. On Sunday, May 24, Brigham Young sounded the horn there to announce a meeting. His record states: "Only a few came out [so I told them] the time had come when I should command them what to do, inasmuch as they were not willing to listen to counsel." The next try was more successful; but there was so much discord, and the mud and madness of traveling through Iowa was still so vivid in memory that the twelve felt the need for divine guidance. They withdrew to the isolation of the limitless prairie, clothed themselves in temple robes, formed a prayer circle, and invoked God for the good of the people and the success of the venture.

All along the trek for the next two years, the leaders held such special group prayers. At one time, close to two thousand people were camped at Mount Pisgah in "bark cabins." Many stayed there until they left for the Valley.

1847–48 Companies

A year later, finally ready to head out across the plains, Brigham discovered that smaller groups did not mean an end to what he denounced as unruly behavior. Young and Heber C. Kimball called the roll to determine if everyone was present, and then Brigham got into the Revenue Cutter (a collapsible boat) to start his complaints and demands. John Brown and William Clayton heard it all and wrote most of it down. According to Brown, Brigham Young announced that "Satan will slip in slyly and steal away the hearts of the Saints with the spirit of mirthfulness, levity and gaming. . . . Young divided the camp, called each quorum separately, and then asked the Twelve if they would repent. . . and the answer was in the affirmative, and he asked each group the same question and all agreed to repent."

Clayton recorded the comments in the first person:

[May 29, 1847 Saturday:] I remarked last Sunday that I had not felt much like preaching. . . . This morning I feel like preaching a little, and shall take for my text 'That as to pursuing our journey with this company, with the spirit they possess, I am about to revolt against it. . . .' Before we left Winter Quarters, it was told . . . that we were going to look out a home for the saints where they would be free from persecution by the gentiles. . . . I have said many things to the brethren, about the strictness of their walk and conduct, when we left the gentiles, and told them that we would have to walk uprightly or the law would be put in force. . . . The gospel does not bind a good man down . . . It does not diminish his kingdom. . . . You can see the result of yielding to the evil itself and what it will lead you to . . . if you do not open your hearts so that the spirit of God can enter your hearts . . . I know that you are a ruined people. . . . I don't mean to bow down to the spirit which causes the brethren to quarrel and when I wake up . . . the first thing I hear is some of the brethren jawing each other and quarreling because a horse has got loose in the night. . . . You never read of gambling, playing cards, checkers, Dominoes &etc in the scriptures, but you do read of men praising the Lord in the dance. . . . The devils which inhabit the gentile priest are here. . . . I think it would be good for us to have a fast meeting tomorrow and a prayer meeting to humble ourselves.

Heber C. Kimball seconded what Brigham Young said. Wilford Woodruff reminded the group about the chaos in Zion's Camp because "they did not obey." Orson Pratt commented: "There are many books in the Camp and worlds of knowledge before us which we have not obtained, and if the brethren would devote all their leisure [sic] time to seeking after knowledge, they would never need to say they had nothing with which to pass away the time. . . . [I] recommend to the brethren, besides prayer, and obedience, to seek after knowledge continually, and it will help us to overcome our follies and nonsense."

The meeting lasted about three hours and fully acknowledged the moral authority of the Twelve. Several repentant men bore their testimonies. Colonel Stephen Markham, weeping, admitted that "he had always indulged himself before he came into the church, with everything he desired." He asked for forgiveness. Probably no more chastened group of adult men existed in all of Mormon history.

The next two days saw a subdued and repentant company. Clayton wrote on June 1: "All is still and quiet as a 'summer's morning' the Camp well and in good spirits and a feeling of peace, union, and brotherly love seems to dwell in every breast." The Saints had a day or two to absorb Brigham Young's sermon before the sights and sounds of Fort Laramie gave them a welcome diversion and a chance to buy supplies and other goods. The leaders also found a secluded spot to robe themselves in their temple garments and have another prayer circle.

More Discord, More Problems

The companies under Parley P. Pratt and John Taylor, which set out in June after Brigham Young's pioneer company in April 1847, struggled from the start with insubordination and rebellion. The men argued and ignored counsel, were hellbent on being first in line, and quarreled endlessly over who had the authority to make which decisions.

Eliza R. Snow, who had led the women in the comforting spiritual sessions employing the gift of tongues all winter, recorded incidents of virtual mutiny. On June 24, "Capt. [Jedediah] Grant's comp start at 7—pass'd J[ohn] T[aylor]'s com. Who rode past us on horseback & order'd J. Grant to stop. Prest. J. Young told him to drive on—J.T. came back & told our capts of tens to stop, their leaders were in rebellion—he soon rode past us again on his way to Parley's camp. We traveled 10 ms. Stop'd at half past one in the rear of P. A. Meeting in the eve—matters adjusted with good feeling."

These good feelings were only temporary since she later records similar scenes. On July 7, "Capt. P[ratt] leads our 50; after starting we were told to leave the beaten track, and each 50 break a new one—it made hard riding for me, yet I felt like submitting to 'the pow'rs that be.' & endure it altho the 2 [main] roads were unoccupied. After our nooning we came to where br. [Charles C.] Rich was baiting . . . we passed them; but perhaps an hour after, br. Lathrop came up telling br. P[ratt] that Rich demanded the road--br. P[ratt] said the command had not come to him from proper authority, it being from Grant instead of Noble the Capt. of our 50." A few weeks later, Snow commented cogently: "My heart was made to rejoice at seeing our 3 head Officers united in one thing–it surely is in accordance with the prayers of the sis. . . . We seem to have the most difficulty when the most officers are with us."

Pratt's autobiography smooths over the scandal with a few generalizations: "There were some difficulties and jealousies during the first few day, on account of some misunderstanding and insubordination in the order of travel. This at length became so far developed that it was found necessary to call a general halt on the Platte River, and a council of the principal officers, in which things were amicably adjusted and the camp moved on."

Brigham Young, returning to Winter Quarters that September, met Taylor and Pratt near South Pass on the Sweetwater. He had heard about the disorder and was furious with both apostles. Once again, Pratt endured the full force of Brigham's tongue-lashing: "A council was called, in which I was highly censured and chastened by President Young and others. . . . I was charged with neglecting to observe the order of organization entered into under . . . the President before he left the camps at Winter Quarters. . . . [The rules from The Word and Will of the Lord.] I was severely reproved and chastened." We don't know what Taylor thought.

Ironically, Brigham Young's company, returning to Winter Quarters, was far from a shining example of unity. On October 8, 1847, Clayton recorded: "Many hard speeches have passed among the brethren, such as damned hypocrites, damned liars, mutioneers &c. and most of those who started ahead are ordered to travel in the rear. . . . This savage, tyrannical conduct was one thing which induced some to leave and undertake to go through alone."

Crimes and Punishments

The vast majority of immigrants on all trails obeyed the law. Camp leaders administered rough justice, with camp councils hearing the more difficult cases and functioning as courts. Jesse Applegate, traveling in the first major company to Oregon in 1843, wrote: "Today an extra session of the council is being held to settle a dispute that does not admit of delay. . . . Many such cases exist and much interest is taken in the manner." The verdicts of these drum-head trials could result in anything from expulsion to hanging. Along treeless portions of the trails, a tripod of raised wagon tongues made a gallows. (There is no record of any Saint being hanged.)

Murders and sex crimes were comparatively rare. (See Chapter 12.) There was at least one Oregon Trail "legend" of a young man slipping into the tent of a young girl in 1850, being discovered by the father and killed. Everyone sided with the father.

Traveling along the Oregon Trail in 1849, a man was acquitted for shooting a man who had raped his wife. In 1851 near Fort Bridger, Mormon "Howard Egan shot and killed James Monroe for committing adultery with his wife." Abigail Scott Dunaway, en route to Oregon in 1852, saw two markers at Devil's Gate. The first read: "Charles Botsford, murdered June 28, 1852." The second belonged to the murderer: "Horace Dolley hung June 29, 1852." Abigail surmised: "It appears Dolley had contracted a grudge towards Botsford with regard to some little difficulty between them [and] while alone with him he dealt the blow."

Without jails, punishment was usually corporal and administered quickly. Flogging was occasionally administered. Hosea Stout wrote about administering "lashes" to some wild boys in Winter Quarters who were out late with some girls. In 1848, a nephew of Heber C.

Kimball's was tied to a wagon wheel and whipped for stealing from Oregonians. Banishment could also be enforced, a serious penalty beyond the frontier.

The Mormon Battalion, of course, was a special case because the U.S. Army enforced obedience with the threat of courts martial. Sixteen-year-old Lot Smith, who was court martialed for unspecified disobedience, suffered an unusual punishment: "They tied his thumbs to the back of one of the wagons and he was compelled to walk for some distance."

The role of social pressure, essential in a democracy, usually worked toward unity. Elijah Mayhew, traveling in 1853, described: "One man swore and threatened the life of another, and even prepared his rifle. This came before the camp council, witnesses gave testimony, and the man was found guilty. The council ordered him to make a suitable apology and humbly beg forgiveness. This the man did, the matter was settled to the approval of the whole camp."

There was much counterfeiting of paper money along the trail in 1846 and in the Iowa settlements. There were also accusations of this activity in Nauvoo and in Winter Quarters. William Hall was involved in one infamous burial that summer. "At Garden Grove [Iowa]. . . we buried two bogus presses, which I carried in my own wagon, with a barrel of rosin and materials belonging thereto, amounting in weight to one thousand pounds."

In such a poverty-stricken environment, theft was temptingly easy. Brigham Young vigorously denounced stealing on February 24, 1847: "I met with the brethren of the Twelve. . . . I swore by the Eternal Gods that if men in our midst would not stop this cursed work of stealing and counterfeiting their throats should be cut." Hosea Stout, as chief of police at Winter Quarters, noted in his diary on June 20, 1847, two months after Young had left for the West: "At meeting today [Orson] Hyde preached his celebrated bogus sermon, denouncing all bogus makers, counterfeiters, thieves & commanding all such & all who knew of any such to come forthwith and tell him & also absolved them from all former acts and covenants to keep secrets. This caused quite a stir and caused some to 'confess their sins.'"

In addition to thefts of food, cattle, and tools, some stole clothes off the line. A couple at Winter Quarters broke into a store and stole some clothing, and were cut off from the Church. On August 25, Stout was visiting some nearby settlements and again reported: "There had been some melons stolen just a day or two before I came & it was rumored by some that I had come to execute the law on those who were guilty. . . . It is a sad thing to see a camp of the Saints thus quarreling and trying to put each other down and more so when they were overwhelmed with sickness & death."

Men on the Oregon Trail were sometimes temporarily disciplined for fighting. James Godfrey, a non-Mormon from Alton, Illinois, wrote July 22, 1850, about his California-bound company: "We had rather an unpleasant altercation in camp this evening in which one man raised an axe to another; no harm was done however, one being afraid and the other dared not strike. Both were soon heartily ashamed of it. The boys have humorously styled it: 'The Battle of the Humboldt,' and the two poor fellows will not hear the last of it as long as we are together." In 1853 a Mormon was "almost disfellowshipped" for carrying away a pier from a bridge. Another unidentified man was cut off because he had "hardened his heart and would not acknowledge his sin"—which seemed to be that he had changed his mind about going west. According to Thomas Bullock, his wagon mate needed to be disciplined for swearing and for being indifferent and lying about Church leaders. Bullock does not specify if that matter was ever settled to his liking or not.

Hosea Stout complained about the weary trail guards in the 1848 Brigham Young Company. [June 24:] "To night W. J. Norten was tried for being found asleep on guard last night." [June 27:] "Seth Dodge was tried tonight for being found asleep on guard." [July 6:] "T. B. Fott & J. Ivie was [sic] court-martialed tonight for being asleep . . . on duty."

Discipline at Sea

The examples above deal primarily with Americans and with events that began in Iowa. Their passage to the new gathering place lasted about three months. But for many Saints, crossing the plains was only the last leg of an arduous journey that had begun in Europe and lasted eight or more months. This extended journey, nearly always undertaken in organized companies of other converts, required even more effort, helped reshape their identity into the "chosen people," and heightened the already acute drama of being persecuted for the gospel's sake. It reinforced their sense of community and gave converts of differing backgrounds a common experience.

English converts had the chance to get accustomed to the rules and regulations at the Liverpool docks. The first immigrant companies sailed in 1840 and continued with barely a pause through the transition from sail to steam, even when the completion of the transcontinental railroad made it possible to ride to Zion. It became common knowledge among seamen that the Mormon groups were examples of orderliness, cleanliness, and piety. Aboard ship the Mormons kept together, selected their own leaders, made their own regulations, set their own night watches, and insisted on moral conduct. Morning prayers, meals, cleaning, worship services, and retiring were at set times.

In perhaps the best-known description of Mormon travelers, English novelist Charles Dickens described the Saints aboard the *Amazon* in 1863: "I go out on the poop-deck, for air, and surveying the emigrants on the deck below [and] nobody is in ill-temper, nobody is the worse for drink, nobody swears an oath or uses a coarse word, nobody appears depressed, nobody is weeping. . . . They came from various parts of England [and] they have their own police, make their own regulation and set their own watches. . . . [Captains] extol the behavior of these Emigrants, and the perfect order . . . of all their social arrangements." They were, in his phrase, "the pick and flower of England."

Artist Frederick Piercy left the best account of this order when he sailed aboard the *Jersey* in 1853. Within twenty-four hours of sailing, the immigrants had received "the regulations deemed necessary for their comfort, health, and safety. The most rigid discipline should therefore be observed. . . . The Presidents of districts also had to see that no principle of morality was violated." Each district gathered at 8:00 P.M. for prayers and for "any general instructions thought necessary. . . . The most scrupulous cleanliness was thought to be necessary; frequent fumigation and sprinkling of lime; and on warm days all sick persons, whether willing or not, were brought into the air and sunshine. The consequence was, that the general health . . . was most satisfactory, only one death occurring, and that of a very old woman . . . who was nearly dying when brought on board."

Not all were this lucky. Thomas Memmott left some terse jottings in his journal in 1862. Between spells of sickness, he worried about dishonesty among the passengers, water shortages and death. Three weeks into the voyage, he wrote "half way across," but it had provided ample time for "some foolishness concerning one or two young women with sailors, counsel was given against it and watchmen set. . . . President [William] Gibson having become addicted to taking too much strong drink, Brothers John Clarke and F. M. Lyman were compelled to take charge of the company." With even greater relief, Memmott wrote on June 25: "Land Oh . . . a most beautiful sight."

Still, most of the Mormon companies aboard ship were models of good conduct, except for minor cases of interpersonal friction that were inevitable in such crowded quarters. As a result, there was little need for severe punishment on most ships. One of the most drastic measures occurred in 1865 when forty-seven converts sailed on the *Mexicana* from Port Elizabeth, South Africa, to New York City. Miner G. Atwood commented that the leaders were "obliged to tie up Samuel Francom [because] he was a very bad boy." Samuel, about ten or twelve years old, promised to be good and was released but had to be tied up for a second time "because he would not obey." Perhaps this trait ran in the family because a few days later, his father, John Francom, the father, called Elder Adolphus H. Noon a liar and got the same punishment.

Crusaders and Kind Captains

Surely the experience of conversion and, quite frequently, earlier gatherings had already done much of the work of disciplining the Saints. The watchful leaders provided immediate recourse in the case of disputes. The personal discipline of daily prayers doubtless did much to deflect disagreements or grudges that could have erupted into violence. The nightly sermons and exhortations of the leaders were daily reminders of how Saints should behave.

John Brown's record provides a look at discipline from the leader's perspective, including the high value placed on unity. A Mississippi convert, Brown returned to the Midwest in 1850 with the assignment of purchasing oxen, cows, and wagons for the Perpetual Emigrating Fund party that would be starting out from Kanesville (Council Bluffs) in July of 1851. He served as the captain: "I . . . left the Missouri River on the 7th of July, with upwards of 50 wagons. . . . We pursued our journey over the plains without anything of great importance or unusual occurrence happening to us. The most remarkable thing to record is that I was able to manage the camp as captain of fifty without any difficulty. There was not a single rebellion against my orders on the whole route, and unlike all other companies, came through without dividing up—notwithstanding we had gentile emigrants in company."

Warren Foote was a company captain in 1850, responsible for "500 Saints." Like John Brown, as he reflected on his experience, it was the company's unity that he prized most highly: "I am certain that a journey through a desert country of a thousand miles, with five hundred souls will try the patience of any man, or set of men who are appointed to preside over them as leaders, especially so, when the company consists of different nationalities, having different customs, and some without experience in driving ox teams and take care of them." Much of this success seems to have come from Foote's philosophy of leadership: "I was determined that every person in the Company should have their rights respected," he wrote. As they approached Utah, Foote asked "forgiveness of others" and also counseled them to seek and extend forgiveness to company members "so that we [can] enter the Valley free from any hard feelings." Proudly he reported, "A good spirit prevailed."

The converts showed their character in many ways, and the trail experience gave them daily chances to give a bit of comfort and food to others. And for those with aesthetic and spiritual sensibilities, the grand scenery provided its own balm.

One handcarter, Hannah Settle Lapish, convert from England, could have defeated the "grim reaper" when she traded in her jewelry at Fort Laramie in 1860 for the benefit of her starving company. She does not specify what it was, but she boldly marched to the fort with her jewelry clutched in her sun-burned hands, and told a man at the fort that she wanted "700 pounds of flour" in exchange for her jewelry. He took the jewelry and sent the flour to the camp. "I gave it to the commissary," she said, "who dealt it out to the hungry . . . the last being distributed on the day we crossed Green River." Help soon arrived from the valley, "our troubles were over and we arrived safely in Salt Lake City August 27, 1860. Our company was one of the last companies to make the journey in that pathetic way—pushing handcarts across the western prairies and mountains. We are the crusaders of the 19th century. . . . We handcart people will never outlive the memory of those experiences." Hannah did not have to get to Zion to establish that she was already a Saint.

Wallace Stegner wrote in *Gathering to Zion*: "For every early Saint, crossing the plains to Zion in the Valleys of the Mountains was not merely a journey, but a rite of passage, the final, devoted, enduring act that brought one into the kingdom. . . . They were the most systematic, organized, disciplined, and successful pioneers in our history and their advantage . . . came directly from their . . . social and religious organization. . . . Far from lessening their social organization, the trail perfected it. As communities on the march they proved extraordinarily adaptable."

If the rules and discipline were a hindrance or nuisance to some, they were a lifeline to others. The success was largely due to the Saints' humility and obedience. Foote's democratic method worked for him. Brigham Young's harsher method worked for him. The demanding doctrine of gathering that pitted the Saints against so many obstacles before they got to Zion helped most stay humble once the journey was over. Brigham Young got his wish. Zion "was a good place to make Saints," but it was a good place for those who were already Saints.

Chapter 6

Young Pioneers

Everyone in the tent began laughing at each other's faces; come to find out we had all of our faces besmeared with tar and waggon grease. Some of the boys from the other camp paid us a visit and left their compliments upon our faces. —Zebulon Jacobs, 1861

Somewhere, sometime on that trek west, most young emigrants witnessed the ebbing and flowing cycle of life and death. The dull thud of dirt filling a hole where a body lay was a sharp contrast to the urgent cry of a new baby. Within this cycle were other beginnings and endings: a marriage was uniting a couple, while a mission or Mormon Battalion call separated an individual from loved ones.

In the mid-nineteenth century, about 50,000 young Mormon pioneers marched toward what they hoped would be a better life in the Valley of the Great Salt Lake. The contributions of young people have been overlooked by most historians. Lillian Schlissel wrote that women's added trail responsibilities forced children "to fend for themselves . . . [and] they suffered from benign neglect." John Mack Faragher echoes her assessment: "The burden of other responsibilities made child care a relatively low priority." While these two historians were appraising Oregon Trail diaries, Mormon accounts corroborate that children received casual supervision. Heber C. Kimball—colorful and direct at times—chided the women with him after little Lucretia Cox was crushed under a wagon wheel in 1848: "It is better for mothers to tie up little children in the wagon than bury them. Mothers don't half the time know where their children are." His company consisted of 662 people, which included wives, children, grandchildren, and adopted families.

Surprisingly, even in trail accounts kept by mothers, children seldom appear. Harriet Page Decker Young, one of the three women in the 1847 vanguard company, kept a diary with her husband, Lorenzo. Neither one mentioned their two sons, Perry Decker Young and Sobieski Young, except to note that they were part of the company. They omit an episode recorded by Thomas Bullock: that these boys were in a wagon that overturned in Echo Canyon.

A few exceptions are Mormons Jean Rio Baker and Hannah Tapfield King, and Oregon-bound Amelia Stewart Knight. Only a few Mormon teenagers (Lucy Marie Canfield, age fifteen, William Pace, age fourteen, and George W. Bean, age sixteen,) kept substantial trail diaries, but hundreds left autobiographies—some of them general and dimmed by time but others as vivid as if they had been kept on the journey. The contributions they made during the trek west were often the difference between a successful or a disastrous ending for their families.

Despite their general invisibility, children and youth frequently showed outstanding heroism, courage, and character as they trudged west. Their life stories reveal how well they performed their chores and responsibilities under adverse conditions. The bravery and discipline of those who were sick, cold, and hungry but who "went to bed without a whimper" is of heroic proportions. Above all else, like their parents and leaders, they dreamed of and hoped to find a permanent Zion.

Getting Ready

In 1845, when the Nauvoo Saints began to accept the fact that another move lay in their immediate future, youngsters helped prepare for the journey. They were released from school classes because "no one could concentrate." They helped repair wagons, repair or sew clothing, dry breadstuff, fruit, and meat, make wagon covers, or earn money to contribute to family necessities. They picked berries, hired out as apprentices, helped tend children, cooked, chopped wood, washed clothes, taught school, sewed and knitted, milked cows, tended cattle, and hunted for food.

Six-year-old Lucina Mecham picked six kinds of berries in 1847 so she could buy shoes to replace the moccasins that she had worn for more than a year. Twelve-year-old Jesse N. Smith chopped corn to earn money for new boots. Joseph Fish, age six in 1845, still remembered Nauvoo as

> an exciting scene. Men and women [and their children] were now making ready for their long journey into an unknown wilderness. The manufacturing of wagons was one of the first things; green timber was procured for spokes, felloes, etc., and kiln-dried; some were boiled in salt water. Iron was the most difficult to obtain, it was gathered up from different parts of the county. All were busy, wagon-makers, wheel-wrights, covers, tents, etc. Provisions, groceries, and implements were gathered as fast as possible. . . . Flour was not plentiful and some families parched corn in large sheet iron drums and had it ground into meal, but it soon got damp and musty . . . and [most] was fed to the stock.

In 1845 fourteen-year-old George Washington Bean "was detailed to go into Iowa to cut and prepare wagon timber of white oak and hickory that grew there in abundance. . . . The timber we hauled nine miles to the river and boated it across." In February 1846, George helped the Mormon leaders across the ice-clogged Mississippi and drove a wagon for several weeks into Iowa, then returned to Nauvoo to assist his parents. When "a little unpleasantness arose between me and Father," George celebrated his fifteenth birthday on April 1 by crossing to Montrose, Iowa, where he got a job unloading a steamboat, for which he "rec fifty cents per hour. I carried four bushels of wheat at a load and would take a 'pig' of lead ore in each hand. I made a few dollars and got more money than I ever had before [then] returned home [to Nauvoo] and took hold of duty as well as ever." Thanks to the rare cash he had earned, George saved his family from "certain death" a few months later on the Iowa Trail because he could buy food when they were all sick and hungry.

At age sixteen, he was on the trail as teamster for his sister and her baby, while her husband was with the Mormon Battalion. He recalled it with an undiminished sense of adventure: "There was I, . . . launched forth on a journey of one thousand miles in charge of a team of four oxen and a family, sensing in part the responsibility, yet full of hope and plans for the future."

Thomas Cropper, who was eleven in 1854, absorbed key survival skills: "I learned to turn with the lathe and ran the mill. I hunted wild turkeys, ducks, and squirrels and did some fishing. I learned from the Indians to paddle a canoe, fish with a spear; and shoot the bow and arrow."

Even those whose trail did not begin in Nauvoo had learned the most important lesson: the necessity of hard work. Heber McBride, whose family joined the Church in England, apprenticed at age nine as "as errand boy in a large Drug and Chimists store. I had to be on the go from 7 oclock in the morning till 9 oclock at night and Saturday nights till 10 oclock. . . . My wages was about half crown perweek, or about 60 cents American money."

The Mays were another convert family who immigrated to the United States. Cash-strapped on arrival, Ruth, "not yet twelve years old . . . went to work" in a Massachusetts cotton mill. Moving on to Philadelphia with her family a few months later, Ruth hired out with a family where she earned "a dollar a week and board. Thus we began to save and prepare for the journey to the Valley."

At Winter Quarters

Orson Spencer left his six motherless children at Winter Quarters in the care of the two eldest, Ellen and Aurelia, ages fourteen and twelve, while he went to England on a mission in the fall of 1846. Back in Winter Quarters in the fall of 1847, Brigham asked the Spencer children if Orson could extend his mission by another year. They agreed. According to Aurelia, "We kept house by ourselves. . . . It was well for us that we had been taught to knit and sew, for we had our own clothes to mend and look after. . . . We really suffered . . . having nothing but corn-meal, which was stirred up with water and baked on a griddle. Many a night I have gone to bed without supper having to wait until I was hungry enough to eat our poor fare."

The Spencer children amused themselves with a potentially dangerous open-knife game "when the weather was cold or stormy and we could not go out. 'Mumble-peg,' [which was played by flipping the open blade into the dirt from the shoulder] was recently introduced and became all the rage among the children at that time," recalled Aurelia. "This we used to play on our dirt floor, which rather marred its smoothness but afforded us considerable amusement." Aurelia tried to earn some money and discovered skill in making hair jewelry and sewing.

In the spring of 1848, Brigham Young assigned a teamster to bring them to the Valley in his company. Once there, they moved into their little log cabin and were again on their own for several months before their father returned.

Eleven-year-old Frances, the daughter of Louisa Barnes Pratt, whose husband was on a mission, "was unusually smart to do outdoor work," as Louisa noted gratefully in her diary. "She could make a garden, take care of the cows in winter [and] sometimes she chopt the wood." Her fourteen-year-old sister Ellen helped Louisa teach school to contribute money to the family pocketbook.

At another location in Iowa, fourteen-year-old Stephen I. Bunnell, a skilled marksman, was the main provider for his own family and five others living near each other in 1848. "We came very near starving to death the winter of 1848. Our provisions was all gone about Feb the 20. I at the time was detained as hunter for the camp on account of my excellent good luck with the gun."

When ten-year-old David W. Hess's father died in 1848 and his older brother, John W. left with the Mormon Battalion, David's mother and his three younger siblings patched together a shelter of elm bark and planted a small crop of buckwheat and corn. David grimly survived a rattlesnake bite to fill, as much as possible, the duties of the man in the family.

On the Trail

In many ways, trail life continued the norm of hard work but added the challenges of sometimes-fierce weather including mud, rain, hail, snow, thunder and lightning. Hunting for cattle, preparing food, and finding water were accepted parts of these daily demands, and children's chores extended to include new responsibilities. Traditional gender roles, for youngsters as for adults, formed the more "desirable" division of labor but, in actual fact, were observed only if there were enough of the "proper" sex to do the necessary chores. Otherwise, both boys and girls drove teams, herded cattle, gathered fuel, hauled water, picked berries, tended younger children, washed clothes, prepared meals, and cleaned up afterward.

I found no cases of girls hunting, but that was probably due to the scarcity of firearms rather than a firm-rooted objection to the "gentler sex" hunting meat for the camp. Also, only boys stood night-guard. Naturally, girls did more of the cooking and child care than boys, if both were available. Joseph Fish recalled that his older sister carried their little brother so much on the trail that it impaired her health.

Rachel Emma Woolley, who turned twelve in 1848, substituted as a teamster when her brother was moved to another wagon. It required courage: "I did so with fear and trembling, as one of the horses was very vicious. She used to kick up dreadful until she would kick the board of the wagon all to pieces, but it made no difference, I had to go at it the next day just the same." Her father, Edwin, also held her to adult standards of responsibility. When she "rush[ed] for the river to bathe off the dust" after a long day, she lingered too long. Her father whipped her with a rope end when she returned, and Rachel meekly confessed, "I got what I deserved." Etta Berry, also twelve and in the same company, was pressed into service as a teamster when "Father came down with [mountain fever] and was sick for two weeks."

Twelve-year-old Matilda Ann Duncan earned bragging rights by driving "the final 500 miles to Utah in 1848 without any mishaps." These miles comprised the entire trail past Fort Laramie, through the Wasatch Mountains, and down steep Echo Canyon where many wagons overturned or broke down.

Sarah Norris was orphaned in 1846 when her father was killed in the Battle of Nauvoo and her mother died in childbirth soon afterwards. Sarah had charge of a wagon and team, and a year later, she drove the same wagon to the Valley.

Young boys almost routinely became expert teamsters and herders on that 1,030-mile journey. Twelve-year-old Jesse N. Smith was put in charge of all the cattle of the "Poor Camp" until they reached Council Bluffs. Henry P. Richards, age seventeen, was in charge of two teams in 1848 in addition to standing watch "half the night every third night for the entire time." Sixteen-year-old John Smith, the stepson of Mary Fielding Smith, and William H. Hill, age eleven, were also responsible for two teams. Thales Haskell, age thirteen, drove the family wagon. Two of the youngest teamsters were nine-year-old Albert Nephi Clements and Brigham Henry ("Harry") Roberts in 1866.

Guard duty was an additional drain on energies depleted by long days. In most camps, the guards worked four-hour shifts, but in a few cases, their duty lasted the entire night. George W. Bean and his company of 1847 had many cattle go astray, and the almost daily, largely unsuccessful hunts must have left everyone exhausted. The guards were not only responsible to keep a lookout for Indians but were also responsible for keeping the animals together. Even awake, they were not always successful, and even the threat of punishment could not stave off exhausted sleep. George W. Bean witnessed a typical scene. In 1847, an adult was on guard with Amenzo Baker, age eight. When some of the cattle started drifting, Amenzo, who was using a sheep hide as a cloak, "shook the skin to scare the animals back. It rattled [and] in an instant, with one snort, the whole herd was on the full run. . . . 46 head were lost [and] this circumstance caused a week's delay."

In a poignant incident preserved about the Martin Handcart Company, Agnes Caldwell recalled that her mother took pity on the young men who were standing guard duty over their few animals "one very cold night." She "prepared some meat broth, and gave each one of the young men a half pint. They often declared it saved their lives and never before or since had anything tasted so good."

Fatigue and even illness did not always earn youngsters a reprieve from their labor. Wallace Stegner wrote that some children in 1846 "sniffled and sickened and had to be whipped from their beds . . . to milk cows and hunt up the teams."

Unusual Adventures

Three young Mormon boys participated in extraordinary adventures in 1846 with the Mormon Battalion. Although the men marched out of Council Bluffs on July 21, 1846, to the tune of "The Girl I Left Behind Me," about four dozen children accompanied their parents. Fourteen-year-old William B. Pace, possibly the youngest "soldier" in the battalion, acted as an aide to Lieutenant

James Pace and marched all the way to California. Then he and his father started for the Salt Lake Valley, arriving October 16, 1847. Three days later, they began the journey to Winter Quarters, hampered by severe snowstorms and short rations. On November 1, they reached " Fort Larrimie." William recorded:

> Here our provisions being exhausted we procured a little Flour and some Hard Bread and some dryed Buffalo meat and proceeded on. . . . After traveling several days without food and not knowing where we would find the next meal . . . we agreed to make a supper out of Old Jack [their mule, as] . . . a repast for some ten or twelve half starved Mormon Soldiers. . . . Some stood off and would not partake while others pitched into it like as many ravenous wolves devouring their Prey.

In fact, before they reached Winter Quarters on December 17, 1847, they actually ate wolf meat, continued to fight their way through storms, and finally "exchanged our camping out for the Soft side of a Feather Bed & snug Log Cabbins." In eighteen months, William had walked more than 1,500 miles, ridden nearly that same distance, and suffered about half the time from inadequate rations.

A week after the Mormon Battalion left Council Bluffs, a young boy named Charles Colton walked into camp. He had left the main body of the Saints to be with his father, Philander. That night, Charles serenaded the camp and apparently made such an impression on Colonel James Allen that he gave permission for Charles to remain. Charles became an aide to one of the officers, reached California, then returned to Winter Quarters by the southern route, in the fall of 1847.

Fourteen-year-old Andrew Shumway was allowed to accompany his father, Charles, to the valley with the 1847 pioneer company, making the round trip back to Winter Quarters in seven months. The Shumways had made history in another way by being the first family from Nauvoo to cross the Mississippi River on February 4, 1846.

Recreation and Toys

Children did not have many toys at the best of times in the 1850s, and they often had to leave those behind. Boys had pocket-knives and marbles and played games of physical skill, such as stick pulling, foot races, and sling-shot marksmanship. Fishing served the dual purpose of providing both food and entertainment. Young B. H. Roberts, fishing along the Missouri River in 1866, "hooked . . . what was called a turtle of terrapin species, rather large and quite disconcerting. . . . This was cut into small pieces . . . and eaten for supper." Boys also took advantage of pauses along the waterways to swim, while girls, in chaperoned groups, "went in bathing, and had a real jollification," as Ruth May recalled of a stop on the Sweetwater.

Mary Jane Mount (Tanner), who crossed the plains in 1847 when she was nine, recalled a novel form of entertainment: "There were a great many ant hills along the road raised to a considerable height where we often found beads which were no doubt lost by the Indians; collected by these indefatigable little workers along with the gravel of which their mounds are composed. If we were hardy enough to risk a bite now and then we found much amusement in searching for the beads to string into necklaces."

Girls could make stick or rag dolls and sometimes had a set of miniature dishes or a real doll. They also chased fireflies at night, generally unknown in Europe, sang, listened to stories, explored, and played games like "I Spy," "Red Rover," jump rope, and tag. Games that required minimal equipment included "Kick the Can," "Hunt the Thimble," horseshoes, and quoits. After baseball became popular in the 1850s, youngsters sometimes played it on the plains. Snowball fights were a way of turning storms into fun.

Children crossing the Atlantic had a choice of diversions if the weather was good. Some attended school, practiced English, learned to knit or sew, and were sometimes allowed to explore the ship. One mother put her children to work drawing colored yarn through per-forated papers (sewing cards) with a needle.

Immigrant parents cared about their children's education; but except for the ocean voyages and during the seasonal hiatuses at Winter Quarters, it was usually squeezed out by circumstances. Fourteen-year-old Ann Cannon, who helped drive an ox team in 1847, later lamented: "When I did not have to drive, I rode with George Q [her brother]. He said: 'Now Annie, get your books and I will teach you.' 'Oh, I have not time; it takes me all the time I get to fix my clothes.' I missed the best opportunity I ever had. I have been very sorry I missed it."

Parties, Pleasures, and Pranks

Margaret Jay Judd (Clawson) and Romania Bunnell (Pratt) remembered their journey across the plains as fun and adventure. In 1849, seventeen year-old Margaret picked some berries and invited the young people to a pie party: "There were several nice young men in our company, which made it interesting for the girls. . . . I asked some of them to come to a party. . . . Pies were a great luxury and seldom seen on the plains." She thought the event was a success until she later tasted one of the pies: "Oh, my, how it set my teeth on edge. . . . That ended my pie making on the plains. . . . I don't think there was enough sugar in camp to have sweetened those pies."

Although the fifteen-year-old Romania did her share of chores in 1855, she recalled the journey as "a summer full of pleasure to me; the early evening walks gathering wild flowers, climbing the rugged and ofttimes forbidding hills—the pleasant evening by the bright camp fire, while sweet songs floated forth." These experiences "gladdened our young hearts." (See also Chapter 5.)

Handcart Children

The young people in the handcart companies experienced distinctive adventures and tragedies. Thomas MacIntyre, an adult handcart pioneer in 1859, recorded: "I am assisted at my cart by three young girls. For pulling the Scot lassie could beat the others and was a team of herself. The Welsh girl, Ann Lewis [age 20] was subject to fainting spells which was very awkward in traveling as I had occasionally to let go the cart to catch her. . . . The English girl Sarah [Pearson, age 20] was quiet and did not care whether the cart came along or not." His record does not say, but Sarah was with her mother; and Ann Lewis was traveling alone.

Emma James, age sixteen, who was in the Willie Handcart Company of 1856, remembered: "It was great fun pulling empty carts and imitating the wagon drivers with a 'gee' and a 'haw.' We got ahead of the slow moving wagons and had to wait for them. We had plenty of time to see the country we were passing through, to run here and there and to explore this and that. There were many things to catch the eye in this strange land. [We ran] after birds, picked flowers, and collected pretty rocks."

Other handcart children had less benign memories. When those traveling with the Martin Handcart Company were ordered to discard nonessential items, fifteen-year-old Mary Williamson was torn between obedience and desire when she had to throw a small keepsake lion in cast iron on the trash heap. She could not bear to part with it. Late that night, she went back to the abandoned items, retrieved her treasure, tied a string around it, and wore it around her neck and down her back underneath her clothes all the way to the valley. Both Mary and her pet made it to Zion, but the imprint of that keepsake was so heavy it left her with a permanent indentation on her back.

When food ran short, and this happened in every company, the handcart children suffered. Henry and Peter McBride, ages thirteen and six "turn[ed] flour sacks inside and out and suck[ed] flour from the creases." (This problem was not limited to the Mormons.)

The Daniel McArthur Handcart Company, which left Florence, Nebraska, on July 13, escaped much of the suffering borne by the Willie and Martin companies, but Theo Didriksson describes the children's treatment as harsh by today's terms: "There were 30 children in the company and every morning they were sent ahead of the grownups, all in one bunch. Some of them had very little clothing, but they all wore hats. They were driven along with willows and had to keep walking as long as they could. No use to cry or complain but along during the day when it was hot they were allowed to rest and were given food. They were often two or three miles ahead of us. It was hard for parents to see their little five and six year olds driven along like sheep." McArthur succeeded in getting his company to the valley by September 22, with the loss of only seven members out of 222. In contrast, about 25 percent of the Martin Handcart Company died before being rescued in late November. Many of those deaths were children.

Two sisters, Nellie and Maggie Pucell, ages ten and fourteen, were among the children walking ahead in the Martin company. Their shoes were in rags, and eventually they were barefooted. Compassionate strangers gave them money for shoes, but Nellie's feet were already frostbitten and she could barely walk. Maggie had the good fortune to be less damaged. Carried to the Salt Lake Valley by covered wagon, Nellie then endured the amputation of both legs near the knees by a doctor who used a "crude saw and knife" and no anesthetic. Despite walking on her stubs with some help from a low-wheeled cart all of her life, she married and had six children.

Stragglers and Lost Children

A constant danger for young children was getting lost, especially when their parents were so preoccupied. Seven-year-old Kittie Simmons, traveling with an 1857 handcart company, fell asleep by the roadside. Her nine-year-old sister Margaret later remembered: "We traveled on, leaving her to be picked up by the wagon which accompanied us as it came by. When we camped at night, the wagon had not brought Kittie. Mother was frantic. A searching party went to seek her and found that a strange company had picked her up. They restored her to us."

At least in Iowa, one sixteen year old, apparently too tired to care, simply stopped at a farmhouse and got work. Only later did his grieving parents learn what had happened to him.

One famous "lost child" story has a special poignancy. About a hundred miles before Council Bluffs, six-year-old Arthur Parker, whose family was traveling with the McArthur Handcart Company, sat down to rest and fell asleep. When his parents missed him, the camp began a search, curtailed before dark. Arthur's father, Robert, elected to back-trail while, Ann, his distraught wife, went on with the other children. As they parted, Ann pinned her red shawl about Robert's shoulders with instruction to wrap Arthur in it if he were dead but to wave it as a signal to her if he were alive.

Robert eventually reached a trading station where he learned that the boy, ill from exposure and fright, had been found and cared for by a farmer and his wife. Taking up his son, Robert followed the trail to catch up with the wagon-train. For two nights, Ann and her children kept watch. On the third night, the rays of the setting sun caught the glimmer of a bright red shawl. "The brave little mother sank in a pitiful heap in the sand and slept for the first time in three days." Captain McArthur in his report to the brethren said only that their group "had the very best of luck all the way."

John D. Lee reported another poignant story on June 23, 1848: "J. Workman . . . came back in much distress having been told that his litle boy lay by the way Side not able to stand being very sick. His co. was then some 5 ms ahead & still going on. J. D. Lee [speaking of himself in third person]. . . , said: 'Take one of my Horse out of my waggon and go & search.' Capt Workman went & found his child lying in the oppen Prairie . . . wept with Joy & gratitude because his child was yet alive."

Immigrants got lost while hunting, gathering berries or fuel, searching for water, lollygagging around, attempting shortcuts, and trying to visit landmarks which were farther away than they appeared because of the clarity of high plains atmosphere. The slow pace of the oxen made it easy for travelers to wander off in boredom, thinking they could easily catch up with such slow-moving trains.

Children's Deaths

Children died from drowning, from being trampled by animals or crushed by wagons. Exposure, fever, diarrhea, starvation, and many diseases took their toll. (See also Chapter 11.) William Barton's little boy died of cholera in August 1850 before the family had even left Kanesville (Council Bluffs). The dying child "put his little fingers first to my lips and them moved them to his mother's lips for a kiss, and moved them back again and kept on doing so for about twenty minutes before his spirit departed, looking up to us with a kind of smile until the last."

In July 1850 just west of Fort Kearny, three-year-old Peter Maughan, sitting on the front of the wagon, leaned forward and fell in front of the wagon wheels. The first wheels missed him. He tried to escape the hind wheels, but the wagon stopped just as the hind wheel ran upon his back. The men quickly lifted the wheel and "we done all that was possible for him, but no earthly power could save him," wrote his mother, Mary Ann. "He did not suffer much pain. We all wept for the dear little boy. . . . I had talked to him many times to be careful and not fall out of the wagon. I did not know that his father had fainted and fell down in the road, for the brethren stood to hide him from my sight. I emptied a dry goods box and Brother Wood made him a nice coffin."

Near Chimney Rock in 1862, B. H. Roberts's two-year-old brother Thomas, died. "He was wrapped in a bed sheet and lowered into the grave." When their mother, Ann Roberts, heard the dirt dropping on her baby's body, "with a groan she sank beside the grave in a dead faint. Capt [Morton] Haight . . . cried out, 'This is too much for me!' He then took a bread box from his wagon and put the child into it." Roberts adds that Chimney Rock "was, in a way, his monument."

It was a modest comfort to the suffering parents to have something coffin-like for a child's burial. In addition to Thomas Roberts's bread box, tea canisters and dresser drawers were pressed into service. When two-year-old Flora Jaques died in the Martin Handcart Company near Fort Bridger, her mother, Zilpah, wrapped the little body in a blanket and carried her into Salt Lake Valley for burial. At least one child was smothered by his mother as they slept in the crowded wagon. Traveling in Iowa to join the main camp an unnamed infant starved to death when all the food that a baby could digest was exhausted. His mother, bedfast for nine months and starving herself, simply could not produce milk.

Some children were miraculously healed after administrations and prayers, but others died. Some children who logically should have died, lived. Some who should have lived, died. Children fell through the railings of the steamers. A crewman opened the trap door to get water for the animals on the Missouri River in 1863 and forgot to close it. During the night a small boy, frightened when mules in the stalls started kicking, got up and fell into the river. His body was never found. That same year, a group of Saints was traveling by flatboat from St. Joseph, Missouri, to Florence, Nebraska. During the night, the boat, which had no side railings, hove to for wood. A boy of about twelve got up, half asleep, and walked right into the river. The swift current swept him away and he was lost.

And of course, parents died. When both of them died, sometimes they were able to make arrangements for their children. Sometimes the decision defaulted to the company's leader. To survive, nursing infants had to be immediately placed with women who were already nursing infants. There were more options for older children.

The Israel Barlow family, for example, brought two orphans across the plains with then in 1848. It is not clear who they were or if the children stayed with the family. A few children whose fathers were marching with the Mormon Battalion were entrusted to other Saints traveling west from Iowa. Perhaps the Barlow orphans were among these children.

In commemoration of the trail experience, some parents gave distinctive place names to children born along the trail. Zina Huntington Jacobs, who gave birth to her second son near the Chariton River in Iowa in 1846, named him for the river. Newborn Platte Pulsipher, rescued when his family's wagon overturned in that river, received the river's name. Sister Covington from North Carolina, after a hard delivery, named her son Robert Laborious Covington.

Some mothers named their children after the ships they sailed in from Europe: Jenny or George McClellan or Christina Enoch Lyon or Enoch Train Hargraves. In 1856 a baby was named Charles Collins Thornton McNeil both for the ship, *Thornton*, and the captain, Charles Collins. Two children born to Sam Brannan's *Brooklyn* company were named Atlantic and Pacific respectively.

Patience Loader, in the Martin Handcart Company, remembered the story of little Echo Canyon. Sarah Squires delivered her daughter November 26, 1856, but there was little to wrap her in. Father Henry Squires "was running around camp inquiring of everybody if they had a pin to give him to pin something around the baby but I don't think he was able to get one [but] one of the relief party generously contributed part of his under linen to clothe the little stranger."

Pets

Sometimes, husbands and fathers tried to make westering easier for their families by letting them bring along favorite pets. When Heber C. Kimball took his second trip along the trail in 1848, the animals accompanying his train read like a small zoo: oxen, horses, mules, cattle, sheep, pigs, chickens, cats, dogs, goats, geese, doves, a squirrel and some beehives! The squirrel, cats, and dogs were obviously someone's pets, although cats earned their way by mousing and dogs helped hunt and also gave early warning of Indians. Some captains discouraged having dogs, fearing that their barking would attract Indians, scare game away, or cause stampedes.

Birds, rabbits, prairie dogs, eagles, chickens, antelopes, and lambs were adopted en route. Horses, oxen, and sheep became pets. Some even tried to tame buffalo calves. Most families gave pet names to their oxen. The most popular were Buck, Berry, Tom, Jerry, Bright, and Bill, but Pink, Duke, Stoney, Susy, Dick, Darby, Leon, Smut, Boily, and Snarley also made their appearance. Any of them could be prefaced by "Old." Cows were christened Lady Blackie, Lady Milky, and Lady Cherry. A particularly cantankerous one rejoiced in the soubriquet of Lady Lucifer.

Pets could acquire almost familial status. In 1853 when William Gibson's captain ordered all the camp dogs shot, Gibson lamented, "My little daughter's dog was the only one shot, although it was the quietest in the company.... It was like burying my child over again."

Granville Stuart, en route to California, recorded a bittersweet story in 1852:

> One evening we camped near five abandoned wagons. Close by were freshly made graves and by one of the wagons was a large yellow dog ... thin and nearly starved.... I coaxed him to me and divided my supper with him, which he devoured ravenously. He then went back and laid down by one of the graves and there remained all night.... [Later when we started to leave] I called him. ... He followed a few steps and then turned and went part way to the graves, stopped and began howling. Oh! so mournfully. We stopped to see what he would do. He quit howling and turned and came slowly to us, and when we started he followed us. ... My eyes filled with tears of sympathy for him ... so I took him up on the foot board of the wagon, where he lay part of the time all the way [to Utah, and on] to California.

Louisa Barnes Pratt and her four daughters mounted a chicken coop on the back of their wagon. She does not record how many hens they started out with, but the last one escaped on August 19, 1847, when a slat was torn off going through some willows. "We did not miss her till we camped at night," recalled Louisa. "When the children found she was gone they could scarcely be restrained from going back on foot to recover the lost treasure. Such an extraordinary hen, that knew the wagon where she belonged and laid all her eggs in and had traveled a thousand miles." Very little is said about chickens laying eggs, so it does prove they were not traumatized by traveling.

Summary

Young people on the trail helped make history. Those who survived, both physically and emotionally, toughened up and were better prepared for the hard years which followed, for tragedies and trauma did not cease when the trail ended. Wallace Stegner wrote that the children "who marched barefoot into Florence . . . hardened into health and from here on would stand the trail better than their elders." One of those children was eleven-year-old Margaret McNeil (Ballard), who arrived barefoot in Genoa, Nebraska, with a sick brother in 1857. When their cattle ran away, her parents sent them ahead with the regular group while the adults searched for the animals. All alone, she tended a four-year-old sick brother for two weeks while they waited for their parents. The family could not leave Genoa until 1859; and by then, Margaret was the main caregiver because her mother was not well. Children experienced the same fears, pain, thirst, hunger, and exhaustion as the adults but with fewer resources to meet these challenges. Those who survived did so because they could, in significant measure, fend for themselves and carry their part of the family burdens.

Immigrant children discovered America, saw their first buffalo, Indians, rattlesnakes, prairies, dust storms, flash floods, mountains, deserts, quicksand, animal and human skeletons, prairie fires, prairie dogs, stampedes, sagebrush, wolves, and bears. They drove their first oxen, often shot their first rifle, met their first foreigner, rode their first horse, witnessed their first birth, and watched as graves swallowed up their friends, siblings, and parents. They played and perished, but many of them felt it was an adventure, especially looking at the journey years later.

Jules Remy, a French journalist who visited Utah in 1856, praised the health and stamina of Zion's young men:

> The Mormons have that confidence of power which is given by religious fanaticism. When we saw the soldiers of the desert gather every week on the grand plaza of Zion experienced in [that is, tempered by] all kinds of danger, accustomed to a precarious and almost a savage

mode of life ... armed with revolvers, with sharp eyes, active bodies, and strong limbs–when we saw them under the order of a general in tatters execute with precision complicated operations of strategy, we could not refuse to believe that an army of these people would certainly beat twice their number of other troops.

Being a pioneer was something to be proud of, especially the handcarters. Oscar O. Stoddard captained the last handcart team in 1860. One little girl, Mary Ann Stucki Hafen, age six, walked the "five million little steps that brought her over the one thousand miles, ... which [left] deep recollections ... the remaining eighty-five years of her life," according to her writer/son Leroy H. Hafen

When the weather was harsh, the children and animals suffered. Bathsheba Smith, traveling on the Sweetwater River in 1849 when a sudden squall dumped two feet of snow on the camp, recalled sympathetically: "It was very grevious to hear the children cry, the ox low, the cow bawl, the sheep bleat, the pig squeal, the duck quack, the chickens cheep, and we could not tell them why they had to suffer."

But in mild weather, the trail could present incredible scenes that the pioneers remembered all their lives. Captain James Brown saw this idyllic real life scene in 1854 somewhere on the trail: "All is life and activity when cooking, washing, watching, singing, talking, laughing, and little girls and boys running, jumping, and skipping about camp. It is truly a great work and a wonder."

Chapter 7

Intimate Mormon Family Life

> *One of the Sisters is ill [about to deliver] so we wait for her—how foolish of women to be in that way on Such a Journey as this! But some people consider nothing but their own appetites. Bah!! —* Hannah Tapfield King, August 31, 1853

Victorian Conventions about Bodies

Victorian women left few comments about intimate relationships or bodily functions, for fear of being thought "unwomanly" or "coarse." Clothing for modest girls and women left nothing exposed between face, neck, and ankle. Sleeves came to the wrists except occasionally when a woman could roll them up to wash dishes or do the laundry. As a result, they were seldom comfortable or cool during the hot months.

It was equally indelicate to refer to women's bodies; but William Coray, a soldier in the Mormon Battalion, apparently felt that the conventions were suspended when the women being described were the Pima Indians of Arizona: "It was truly surprising to see the . . . women [who] looked very baudy indeed with nothing but a breech cloth. Many of them were singularly formed. Their bubbies was nearly 18 inches long and looked unnatural."

Henry Standage, another battalion soldier, was disconcerted by the sexual commerce being carried out in Los Angeles and commented in his diary on May 2, 1847: "The Spaniards' conduct in the Grog shops with the squaws is really filthy and disgusting even in the day time."

However, with rare exceptions, the silence in trail accounts about sex, elimination, and other usually private matters is profound. Sometimes, individuals did not undress for days. In 1861, one company traveling by train from Boston to the Missouri did not take their clothes off between June 1 and 23. Thomas G. Griggs wrote in 1861 that he had not changed his clothes for two weeks.

On April 19, 1852, Lucy Cooke, en route to Council Bluffs on a slow boat, wrote to her sister Marianne, "I have now got through having washed 12 diapers, sundry aprons, night gown & petticoat. I've not yet changed my own under clothes."

Bathing, which was far from the daily necessity that modern Americans consider it, was a rare pleasure on the trail. Sometimes they could bathe during "nooning" stops, but night was the more common opportunity. When A. P. Rockwood arrived at the "bank of the Platt" on April 20, 1847, "several of us went to the river and washed and bathed this Evening. We have need of this Every night for it is verry dirty." But Heber C. Kimball chastised the women in his camp in 1848 for bathing at night since "several are sick as a consequence."

Mary Ann Winters recorded the women's experience of bathing in the Platte "by starlight" wearing "a bathing suit of some kind." Because of the quicksand, "we were afraid to go far from the shore. . . . We would make a line from the nearest to the shore to the fartherest ones out. We could get a good ducking without much danger. We were very still about it all, for we never could tell when Indians might be lurking around."

Lucy Cooke, usually wearing an old gown, bathed as often as she could. "On the Plains of Nebraska" in May 1852, she wrote to Marianne: "I went in the river to bathe in the evening could not get any one to go in with me as there was such a cold wind blowing but I enjoyed it much." Camped at Independence Rock in mid-June 1852, she again wrote Marianne: "I have just been bathing in the sweetwater but Oh it was cold as ice. We could only take 2 or 3 dips & run out again. . . . . Really what a strange country we are in here, we bathing by the side of snowbanks & in sight of mountains covered with it whilst at the same time grass is good & gooseberries are growing in abundance."

A special treat was the warm springs near present-day Guernsey, Wyoming, which were usually about 70 degrees. (Most indoor pools today are 80 to 84 degrees.)

In 1862, soon after leaving the campgrounds in eastern Nebraska, Henry Stokes took advantage of the opportunity to bathe at the Elk Horn River. "In the afternoon I went with one teamster and some brethren down to the river and had a good bath."

In the hundreds of accounts I read for this book, only one or two mentioned brushing their teeth or oral hygiene in general. Some of the Saints lost their teeth and hair at Winter Quarters to scurvy. The omission of mention, however, does not mean that the travelers did not brush their teeth. It may simply mean that such a minor chore was not worthy of mention. The history of brushing teeth with the soft stem of a bush, perhaps augmented with a bit of baking soda, is well known.

Another unavoidable human "chore" that is conspicuous by its absence from the trail diaries is elimination and, for women, menstruation. Such physiological demands are far less optional than bathing. Chamberpots and a screened-off corner probably served this need aboard ship and on trains.

According to Robert Williams in 1850, an exceptionally lazy pioneer named George "sat in his wagon, playing some music and appeared a dandy gent." Too lazy to get out of his wagon to accommodate calls of nature, lazy George "had to toil through much slush and empty his dirty s—t p-t."

On the trail, the universal rule as part of the morning routine was: "Gents to the right, ladies to the left." Women could retire from the camp in small groups and, by spreading their long skirts, provide screens for each other. Immigrants were frequently advised, rather decorously, to remember the "Law of Moses," meaning the restriction decreed in Deuteronomy 23:13: "And thou shalt have a paddle ... when thou wilt ease thyself abroad, thou shalt dig therewith, and shalt turn back and cover that which cometh from thee."

According to trail lore, one wagon had enough room inside "for a small privy" in it; but this reference is unique. Given the number of immigrants confined to the narrow trail, the stench of many campsites must have been most disagreeable, but it is almost never mentioned in trail accounts. Oregonian Amelia Stewart Knight, who was pregnant, noted the stench caused by dead cattle but did not comment on human waste. On July 22, 1853, she recorded: "Crossed the river before daybreak and found the smell so bad that we left as soon as possible. . . . The dead cattle were lying in every direction. Still there were a good many getting breakfast among all the stench. I walked off among the rocks . . . and we drove a mile or so, and halted to get breakfast."

John Jaques noted an atrocious smell in the Martin Handcart Company "because so many had dysentery." John Chislett, in the Willie company, corroborated: "Before we renewed our journey [from Willow Creek], the camp became so offensive and filthy that words would fail to describe its condition and even common decency forbids the attempt. . . . It was enough to make the heavens weep."

All trail accounts are silent on the topic of menses. Jeanne Watson, an Oregon Trail expert, wrote:

> Neither is any thing said [in trail journals] about menstrual periods and what was done at this time, aside from indicating that some protection was available through use of cloth tied from the waist, probably an age-old feminine practice. Some women's diaries are marked in code to indicate days between periods; since researchers seldom have access to the manuscript itself, but must work from typed versions, such symbols may not have been reproduced on these copies. . . . Perhaps a number of women developed amenorrhea during the long, arduous trip and so skipped menstrual periods, as occurs today with some women athletes and ballet dancers due to exercise and stress.

In 1853 near Keokuk, Iowa, Arthur Christopher considered it a wonder "that with all the trouble, lack of privacy, lack of goods and outfits, that there was not much more quarreling and fussing in the camps and on the trails."

Traveling Flirtations

Young Mormon women, to the dismay of their elders, flirted, not only by singing hymns with the elders of Zion but with decidedly unsuitable crew members during ocean crossings and teamsters and soldiers on the plains. William Clayton wrote disapprovingly September 29, 1840: "This night Elizabeth Wilson, Elizabeth Lambert and Eliza Prince all from Manchester and Sister Crampton from Bolton was making very free with one of the mates and 2 of the cabin passengers. Brother Cope says they were drinking wine with them. Elder Turley sent Sister Poole to request them to come [away] but they returned very indifferent answers and said they could take care of themselves."

In 1851, English convert Jean Rio Baker primly summarized efforts to restore discipline aboard ship: "Held a meeting this afternoon at which three of the sisters were cut off the Church for [unclear] behavior with some of the officers of the ship, and continued disregard to the counsels of the president." In this case, "Elder Booth and Sister Thorn" were also guilty of misbehaving, and Jane recorded, scandalized: "The conduct of these two has been most shameful ever since we came on board the ship. . . . Brother Thorn is deeply grieved at the conduct of his wife [but] such a woman deserves no place in the remembrance of a man of God."

Once Mormon immigrants reached the campgrounds, they might have to wait four or five weeks before leaving; and except for chores, young women had more leisure than during the actual travel. In 1862, fifteen-year-old Lucy Marie Canfield, who would be traveling with a down-and-back train, kept only a sketchy diary, but about 20 percent of her entries mention the young men at Council Bluffs and on the trail:

> July 2, 1862: We went down to the boat. . . . Al West came and brought us some perfumery.
>
> July 8: It is a pleasant day. Alvin West and I gathered some wormwood to use for Mr. Young.
>
> July 11: Al went to Omaha and bought Rose [her cousin] and me each a fan.
>
> July 22: Brigham Kimball sent Rose a circle comb to cheer her.

On the trail, Lucy was still alert to male company, and Al West was still alert to her:

> July 30: Some boys from Ogden, Utah, camped near us. Al was up twice today. His company is about two miles away.
>
> Sept 28th. Camped near a military station, the soldiers invited us to take dinner with them.

Other single Mormon women flirted with soldiers at Fort Kearney, Fort Laramie, Fort Bridger, and on the trail. According to Thomas MacIntyre, the girls were reproved for "giving encouragement to strangers to lounge around camp; for trimming up and entering into conversation with gentiles no matter how obscene their language was," for wanting to attend a ball at Fort Bridger to be "treated with raisins and sugar," and for "taking dinner with soldiers."

In contrast was the experience of Christena McNeil, traveling with the 1856 Willie Handcart Company in which rations were already short. Agnes Caldwell recorded that a smitten officer at Fort Laramie proposed marriage to Christena, who turned down the chance for a financially secure marriage with him for the uncertainty of Zion. He "showed her the gold he had, telling her what a fine lady he would make of her [but] she told him she would take her chances with the others even though it might mean death. The officer . . . seemed to admire her . . . and gave her a large cured ham and wished her well in her chosen adventure."

Either less constant or more realistic, Sarah Jones, another woman in a handcart company, married a rancher near Devil's Gate. Whatever her religious feelings, she certainly spared herself much physical suffering.

There was even flirting in the handcart companies, despite the much more strenuous labor—at least during pleasant weather. Cold weather put a damper on Albert Jones, age sixteen, in 1856. "At the first fall of snow, [we felt] a great gloom upon us. We boys that up to this date rendered attentions to the Girls, had our spirits checked to [the] freezing point and the little God Cupid sped off for warmer climes."

Another Victorian convention was that women were both physically fragile and morally weak, so honorable men must step forward to protect the womenfolk. And certainly the potential for assault was present. Zebulon Jacobs left a detailed account in 1861 of intervening when some "rough fellows" made overtures to the women in Jacobs's company:

> Came to Old Fort Hollock and camped for the night. Here we found a rough lot of fellows. They wanted some of our sisters to go and get a glass of wine with them about 1/4 mile away. I quietly told them anything they [the sisters] wanted there were gentlemen [who] could get it without the Ladies leaving the camp. They got quite offended and tried to "score" me. Told them to go slow or some of them would get trip[p]ed up. One fellow bristled up, said he was an interpreter and knew where the Indians were. (Told him so did I) & some time set them on the immigrants out of spite. Told him could not help that & he was a d— rascal, did not wish to offend anyone but intended to take care of our women at any risk.

Zebulon's chivalry seems all the more notable because he apparently had no personal interest in any of the women he was protecting with such care. William Woods, who was conducting a genuine courtship, was forced to join an all-male team taking freight wagons to Salt Lake in 1862; and his fiancée, Elizabeth, was handed off to another wagon, much to his sorrow. In their farewell moments, he transferred her luggage with gloomy thoughts: "I think this was the greatest trial I ever underwent—to leave my betrothed. . . . However, I submitted and kissed my girl goodbye and gave her a half sovereign, all the money I had with a sorrowful heart and a mind full of reflections as to the outcome of it all."

He spent that first day with the freighters withdrawn and abstracted. "My mind was rambling over many things, especially as to when I should meet my dear girl again. As the shades of night closed down . . . I had occasion to go to my bag for some clothes and in taking out what I expected to be white duck sailor overalls and holding them up . . . they turned out to be some sort of ladies' unmentionables trimmed and adorned with lace. . . . I had made a mistake and got my sweetheart's bag. . . . Of course you can imagine the remarks that followed."

The sore-hearted lover had to put up with teasing till the trail's end. When Wood arrived a few weeks later in Salt Lake City, the family with whom Elizabeth had traveled told William she had gone off with an old polygamist. He was stunned. The woman, furthermore, told him that Elizabeth had also made love to her son and was no longer worthy of his devotion. She encouraged him to think no more of Elizabeth and instead to court her own daughter, Emma, who thought the world of him. Depressed and angry, he refused and went north twelve miles to Centerville to live with some friends. To his sublime joy, there he found his fiancée. Apparently she had not "gone off" with an old polygamist; but when the woman's efforts to match-make between Elizabeth and her son failed, the family sent her away. The reunited couple soon wed and had a long, happy married life.

Not all trail romances had prickly outcomes. After three months on the trail with Thomas Rogers, sixteen-year-old Aurelia Spencer formed a strong attachment to him and married him "in my seventeenth year," she wrote. Despite the difficulties and problems of Mormon immigrants, the sources contain a good number of pretty and tender stories of love and romance.

A brave girl might sing this 1840s song to her beau:

I'm Talking In My Sleep

By Mrs. F. S. Osgood

I have something sweet to tell you,
but the secret you must keep;
And remember if it isn't right,
I'm talking in my sleep.
For I know I am but dreaming
when I think your love is mine,
And I know they are but seeming
all the hope that round me shines.
I have something sweet to tell,
but the secret you must keep;
And remember if it isn't right,
I'm talking in my sleep.
So remember when I tell you,
what I cannot longer keep,
We are none of us responsible
for what we say in sleep.
My pretty secret's coming,
oh, listen with your heart,
And you shall hear it humming,

So close 'twill make you start.
Oh, shut your eyes so earnest,
or mine will wildly weep;
I love you! I adore you!
But I'm talking in my sleep.

Weeks and months spent in close quarters permitted people to get well acquainted. For teenagers who were not cripplingly burdened by camp chores, driving teams, inclement weather, illness, and caring for young siblings, the novelty of the surroundings lent an air of romance. Kezia Carroll recalled: "The thrill of the pleasant hours spent together and . . . nice little conversations . . . helped to shorten the journey." Many wrote of laughing, joking, gathering flowers, picking berries, and other pleasant activities. A few deemed it novel and romantic to travel in wagons. Riding double on horseback, singing, dancing, and conversing by moonlight were considered thrilling, especially with the addition of bouquets of sweet-scented wild flowers. Such pleasant activities lightened the trials and helped to shorten the journey—psychologically at least.

Although no pretty face or well-turned ankle went unnoticed, several of the eligible young men soberly took note of young women who adapted well to driving oxen, could make a good fire, did not waste food, and didn't flinch from gathering buffalo chips. Perhaps they thought such young women would make hardworking wives.

Another tale of sweet union came from a young man who had preceded his fiancée west, then, having made plans for them, traveled back east along the trail at the same time as George Rowley's 1859 handcart company. At Devil's Gate, much to his joy, he found his fiancée and her parents. According to William Atkins, they were married on the spot by the company captain.

Of all the tales of romance and love on the trail, the most romantic was surely that of seventeen-year-old Margaret Judd from Canada. Prior to going west in 1848, she and her true love "vowed eternal constancy for at least four years. When we were of age he would claim me, even though it was at the ends of the earth." Therefore, she traveled happily. Everything was "bright and beautiful. . . . I was young and healthy." At night after chores, Margaret and the young people generally made a bonfire and encircled it, telling stories and singing. Margaret enjoyed the attentions of several nice young men in her company. On the 4th of July, a "dapper young gentlemen from New York . . . brought a bottle of wine and a large piece of delicious fruit cake which was made to celebrate the fourth on the plains."

Thereafter he started calling at her wagon, said a lot of lovely, romantic things and eventually proposed. In the Valley, however, they had a lover's quarrel and did not make up. She later recorded that he married "a useless ignoramous he had ridiculed to me many times while on our journey. Such is the constancy of men!" The story is not clear whether she found her "forever love" or not.

LDS girls were not above playing games with unwanted suitors. In 1847 an old tailor at Winter Quarters thought he still had charms and tried to court two younger women, unaware that one was already married. The two friends let him continue with his dogged courtship for some time, to the amusement of those in on the matter.

Marriage on the Trail

There were two kinds of marriage among Mormons during the exodus: first marriages and polygamous marriages. Either kind could occur at any point: crossing the Atlantic, on the Mississippi and Missouri rivers, in camps and tents along the trail, on sunny afternoons, during rainy nights, and at Chimney Rock, and Independence Rock. At Winter Quarters on March 8, 1848, "Mother Calkins . . . and Brother Fisher were married, both over seventy, but peart and lively." After an explosion of endowments and sealings in the late winter of 1845-46, Brigham Young also performed a number of sealings in Winter Quarters and en route, since it was hardly possible to go to a temple. Other Church leaders also performed marriages on request, although, from the record, only Brigham Young performed sealings.

George Whitaker drove a team across Iowa in 1846, then waited for his fiancée "Miss Robinson" to arrive from Nauvoo that July. It was very proper and dignified: "I took my horse and carriage, crossed the river and found [the Robinsons] camped on the bluffs. I made my errand known to them and she was willing to go with me and share with me in anything we would have to go through. . . . On the evening of 27 of July, 1846, all of the family dressed in their best, and Brother Parley Pratt performed the ceremony. Hymns were sung, a good supper was served, and we all felt happy." The newlyweds spent their honeymoon herding cattle about thirty miles from Winter Quarters.

Shipboard marriages were common. In 1859, Robert F. Neslen helped organize an Atlantic crossing for 725 Scandinavians and English converts who among them spoke nine languages. "In the matrimonial department we did exceedingly well," he reported. "We had nineteen marriages, five couples of which were English, one Swiss, and thirteen Scandinavians—all of which were solemnized by myself."

Trail life disrupted many of the standard procedures of courtship that acted to integrate the young couple into the community. Such rites included long courtships, intricate family arrangements, and the posting of marriage banns. There was neither time nor money for such arrangements on the trail, which saved a lot of both. On the other hand, because of the closeness of trail travel, people got to know each other during the good and the bad times with the possible result of fewer unpleasant discoveries after marriage.

Even the Mormon Battalion soldiers spent some time on the trail courting and marrying. The detachment of soldiers with various family members that had not continued to California in early 1847 went into camp at Pueblo where some Mississippi Saints also wintered. According to Abner Blackburn, "Their was a coupple spooning"—Harley Mowrey and Martha Jane Sharp, a young widow. "The whole company weare tired of it," recalled Blackburn, "and they weare persuaded to marry now, and have done with it and not wait until their journeys end. The next evening we had a wedding and a reglar minister to unite them. Then came the dance or howe down. The banjo and the violin made us forget the hardships of the plains."

As Abner reports, music, where available, played an important role, and so did the musicians. On September 28, 1862, Henry Stokes solemnly recorded that "Brother Wm. F. Critchlow officiated" in the marriage of William Fuller and Emma Happen. Then, "Brother Critchlow sang two love songs and played some lively tunes on the fiddle" for the dancing. The lack of an officiator did not cause the lack of a wedding. Dan Judd, en route to Oregon in 1847, wrote about the democratic solution to "a wilderness wedding" when "there wasn't a minister available." The other travelers "deputized a man to say the ceremony."

Polygamy

According to George D. Smith, there were at least 153 polygamous families in Nauvoo at the beginning of the exodus in 1846—that is, 153 husbands, 587 wives, of whom about 500 were plural wives, and 734 children, for a total of nearly 1,500 people. If we add to this figure the number of plural marriages through 1848 before Winter Quarters was abandoned, we have (by one count) 653 wives and an unknown number of additional children, or something like 1,600 individuals. Since most of these husbands and wives went west, polygamy was an important and unique dimension of the Mormon migrations.

All of the Twelve and most of the leaders at that time were among the polygamous families who went west during 1846-48. At the beginning of the exodus in 1846, some husbands took all of their wives and children with them, while some families followed. Many returned to Nauvoo later for the other family members, or the plural wives and children subsequently joined their husbands on the Missouri River or even in Utah. Some did not join their husbands for years. Some wives never did go west, which resulted in more fractured marriages.

Since polygamy was not openly preached in Europe, some converts did not learn of the doctrine until they reached the United States—sometimes not even until they reached the Salt Lake Valley. Not all of them embraced the new doctrine, although not all of those who rejected it were economically able to leave Utah and seek another home.

Sophia Whitaker, who emigrated from England in a party led by Apostle John Taylor, married him in April 1847. Parley P. Pratt brought back two "young ladies from England whom he intended to make his wives." He married them on April 28, 1847. Mary Ann Stearns Pratt, his second monogamous wife for several years, was so upset by these seventh and eighth marriages that she went east from Winter Quarters to live with relatives for a few years. When she rejoined Pratt in Utah, the marriage ended in divorce.

Pioneer John Pack left three wives in Winter Quarters. On May 4 near present Grand Island, Nebraska, he wrote them: "Dear Julia, Ruth, and Nancy, I take this moment with the greatest pleasure and take my pen with more anxiety than I ever had before in my life. I am well, thank the Lord, but I never missed the society of my family more than I do at this time. I feel so lonesome.... There is no society so dear and so sweet as my kindred ... but it is good to be deprived of the sweet so as to no [know] how to prise [prize] it."

Martha Spence Heywood, a convert school teacher from Ireland, learned about polygamy en route to the Valley in 1850 from Sarah Lawrence, a plural wife of Heber C. Kimball: "I visited Sarah Lawrence [and] some knowledge imparted was calculated to make me feel sober and that the light heartedness and buoyancy of spirits I have been wont to feel will have to be given up for a variety of perplexities that are not known amongst the friends I have left. How much I have thought today of the freedom that for years I have enjoyed ... a freedom of thought and action that will never be known again." After reflection, Martha agreed to become the plural wife of Joseph L. Heywood in 1851.

Hannah Tapfield King, though a staunch believer, was troubled by the blatant attentions of her son-in-law, Claudius Spencer. He was married to her twenty-two-year-old daughter Georgey but also openly courted Georgey's younger sister, twenty-year-old Louie, on the trail. Hannah recorded on August 13, 1853: "Left our encampment near Fort Laramie ... felt low—mournful & worn down—I see the determined attention Claudius keeps to Louie, and it takes away my Soul—drinks up my Spirit. I feel too that it affects Georgey. Surely he might wait till he gets to The Valley.... I cannot reconcile myself to this new doctrine coming in such a form—I feel that it works upon Georgey's feeling also—Oh! My Father—help me & give me not up to my own dark thoughts.... Went to bed unhappy and dejected." Claudius married Louie soon after they got settled in the Valley.

One family who seemed to cope well with a polygamous household was that of Joseph Lee Robinson who undertook his responsibilities thoughtfully and made strenuous efforts to deal successfully with his three wives in Winter Quarters: "As to plural marriage's effect upon our wives and sisters," he commented, "now with the tradition and human selfishness to contend with, it could not be expected that they could enter into this order. . . . For the nature of this law would severely try any woman—even to nearly tearing their heart strings right out of them. And also, it would severely try the men as well. Surely a man has to possess an abundance of grace, wisdom and patience to be the husband of several women and treat them all with equality, and in a way whereby he would stand justified before the law."

Although polygamy would not be publicly acknowledged until 1852, many men traveled with plural wives; and these more complex households did not seem to have more stress than monogamous travelers. Perhaps those who had trouble with polygamy did not record it or did not wish to appear unfaithful. Or perhaps the journals did not survive or were edited by descendants who were trying to preserve the family's reputation for harmony.

Heber C. Kimball took twelve to fourteen wives with him from Nauvoo, two of them in 1847. Sarah Ann Whitney and Ellen Saunders were both pregnant. The rest of his extended family, traveling with friends and relatives eventually joined him on the Missouri River. At least four of his total of forty-three plural wives never went west and sixteen others separated themselves from him at one time or another. There is little indication that Kimball considered plural marriage as more than a religious chore to raise up numerous children and provide for widows.

Kimball was dutiful but discreet with his other wives. They all knew that his first wife, Vilate Murray Kimball, was his greatest love. About a week into the journey of 1847, Heber got a chance to write her. This letter so moved Howard Egan, that he mentioned it in his journal on April 18, 1847: "H. C. Kimball wrote a letter to his companion this morning and sent it by Brother Ames, the contents of which I heard read and it done my heart good. It portrayed the feelings of his heart and his affection for his family, in the most simple and beautiful language that would touch the soul and cause the heart to rejoice." At that point, the Kimballs had been married for more than twenty years.

William Clayton traveled with three wives and a mother in-law in 1846. His fifth and youngest wife, seventeen-year-old Diantha

Farr, stayed in Nauvoo with measles and the last stages of pregnancy. When he heard that she had safely delivered a son, on April 15, 1846, he wrote the most famous of all Mormon hymns, "Come, Come, Ye Saints." Clayton's other wives were two pairs of biological sisters: Ruth and Margaret Moon, and Alice and Jane Hardman. Jane died in Winter Quarters. Diantha died soon after they got to the Valley.

July and August of 1848 saw the births of an extraordinary number of babies en route, children who had been conceived at Winter Quarters in October when the brethren returned from the Valley. On July 23, Louisa Beaman Young delivered twins. Helen Mar Kimball Whitney gave birth on August 17, but the baby died. Sarah Ann Whitney Kimball, Heber's plural wife, delivered her baby on August 26.

Midwife Patty Sessions wrote extensively on her experiences in plurality—all of it negative. Her husband, David, married a selfish young woman, Rosilla, as his plural wife. Many wives must have experienced similar anguish. Crossing Iowa in 1846, Patty recorded: "Mr. S. has said many hard things to me. I have slept but little. I feel as though my heart would burst with grief; Sorrow of heart has made me sick; I am too full of grief that there is no room for food. I soon threw it up; Mr. Sessions has found fault with me and we are here alone mostly, in tents. . . . I have slept but little. I feel as though my heart would break. I cannot eat. Sorrow of heart has made me sick." This kept up all across Iowa.

At Winter Quarters Rosilla proved to be obstinate, lazy, saucy, and abusive toward Patty. She was also decidedly possessive about David, gloating about his obvious preference for her. In an unconsciously insulting offer, Sessions told Patty that he would sleep with her when she was not off delivering babies if she would make peace with Rosilla. But by November 1846, either David tired of Rosilla or vice versa. She went back east, dropping out of the Sessions family.

Bathsheba Smith explained how her husband, George A. Smith, managed his household of five wives, four children, and eight teamsters. "Sister Lucy," Bathsheba notes, "occupied one wagon; Sister Zilpah another; Sister Sarah and her babe, John Henry, and sister Hannah Marie and her babe, Charles Warren, another; myself and children, George Albert and Bathsheba, occupied another." She does not describe where George A. headquartered. Presumably, he rotated among his family units.

Not all women had trouble with the system. Vilate Kimball recorded how the Lord revealed to her the "rightness" of polygamy. Sarah Studevant Leavitt, also had a vision that moved her to exclaim: "I saw the order there and oh, how beautiful. . . . I waked my husband and told him of the views [of polygamy] I had . . . but [I said] it would damn thousands. It was too sacred for fools to handle, for they would use it to gratify their lustful desires."

Domestic Strife and Divorce

Marital difficulties, separations, and divorces also occurred along the trails and way stations. For example, soon after Peter McIntyre reached Sugar Creek in February of 1846, his wife suddenly announced that she intended to leave him, the immigrant company, and their three daughters. They were within walking distance of several small communities; and Peter, hoping to prevent her from leaving, refused to let her take her clothes. She left him anyway and sent him a postcard when he was in Council Bluffs requesting that he send her clothes to a grocer in Boston, Lee County, Iowa. He did so, hoping she would come back, but they never heard from her again. Later in Utah, McIntyre recorded. "I feel very sorry for my poor wife Margaret. . . . When I open her chest and see a few things of hers my heart is sorrowful."

In 1846, according to Henry Emery: "a man became so furious with his wife for having sold six plates for 48 cents that he accepted an offer of $1.00 for her." *Women of the West* preserves an account, possibly apocryphal, that a man bought a wife from a Mormon for a horse, a revolver, and six hundred dollars.

The Thomas Cooper family history recounts how the husband and his mother-in-law quarreled frequently during their trek in 1864, but he and his wife did not have an untroubled relationship either. Once, during a domestic squabble, the husband began to choke the wife, the mother-in-law tried to drag him off, and another member also came to the wife's rescue. They threw the husband out of the wagon. He began to cry and blustered: "I'll leave you, and you'll never see me again!" He left and the wife turned on her mother, blaming her for driving the husband off. Later that night, the husband crawled back into the wagon, begging forgiveness.

According to Henry Emery, a sister in Kanesville demanded a divorce during the winter of 1848–49. She had nothing against her husband but wanted to marry another. Later she wished to return to her first husband, but "he would not hearken to her any more."

Jacob Hamblin's wife not only stole from him and his friends but also lied about him and sought to prejudice others against him. He finally appealed to Elder Orson Hyde at Kanesville to give him a "writing" (meaning, a divorce), so he could take his children and leave his wife—which he did.

Childbirth

Hannah Tapfield King's epigraph, which opens this chapter, communicates nothing but scorn for a woman who would start across the plain in such an advanced state of pregnancy that she was sure to deliver en route. Although Hannah sounds censorious and blames the woman for her plight, she conveniently ignores the role that a husband's desires may play and the fact that conception could not, except in rough and not always reliable ways, be deflected. The result, however, was indeed childbirth.

Patty Sessions, one of Mormondom's most experienced midwives, delivered about four thousand babies before she died. Within a month after leaving Nauvoo in 1846, she had assisted at four births and three miscarriages. One of Patty's pregnant patients in Winter Quarters was unmarried, which prompted Patty's mixed reaction of condemnation and kindness: "Called on Hannah Jones to talk to her for her bad conduct. Then I went to the bishop to have a bedstead fixed up for her and to make her comfortable. Altho I thought she was a bad woman, yet she lay on the ground and about to be confined and I pitied her."

Since pregnancy and childbirth were not considered cause to delay a journey, the women made do with makeshift care and few comforts. A surprising number of babies were born under trying circumstances, and the outcome for both mother and child was often harsh. Given the difficulties of trail travel and little medical knowledge and practices, the wonder is that more tiny graves did not line the trail west.

Women gave birth on the ground, in log cabins, in tents, in wagons, under makeshift umbrellas, and under bushes. Patty Sessions noted that one woman rode thirteen miles "after she was in travail." Victorian conventions also suppressed the recording of labor and birthing. One woman appeared one morning in an 1857 handcart company with a new infant in her apron; she had delivered the child alone in the bushes unknown to the others. Twelve-year-old Rachel Emma Woolley boasted that the birth of her sister in 1848 "did not hold the camp up at all," but it was rare for a whole company to stop for a delivery. The John Brown Company of 1848 stopped for two days for Brown's wife to deliver. Not many women had that luxury. All went well with the birth and perhaps the whole camp also rejoiced in the chance to rest for two days.

Infant and Child Care

While Mormons were typical parents in the homes of pre-Civil War America, they were unique in their belief in an unending family life in this world and the next. In such a belief system, children take on even greater importance. Child care was greatly complicated by traveling, but pioneer women were quick to find substitutes for cradles and beds. Diapering infants was a constant problem, especially when water was scarce. Although references were scarce, it was probably common to dry, scrape, wash if possible, air, and reuse the cloth diapers. Many women probably learned from Indian women how to use grass, moss, and even pulverized buffalo dung, which was absorbent. Most camps allowed the babies to sleep in the wagons as long as possible. A few secured baskets or sacks as saddlebags in which infants and small children could be carried with a riding parent. But most small children were carried by sisters or mothers. Louisa Charlotte Graehl, the first woman in Geneva to join the Church in June 1854, migrated to Zion a year later with her husband, three young girls, and a baby boy. One daughter, Eliza, died en route. Their wagon came near wrecking, the horses were unruly, and they were forced to walk to camp; Louisa had to carry two of her children but never once complained. " I had to carry a little girl in one arm and a baby in the other and to find my way through the high grass. I was very much afraid that I would trample on a rattlesnake. My husband had not been well since we left the old country and now he became even worse and had to stay in the wagon so I had to drive." They arrived in the Valley in October 1955.

Regardless of how careful parents were, bizarre accidents happened to children. A little girl was kicked out of the wagon accidentally by the mother, but not hurt. Kicking animals broke children's arms and legs. More adventuresome older children would balance on the wagon tongue with both hands resting on the backs of the oxen. This very dangerous practice resulted in some deaths. Some children, especially boys, would hang onto tent poles and extra axles lashed beneath the wagons. Some children were accidentally shot.

Illness on the Trail

Dysentery apparently came under the heading of illness and could be acknowledged more openly. In 1853, the well-educated Martha Spence was nursing a sick young man, Frank Heywood, the young son of Martha's future husband in polygamy. She recorded: "[Frank] had a passage about three o'clock and another tonight . . . was very weak this morning—had two passages during the night but other wise rested well. The laudanum that was given yesterday afternoon caused these symptoms." Forty-niner Jesse G. Hannon, quoted one buddy who was "taken with the diarrhea; common now on the prairie, and have been kept quite busy attending to the wants of nature, having 25 passages today."

Eighteen-year-old Abigail Scott, en route to Oregon in 1853, wrote that her mother "was taken about two o'clock this morning with a violent diarrhea attended with cramps. She, however, aroused no one until daylight when everything was done which we possibly could do to save her life, but her constitution long impaired by disease was unable to withstand the attack."

Hannah Tapfield King, an English convert crossing in 1853 with her family, nursed her thirteen-year-old son, Tom, through an unspecified illness, and commented in early August: "I hope Tom is better. I washed him all over in vinegar and water—changed his bed & put on all clean Linen—he looked comfortable and comforted—my poor wounded heart." On August 20, she "sat in the Carriage all the afternoon with T.O he's no worse. . . . Slept in the carriage with T.O."

Summary

Young people could become well acquainted from being around the same person for three to eight months. If romantically inclined, a couple could spend a lot of nights together talking, holding hands, singing, teasing, and meandering around the camp. And if the rain kept sweethearts apart, they were even more excited to see each other afterwards. Being close and surveying the billions of stars would tend to make lovers more than "star struck." Sometimes a tender touch or a smile was all that was necessary.

While many Mormons crossing the plains, recall it as an ordeal to be endured, others—particularly those who were well-equipped and traveling in good weather with well-organized companies—remember the experience as delightful, a romp across flowered prairies with colorful Indians and novel animals and plants to beguile the hours. There is no way to know if they ever constituted a majority. And certainly the accounts of those who grimly endured or cracked under the strain abound. For some, the harsh reality "tore to shreds" natural feelings. A few men abandoned their families. A few women went berserk. Too many men and women starved and simultaneously worked themselves to death in the handcart companies, exacerbated by other hardships, according to John Chislette, who traveled with the Willie Handcart Company. Those hardships often destroyed "all romance and deadened the natural feelings of the most manly and affectionate" and also produced a "fearful amount of selfishness, not to say brutality."

But the opposite experience is also true. Many of those nineteenth-century romances and marriages became a lifetime commitment, whether they had their origins in romantic ideals or whether a desperate man was trying to find a new mother for his young children. Although there were some arranged marriages among the Saints, Cupid was present and made his influence felt wherever young people were assembled. Love, then as now, always finds a way.

Chapter 8

Interactions with Fellow Travelers

Mr. Meeks and wife treated us with the greatest kindness; [we] were invited to take supper with them. We accordingly went and had a rich repast, consisting of beacon [bacon] and lettuce, short cake and butter, a . . . baked Pudding Custard stirred cake, and a good Cup of Coffee. . . . They have noble hearts and may the Lord bless them. — Harriet Decker Young, Friday, July 21, 1846.

The Saints were not alone on the trail west but met many other pioneers over the years at their various points of departure and along the trail—traders, freighters, trappers, mountain men, missionaries, Indian agents, Oregonians, and argonauts, as prospective gold-miners were known. Another group was the military, including discharged soldiers.

In 1846

A majority of the Saints evacuated Nauvoo in February 1846. Iowans were curious as these religious refugees pressed into the territory in early March 1846 but seemed kindly and helpful for the most part. On March 6, Brigham Young's history recorded that Dr. John D. Elbert visited their camp and "stated that when the first news reached them that the Mormons were about to pass through . . . there was great excitement . . . on account of the prejudices which had been created by false and alarming reports, fearing that they would be swallowed up alive, but the more recent reports of the honest dealings of the Camp had caused those feelings to subside and [they] had concluded to let the Mormons pass in peace."

Helen Mar Kimball Whitney also recorded that "there was a great amount of sympathy manifested by the people as we traveled through Iowa. Many visited our camps, and wherever the companies stopped our men were able to find employment. The splendid music made by the Nauvoo Brass Band quite surpassed anything that had been heard in that part, and they were cordially invited to play at every settlement."

Brigham Young's brother, Lorenzo Dow Young, said they asked for shelter at a farmhouse when his wife, Harriet Decker Young, "was very sick and could ride no further. The people were very kind indeed to us, and did everything they could. The name of the man was Farmer where we staid. He has a noble family." Similarly, when Catherine Spencer got too sick to travel in Iowa in 1846, a kind family took her and the children in. She died soon afterwards, and Orson Spencer took his wife's body back to Nauvoo to be buried.

Hosea Stout recorded on June 12 that "a company of Gentiles came in and it created a great excitement as all the guns lay in the yard by my tent but we covered them up and placed a guard over them. They came to see if we were preparing for war as they had heard but went off well satisfied that we were not." The fact that a committee came to investigate, instead of accepting the rumors at face value, was gratifying.

A little farther south that spring, Francis Parkman, a wealthy, educated young man from an aristocratic eastern family passed through St. Louis. He knew little and cared less about the troubles of the Saints. Possessed of great curiosity, he had a snobbish disregard for anything that he wasn't "on the best terms with." Although he apparently did not meet any of the Saints as he left to study the Plains Indians, he talked to others while he assembled his outfit at Independence and recorded some of the gossip in his famous book: *The Oregon Trail*:

> The . . . Oregon and California emigrants . . . had heard reports that several additional parties were setting out from St. Joseph [and] the prevailing impression was that these were Mormon . . . and a great

alarm was excited in consequence. The people of Illinois and Missouri, who composed by far the greater part of the immigrants, have never been on the best terms with the "Latter Day Saints;" and it is notorious through the country how much blood has been spilled in their feuds. [The immigrants] sent to Colonel Kearny, requesting an escort of dragoons as far as the Platte. This was refused; and, as the sequel proved, there was no occasion for it. The St. Joseph emigrants were as good Christians and as zealous Mormon-haters as the rest; and the very few families of the Saints who passed . . . remained behind until the great tide of emigration had gone by, standing in quite as much awe of the "gentiles" as the latter did of them.

Parkman did meet some Mormons eventually and termed them "blind and desperate fanatics."

Thomas L. Kane, a man of small stature and great compassion, found a new cause in 1846 when he hurried to help those whom he believed had been denied religious freedom. He could do little about the anti-Mormon press and public sentiment, which had spread even further around the country in mid-1846, but he could and did act as a compassionate intermediary extraordinaire. Wild rumors and exaggerations against the Saints, printed as fact, created headlines that sold papers.

Not everyone was compassionate. Franklin D. Richards had been sent to England on a mission, leaving his two wives in deplorable shape. During the summer, Jane Snyder Richards inched across Iowa with her desperately ill sister wife. Jane had just given birth, but the baby did not survive. Her little daughter, Wealthy, saw a field of potatoes, and asked for some potato soup. Jane's mother went to the nearby farm and asked if she could have some potatoes for a dying child. The housewife refused angrily: "I won't sell or give a thing to one of you damned Mormons."

In September 1846, a few Mormons still remained in Nauvoo. Some lacked the health or financial resources to depart. Others no doubt hoped that, with most of the Saints out of the state, the situation would stabilize. They were wrong. Mobs attacked those who still remained in Nauvoo; and in the three-day battle, two Saints were killed and several wounded. The mobs told them if they would renounce their faith, they could stay; but otherwise, they had to leave immediately.

The Fields family was driven out, remembering once they were on the other side of the river, that they had left a warm loaf of bread on the stove. "We could look upon our beautiful Nauvoo and the grain and other crops in the fields rotting while we were going hungry," Mary Field Garner wrote.

Many of the mob considered the abandoned property to be their due as the spoils of war. To add insult to injury, they celebrated their "victory" drunkenly in the temple, desecrating what they could not destroy.

Deep Suspicions

On the trail, both Mormons and Gentiles had suspicions of each other. Mormons, wary because of a history of persecution stretching back to 1831 in Ohio, recorded some of their uneasiness. Sarah Maria Mousley remained rigidly suspicious: "I never knew or appreciated the merits of Mormonism [before starting west]," she wrote en route to the Florence camp. "In wisdom of God's providence I have been thrown . . . continually amidst the enemies of truth. Consequently I am not priviledged to withdraw from their society. Joyful were my feelings [in 1857] . . . when the time rolled on to again mingle with the people whose aim was to do the will of God and obey his command. The day on which we reached the camp our spirits were enlivened by the presence of President Erastus Snow . . . and [we] listened to the words of truth that . . . fell from his tongue."

For their part, some Gentiles were equally wary. In April 1852, a young mother with six children left St. Joseph County, Michigan, with a hired driver to join her husband who had left for California two years earlier. About seventy years later, one of the children, Elisha Brooks, recollected his trail experience as an eleven-year-old boy:

> We spent two days attempting various schemes for crossing the Platte river but the treacherous current and . . . quicksand baffled all our efforts. . . . Two Mormons arrived with timber for a boat, and we all lent a hand in its construction. In a week it was launched and we prepared to cross, when the ferrymen, ignoring our labor on the boat, demanded a price for [ferrying the wagons across]. We compromised the matter by posting a guard of our roughs over them with cocked rifles while we ferried ourselves across . . . then treating those profane ferrymen to a bath in the Platte to cool them off.

Anna Marie Goodell recorded another negative encounter in 1854: "Today we crossed Smith's fork. It was bad crossing. We came to the Mormon toll bridge but the company would not pay him anything. Then he started to steal our cattle." Doubtless this hard-working Mormon bridgekeeper would have told the story differently.

According to young Elisha Brooks, his company's mistrust of the Mormons was so deep that they lengthened their journey rather than pass through Salt Lake City: "North of Salt Lake we were harassed by the hostile Shoshones spurred on by the Mormons. . . . We dared not go through Salt Lake on account of their hostility, but passed to the North by way of Sublette's Cutoff."

Roxanna Foster, a California-bound traveler in 1854, frankly confessed: "I had such an aversion to the Mormons that I did not want to go to Salt Lake." She recorded the rumor that travelers who had to winter over in the Salt Lake Valley "were compelled to become Mormons." Rather than risk the "dangers" of such a place, several wagons left the main company to travel by a different route.

Sandra L. Myers in *Westering Women and the Frontier Experience, 1800–1915* also mentions Mormon price-gouging as a source of conflict. Some travelers were "so disgusted by what little they had heard about Mormons, they deliberately bypassed Salt Lake City and the opportunity to rest their teams, repair wagons, and purchase needed supplies. . . . [They thought] Mormons made it a policy to steal from travelers . . . and deliberately overcharged for goods and service." While instances of gouging no doubt occurred, much of it must be attributed to the simple scarcity of goods. In 1847, prices doubled between Fort Laramie and Fort Bridger according to Mormon journals, and they grumbled about being cheated by Gentiles. Wallace Stegner said that the Saints later enjoyed "skinning the Gentiles."

Brigham Young's unvarnished sermons combined with rumors of Danites and the all-too-obvious satisfaction of the Saints at having a buffer between themselves and the Gentile East. Heber C. Kimball voiced the opinion of most Mormons when he said: "The whole people of the United States are under condemnation." Consequently, it was easy to blame the Mormons for anything fearsome or unpleasant on the trail, nor did the historical fact of the Mountain Meadows Massacre lose any of its grisly effect in the retelling.

Martha Moore, en route to California wrote in 1860, apparently referring to the Mountain Meadows area: "This is the noted Mormon range where most of their deeds of horror have been transacted."

Mutual Kindness

Although such negative encounters are certainly part of the historical record, so are instances of mutual kindness and cooperation. Thomas Bullock, traveling with the vanguard company, noted that the Saints quickly worked out an exchange of labor for provisions with Oregon-bound pioneers. The Mormons built a ferry for crossing the Platte River. The Oregonians were initially suspicious enough to keep their knives and guns at hand, but relationships rapidly changed. On Sunday, June 13, 1847, the Mormons

> saved the life of a young man belonging to the Emigrant Company & ferried over 24 wagons [and the emigrants] invited [them] to take coffee & biscuits; & when the job was finished made quite a feast of Tea, coffee, Biscuits, Butter, Meat & the good things. . . . The Flour & Meal was divided amongst the brethren—6 pounds of Flour and 2 pounds Meal to each person, which was quite a blessing to the Camp.[June 18, 1847] . . . Captain Ashworth invited us to breakfast with him on Bacon, Warm Biscuits & light fried biscuits, good Coffee with Sugar & then Milk. Eating a good breakfast from a Woman's Cooking is a remembrance of past times and renews the desire for such times to come again.

Jean Rio Griffiths Baker noted a special favor on May 8, 1851, when her company was traveling in the Iowa area:

> Nothing can exceed the kindness of the people as we pass along. Any time when our wagons have been in a mudhole, the men working in the fields have left their ploughs to come and help us out. Men, too, who in our country would be called gentlemen, coming from five hundred to one thousand acres of land. It seems to be a rule among them to help everyone who is in need, and they are ready at all times to impart any information which they think useful. [When] we encamp near a farmhouse for the convenience of supplying ourselves with butter, eggs, and milk, we are sure to be invited to their houses in order to partake of their hospitality.

Two months later, Jean Rio Baker wrote on July 12, 1851:

Nine wagons have overtaken us and the travelers have requested to be allowed to join our company. We now number fifty-four.... These newcomers had started for Oregon but had been attacked by Indians who had stolen some of their oxen and driven away the rest. They had recovered some few of their cattle and were returning to the frontier when they saw our company and turned back.... (The brethren) found ten of the strangers' missing cattle, which was quite a Godsend to them.... One of the strangers in our company spoke at our meeting this afternoon and pleased us very much by his testimony in our favor.

In 1859 a well-equipped party bound for "Pike's Peak or Bust" passed the George Rowley Handcart Company. Handcart pioneer William Atkin gratefully recorded that this company killed a large buffalo: "They took one quarter of it, and covered the three-quarters carefully with the hide and put up a notice that read 'This is for the handcarts.' We found it in very good condition and it was divided out, giving us from one to two pounds each. This was the only good mess of fresh meat of this kind that we had obtained."

This same company struggled on and was "in the heights of despair when we met some rough mountaineers" at Green River, according to Sarah H. Beesley's account. "They felt very sorry for us and told us if we would come over to their camp they would give us some breakfast. I never tasted anything better in my life and it was cooked by squaws.... The first thing they gave us was milk and whiskey and we had to drink it out of gourds.... Then they gave us a sort of bread or cake [and] it was all so good. When we were through, we carried some back to the ones who were too sick to come with us. I remember one Scotch girl stayed there with them."

Rescues along the Trail

The trail provided examples of both extremes—a quick and kindly reaching out to whoever was in need but also a callous disregard of human suffering.

One heartless and bizarre incident occurred in 1849 along the Sweetwater near Register Cliff. California-bound Alexander Bear was shot in the knee when a mule accidentally stepped on a gun. He could not bear the pain of riding in a wagon, and he refused to have his leg amputated. Another member of the company, John Markle, laconically recorded: "We had to leave him."

Mormon Twiss Bermingham, traveling with a 1856 handcart company, wrote on August 14: "A few days previous . . . we met a man coming from California. He was deserted on the plains by his companions who left him with nothing but a shirt and trousers which he had on. . . . We gave him some bread." The Oscar O. Stoddard handcart company of 1860 also picked up a sick Mormon family near Green River that had been abandoned by their company. The young daughter died a few days later.

Unfortunately, at least two Mormon captains were guilty of abandoning or mistreating families entrusted to their care. Sarah M. Mousley reported on July 11, 1857: "Early this morning a committee of Elders came from Genoa or Beaver settlement [in Nebraska], was accompanied by the man whom was left on the plains yesterday. A council was called; the captain was forced to acknowledge the great wrong he had done and promised to do better . . . and lead the people with more gentleness."

The Role of Plural Marriage

Julie Roy Jeffrey, writing in *Frontier Women*, explains the difficulty that most Americans had in viewing Mormons with anything but suspicion and fear: "Not able to see the Mormons as persecuted defenders of religious freedom . . . [Gentile] women perceived [them] as threats to domestic culture. . . . [Plural marriage has] destroyed the family and woman's unique place in it and made women unfit for their moral and social responsibilities."

Jeffrey wrote that American women's commitment to monogamy resulted in their assumption that "polygamy exploited women sexually without giving them anything in return." Women, outraged by the idea of "one third or perhaps one twentieth share of a man," considered this bargain "hardly worth the hard work expected of wives." They assessed Mormon women as a "poor heart broken and deluded lot [who] are made slaves to the will of these hellish beings who call themselves men. . . . [The women] have not so much liberty as common slaves in the south." Mormon women were "exploited drudges to religious fanatics."

Public outrage became particularly strong in 1852 when Brigham Young had Orson Pratt publicly announce the practice of plural marriage and defend it in a special conference, then send out dozens of missionaries to defend the practice in the East and in Europe. The newly formed Republican Party of 1856 campaigned against the "twin evils of barbarism"—slavery and polygamy. This political attack was deferred but not eliminated by the Civil War of 1861–65.

Hannah Clapp, an early feminist, was traveling to California in 1859, in bloomers and carried a gun. When she entered Salt Lake City, she attended Sunday services and left a lively account: "The Prophet Brigham and his counselors, Kimbal [sic] and Wells, came in a back way, well guarded by soldiery. The Lord does not always take care of his Prophets, and they are a little afraid of their heads. . . . The appearance of the congregation was after their own peculiar institution—barefoot and no hoops; the men in shirt-sleeves; emigrants in old hats, and clothes; all armed—[with] bowie knife, and revolver. . . . The buildings are made of adode . . . all unpainted except Brigham's Harem."

Clapp went a step further by sending Brigham "a note saying I would like to see him—curiosity of course—and if he would name the hour, I would call. . . . After much questioning, the messenger brought me word that his Superior, Prophet-like Majesty would attend to my call at my earliest convenience." Ms. Clapp admitted that the meeting was pleasant and that Brigham invited her to call again.

She also encountered a determined Saint who felt it his duty to preach to her despite her unwillingness to listen. He completed his task with the explanation: "In another world, [Mormons would] teach those of the gentiles that had not heard the gospel in this life; but he had preached to me, and he feared if I did not embrace the doctrine I would go to hell."

Pausing in Salt Lake City

Since Salt Lake City was, beyond Fort Bridger, impossible to avoid, many travelers whose ultimate destination lay elsewhere entered the city and recorded their temporary stays with interest. On June 18, 1854, California-bound Charlotte Allis recorded visiting a Sunday morning preaching service: "The house will seat 3000 people and it was crowded to overflowing—and a pretty good stock of babies too was present—from 3 to 12 months old which made some musick on the occasion. I thought there was a good deal of a lack of intelligence among the Congregation more so than any other crowd I have saw."

An early piece of negative writing that influenced Gentile trail travelers was a biased account by Mrs. Cornelia Ferris, who lived in Salt Lake City for a few months in 1852–53 because her husband, Benjamin, had been appointed Secretary of the Utah Territory in 1852. They both wrote critical articles, and their book, *Utah and the Mormons* was published in 1854. Cornelia Ferris called the Saints "vulgar," "spiteful," "ill-natured," and "gross" and announced that she could not wait to escape from "its wretchedness, abominations, and crimes." Interestingly, she recorded a scene of sincere faith, when, after a meeting she attended, "the sisters crowded around [a sick woman], and with the two brothers, laid their right hands upon her, and prayed."

Some diaries comment on the "hard looking" Mormon men and "homely," "ill-kempt" Mormon women. One backhanded compliments expressed reluctant admiration: "If you could divest yourself of the idea that they [the homes] are inhabited by Mormons, [they] would in some instances be beautiful," one traveler wrote.

"I thought the inhabitants were fine people," another woman concluded. "Setting aside their peculiar doctrines, I believe as a community they are as good as are usually found . . . [and] not as black as they were painted." Baron Arnold de Woelmont of Belgium in 1870 critically observed: "Most Mormon women are far from being pretty, and in a country where beauty is so common, the contrast is all the more striking. One could not help but think that Utah was a refuge for those women who could not find a husband elsewhere."

In contrast, other travelers "did not find women abused or downtrodden or depraved." They described Mormon women as "clean, wholesome, pious, chaste, and virtuous" and exemplary housekeepers. John Unruh quoted an emigrant who corroborated: "There is so much prejudice existing in the world against them, I can scarcely expect to remove it from the minds of any, but . . . they are the most peaceable, law abiding, and moral people to be found anywhere."

In 1856, Jules Remy called the children "beautiful and strong." Irish journalist William Kelly, who paid the Saints a visit in 1849, found a hearty welcome:

> They were neat and well clad, their children tidy, the rosy glow of health and robustness mantling on the cheeks of all, while the softer tints of female loveliness prevailed to a degree that goes far to prove those Latter-Day Saints have very correct notions of angelic perfection. We politely declined several courteous offers of gratuitous lodging . . . but had not our tents well pitched when we had loads of presents—butter, milk, small cheeses, eggs, and vegetables, which we received reluctantly, not having any equivalent returns to make, except in money, which they altogether declined. . . . [Later] we found a very large and joyous throng assembled; the gaiety . . . making me almost fancy I was spending the evening amongst the crowded haunts of the old world perfectly enraptured with the Mormon ladies, and Mormon hospitality.

Lucy Cooke, who was traveling to California with her parents in 1852, was "very much pleased with the appearance" of Salt Lake City:

> Pa engaged dinner for all our own family & Oh never did vituals look so nice before. We had green peas potatoes, roast beef, chicken, bread, butter, cheese & pie. The bread & butter seemed the greatest treat it looked so clean to what we had been having & then the house was as trim as a little palace. . . . I suppose you are aware that this valley is entirely occupied by Mormons. . . . Much has been said about them making them out to be a disgrace to the earth but as far as we have seen they are as hospitable & kind as any people I ever met.

Adding to the color of Salt Lake City—and the shock of some visitors—was Brigham Young, who thundered in the Tabernacle on Sundays about whatever was on his mind. His sermons, frequently filled with anti-Gentile vindictiveness and threats of violence, shocked visitors and played a role in increasing Gentile suspicion and fear. One Sunday in 1856, Jules Remy wrote, Brigham threatened: "Tell the Gentiles that I am fully determined to cut off the head of the first one of them who attempts to seduce our daughters or our wives." Some writers thought him "vulgar and coarse," A few, like Baron Arnold de Woelmont thought Brigham "tall, well built . . . clear eyes, the forehead high, the gaze piercing . . . [He] appeared twenty years younger." Even though he found Mormonism a "detestable religion," he praised the "strong-mettled character and sagacity of the prophet Brigham Young ... one of the most astonishing figures of our time."

Young did not confine his colorful rhetoric to Gentiles only. When the extent of the 1856 handcart tragedy became known, he roared at those who dared criticize him: "Men who love competition, contention ... I curse you in the name of Lord Jesus Christ. I curse you and the fruits of your land shall be smitten with mildew, your children shall sicken and die, your cattle shall waste away and I pray God to root you out from the Society of Saints."

Military Encounters

Even though the U.S. Army of the West was sent to Utah in 1856 to deal with the alleged Mormon insurrection, almost without exception, their trail encounters were not only peaceful but helpful. Generally speaking, the soldiers provided far more protection and help to the Mormons than interference.

Martin Luther Ensign, a returning missionary, recorded the most dramatic Utah War experience: "When they [the soldiers] left the [St. Louis] wharf they fired a cannon and hurrahed for Utah and the G. D. Mormons and said if they knew there were Mormons on board they would throw them in to the river, but we kept mum and they did not find out we were Mormons or give us any trouble." Some soldiers gave a wounded ox to a struggling company of handcart pioneers, who credited it with "saving our lives."

When the army went into winter quarters near burned-out Fort Bridger during the winter of 1856-57, they did nothing to hinder Mormon immigrants in 1858, but most immigration stopped that year. One group of returning missionaries was halted at the Green River where four elders were taken prisoner by the soldiers and charged with a murder committed several years earlier. When the missionaries were able to clear themselves, they were released.

The Mormon Battalion was a special case. After only a couple of years in the Valley, Brigham Young described raising the battalion as a fiendish plot on the government's part either to test their loyalty or to leave them unprotected. The Mormons, for their part, had responded with unparalleled loyalty and nobility. In fact, the government had responded to urgent pleas from Mormon leaders for help in their move west, and Brigham personally had applied great pressure on the Mormon men to enlist. Among arguments that the leaders used to persuade members to enlist were material benefits from the pay (most of which went to the Church for broader benefits than only to the enlistees' families), their government-issued arms, which the men were allowed to keep, the allotment for uniforms, which also went to the Church while the men wore their own clothes, and from the fact that many men would be transported west at government expense. This last point was only partly realized. After being discharged, members of the battalion had to transport themselves back from California, either to the Salt Lake Valley to meet their families or, more frequently, to Winter Quarters to be reunited with their families and to cross the continent for a third time.

In 1847 at Fort Laramie, the returning pioneers met Commodore Robert Field Stockton of the U.S. Navy. He and his men, who had recently fought in the Mexican War, joined the Mormons returning to Winter Quarters and traveled with them to within six miles of Chimney Rock, where Stockton crossed the Platte to the Oregon Trail.

That same year Mormons noted seeing Captain John C. Fremont whom General Stephen W. Kearny placed under arrest for conspiracy and who returned to the United States with Colonel Philip St. George Cooke, leader of the Mormon Battalion. Hosea Stout wrote on September 5. 1847: "Joseph Taylor . . . returned from California [and] came to see me. He came home with Genl Carney [Kearny] as one of his guards. The Genl chose his guards all from among the Mormons as most faithful."

Encounters during the Civil War

Despite the major interruption to the construction of the transcontinental railroad posed by the Civil War, the Mormons were quick to take advantage of the gradually lengthening lines. But what these experiences offered in speed, they often made up for in discomfort—although admittedly, Mormon immigrants occasionally stressed trials and tribulations to accentuate their faithfulness and sacrifice for "the gospel."

In 1867 Johanna Kirsten Larsen, a Danish convert, recalled: "We traveled through the states partly on steamboat and on the railroad [and] all our belongings were dumped in the wilderness, there to await another train." Part of the time she traveled on a steamer with cows on one side "who got as sick as we did." By the time she arrived at the Mormon outfitting camp in Nebraska, she was feverish with measles.

More than one company was rerouted and changed about a number of times and finally hustled on board a freight train. The cars had previously transported hogs, and no one had bothered to sweep out the filthy cars. The passengers were choked with the dust and could taste it for days afterwards. Still another party traveled nine days and nights in cattle cars. The doors were locked at night, and they had to sleep on straw-covered floors. In 1861 some soldiers tried to force their way into the women's section.

Relations between Mormons and railroad personnel were mixed. Some immigrants complained of a "bitter spirit in Chicago," and "cross conductors"; one even opened the throttle to 60 mph and said he would drive the "Mormons to hell."

In contrast, F. W. Blake recorded in 1861: "The conductors are very gentlemanly in their behavior. I have had conversations with several of them and answered their inquiries and objections. . . . A spirit of friendship has been shown by all the people." William Yates wrote that "railroad people were very kind to us in Toledo, asked many questions about the gospel."

By far the worst immigrant train travel during the Civil War was in Missouri on the Hannibal and St. Joseph line. Missouri not only fought on the Union side but had its own private civil war and, consequently, suffered more war action than all other states save Virginia and Tennessee. Because Missouri controlled much of the Mississippi River, its railroads were exceptionally important to the Union. Southern sympathizers in Missouri made efforts to destroy Missouri's three main rail lines—the Missouri Pacific, the Hannibal and St. Joseph, and the Missouri Northern. Mormons used all of them. Bushwhackers tore up the tracks, shot at trains, ditched cars, and burned railroad bridges. They also built barricades on the tracks; and when the trains hit them, immigrants were thrown about, women and children screamed, and some were hurt. To protect the railroads, 10,000 Union troops were stationed at major bridges, trestles, and railroad facilities.

Jesse N. Smith recorded in 1864: "Crossed the river to Hannibal [Mo] and commenced the weary journey to St. Joseph by the wretched railroad. The engine gave out several times. Saw Union soldiers at all the stations; heard that the country was full of rebel guerrillas. Reached St. Joseph, country full of ruffianly looking soldiers." Immigrants also had to guard their baggage for soldiers would try to steal it.

Sometimes male LDS immigrants were in danger of being drafted by the Confederates since soldiers could get a $1.00 bounty for each man dragooned into service. In St. Joseph, which contained many Confederate sympathizers, the preferred method was to pin a ribbon or a badge on a man, who was thereafter counted as a draftee. Apparently the Mormons declined to accept the honor.

Quantrill's Raiders, Bloody Bill Anderson, and other pro-southern forces in Missouri sometimes fired on riverboats. In 1862, some deck hands refused to man a riverboat along a stretch of the river where they could hear gunfire, so the captain ordered them off and replaced them with Mormons for $1.00 a day and board. They were disliked for being scab labor. Before that, they were disliked just for being Mormons.

A party of Saints left St. Louis, traveling upriver to Omaha in 1863. On board were 500 mules and horses, one cannon, and troops to protect these military supplies. The troops secured the boat as best they could by erecting breastworks of sacks of grain and tobacco.

Despite these dangerous and discomforts, other Mormon travelers recorded the natural beauty along the water routes, religious services, kindness from the officers and staff, and the occasional excitement of steamer races. (See also Chapter 14.)

Encounters with Argonauts

About 100,000 individuals were drawn to the California gold fields, beginning in 1849, and in Colorado, beginning in 1859. It was inevitable that the paths of the Zion-bound Mormons and the goldfield-bound seekers should cross. On May 21, 1850, Jesse Crosby's company met "a man with a wheelbarrow, which he had rolled some 800 [miles] and was still in good spirits moving on, having some 1200 miles before him yet through the wilds of nature, carrying with him his scanty supply of provisions, bedding, arms and ammunition, etc." (It is highly unlikely that this man was equally cheerful by the time he got to the Sierra Mountains.) Crosby mentioned three days later: "The road thronged with gold diggers." Nor was the wheelbarrow argonaut alone. In 1852, an Irish company traveled with five wheelbarrows, so desperate were they for wealth. They arrived safely. It is possible that this unconventional means of travel gave Brigham Young's thoughts about handcarts some forward momentum.

The 1859 handcart company encountered some returning '59ers whose wagon had originally born the inscription "Pike's Peak or Bust." To this optimistic motto, the disappointed party had added "Busted by God." This party also said they wanted to "hang some editors for having over sold the Colorado rush."

In July 1849, John D. Lee recorded the hasty and financially beneficial visits of would-be gold prospectors:

> Emigration for Ca or Gold regions commenced rushing in the Valley, bringing in with them groceries, clothing & Provisions in great Abundance. Much of which were sold & exchanged to the Saints for Butter, cheese, Milk, garden Vegs & at verry low rate. . . . Most of the Emigrants abandoned their waggons when they reached the valley . . . and proceeded with Pack animals. Coffee & Sugar which had been selling at 1.00 per pint was frequently sold at from 10 to 15 cents. Bacon the Same. Firstrate Sacked Hams at 12 ½ cts lb & Dry goodes & clothes below the State Prices.

Those travelers were shocked at the prices when they got to California where eggs were a dollar apiece.

Mail Stations, the Pony Express, and the Telegraph

In 1850 when regular mail service across the plains commenced, the government began to construct mail stations; and Mormon trail accounts include them in their litany of place names: Willow Springs, Wood River, Fort Bridger, Devil's Gate, La Bonte, Mormon Grove, Deer Creek, Big Sandy, Bear River, Hardy's, Hanks', Sun Ranch, and others. Some mail stations provided other services such as blacksmithing and some Mormons, like Ephraim Hanks and Charles Decker, also carried the mail.

During the short life of the Pony Express (April 1860–October 1861) "skinny, wiry" Mormon boys rode some of the routes. Two of Howard Egan's sons, Richard E. and Howard Jr., were among this group. Mormon travelers on the trail watched the hard-riding men race by in both directions. Mary Ann Hafen admiringly described: "When the Pony Express dashed past it seemed almost like the wind racing over the prairie."

Thomas Slight, who was on stock guard "about midnight" near Pacific Springs, "heard the clattering of the hoofs of a horse a long distance off. Our wagons were in a circle on each side of the road. The night was still as death. When in hailing distance, I shouted 'Who comes there!' The clatter stopped immediately. A voice was heard 'Pony Express!' [I answered] 'Come on.' The clatter started afresh. He rode on a gallop through the camp, many wondering what was up."

The time span during which Mormons would have had any encounters with those constructing the Western Union Telegraph Company would have been between July 4 and October 24, 1861—only three months and twenty days. The teams worked at a feverish pace—averaging twelve miles a day and setting twenty-four poles a mile. They started east from Carson City, Nevada, and west from Omaha, linking up in Salt Lake City. A few trail journals mention seeing wagons loaded with telegraph wire, men digging postholes, setting posts and stringing wire, passing many stations, and even sending telegrams. Some Mormons hauled telegraph poles east of Salt Lake City and set them up, especially in Echo Canyon. After the line was completed, Mormon immigrant companies routinely used it to keep in touch with Salt Lake City.

Back-Trailers

Although exact figures are not available, a significant percentage of gold-seekers gave up their quest, either on the trail, after reaching California, or after having spent some time actually prospecting. Quite frequently, their trail back home led through Salt Lake City to the benefit of the Saints in the Valley and those still on the trail toward Zion. Some had been defeated by the rigors of the trail or their own lack of preparedness, occasional Indian trouble, death, loss of draft animals, and "having seen the elephant." John Unruh Jr. wrote that back-trailers were "notorious rumor-spreaders" who magnified their grievances to justify their turning back. Lloyd W. Coffman concurs. "Psychologically, those who turned back knew they could be branded as quitters, if not cowards; so, they had to find a satisfactory explanation for their actions." Hence they freely spread false tales about epidemics, Indians, Mormon atrocities, and the like.

Others were missionaries or men returning for their families in California or Oregon, and some were disaffected Mormons. Westbound Mormons interacted with these back-trailers in various ways. They sent letters back east, pumped them for travel information, and sometimes helped those who were "busted."

Disaffected Mormons went back east usually because their faith and hopes faltered. Perhaps it was trail hardships or dashed expectations regarding Utah, the polygamy factor, and disillusionment with Mormon leaders. The Mormon leaders acted to stop some of those who were fleeing because many of them benefited from the Perpetual Emigrating Fund, and still needed to repay all or part of their trail expenses. Some once-zealous Saints found that their questions were met, not with reasonable answers and support, but with accusations of enmity and apostasy. For some, the homes they had left behind became too alluring in memory. Some lacked the flexibility to adjust to new conditions, especially if those conditions involved a second move to an even harsher location.

In conclusion, Mormons took some pains to travel in their own camps, to maintain their own leaders and customs, and to protect themselves from the uncertainties of meeting Gentiles in much the same way that they were wary about meeting Indians. Some of their caution was justified as reports raged on the trail, especially about polygamy and Mountain Meadows. But in other cases, the noble virtues of compassion for the wayfarer and aid for the unfortunate made the trail an extension of their congregational principles. Briefly, Gentiles were welcome in the Mormon villages on the trail and vice versa.

Although many doubted that the Mormons would tame that desolate spot, the Mormons of modern days have vindicated the early boast that the desert would blossom as the rose and that the mountains—and human voices—would shout for joy.

Chapter 9

Social Interactions with Native Americans

We lived only a few rods from the Potawatomi Chief [Chief Riche.] He told [my] boys if there was anything they wanted that he had, to come and get it and he would wait until they could pay him. They were all a great help to us. —Sarah Studevant Leavitt, 1846

The pioneers were sure to hear frightening stories about Indians at all the jumping-off places and all of them, except those who had come directly from Europe, came from states that had histories going back to first contacts with Indians. Most of the tales were hostile, and fear of Indians threaded through the accounts of many pioneers going to Oregon and California. Despite initial fears, however, many pioneers were pleasantly surprised by their actual encounters; and in many cases, their fear became fascination.

Sara Alexander, a young Saint on the trail in 1859, viewed the natives as works of art; and perhaps the pioneers and Indians could have lived and worked together in peace and harmony if more people had been as sensitive. She admits she both admired and feared them.

> The Indians are picturesque and magnificent only in their primitive habitat. . . . I have watched with wonder and delight, as far as the eye could reach, seeing them disappear in the horizon. It is one of the grandest sights my memory recalls. . . . They were my admiration and fear. I pity their humiliation in compelling them to become civilized. So much has to be crushed in the march of improvement and in the

making of a nation. . . . I shall always be glad I have seen the Indians in their primitive grandeur.

Young Charles True, camping en route to California in 1859, was impressed with some he saw in Sioux territory:

> Suddenly, without warning, there stood at the edge of our circle near a bunch of willows, a splendid athletic specimen of an Indian, wearing a jaunty beaded buckskin suit. . . . [The next one] seemed quite a young man. Fringed leggins of antelope skin encased his limbs, leaving his lithe figure bare to the waistline. His moccasins were profusely decorated with the porcupine quills. Above his forehead there was an elaborate plume of bright colored feathers–the badge of a chief. Small ear pendants of shells were attached to each ear. His bearing was noble, impressive and wildly picturesque. . . . The group presented a scene eminently attractive for its wild and graceful beauty.

The Captivity Narrative

The captivity narrative, one of the oldest—if not the oldest—literary genres of the New World, left a thousand known accounts in the sixteenth century. For obvious reasons the focus has always been largely on women, and few other purely American incidents ever so caught the public fancy or fired the imagination of fiction writers. Here was dualism, a drama of fear on a cosmic scale—a whole continent, a whole New World peopled by "red savages" standing against a few stout-hearted Christian whites, especially the Puritans and French and Spanish padres who were, in part at least, dedicated to redeeming the "savages" and regenerating the wilderness.

Among the Puritans, being captured by Indians meant a "fate worse than death" for women and their children—one long agony of horror and shame as the victim of the lust of successive chiefs and as the tormented slaves of their jealous women until death mercifully ended these Christian women's sufferings.

One of the most sensational accounts, written in 1879 and published by Philadelphia's Old Franklin Publishing House, reveals some spicy details about Miss Josephine Meeker's capture by the Ute tribe. The book promised "further thrilling and intensely interesting details" about her twenty-three-day ordeal. She claimed she was raped repeatedly, and one of the chiefs had insisted on "having connections" with Josephine's mother, who was also captured.

Mormon Exceptionalism

Mormons feared association with Indians less than their Protestant counterparts; and in more than a thousand Mormon Trail accounts, very little fear was recorded. A few foreign converts who were more susceptible to the tales recorded in greater detail their apprehensions about galloping ponies and war-painted faces. Here are two examples of children who recalled their fear at the first encounter with Indians.

Elisha Brooks was eleven in 1852 when his company met the harmless, friendly Potamatomi: "As we drew near Council Bluffs on the Missouri River, the cry of 'Indians, Indians' turned me to stone. Just ahead, a band of blanketed, feathered, beaded, fringed, wild looking objects barred our way. I thought our days were numbered. I slunk under the wagon in abject terror, peering through the wheels to watch the proceedings."

Young Brigham Henry Roberts, fresh from England, wrote about his first real contact on the trail in 1867, as he picked currants away from camp:

> Our contact with the Indians . . . had not been sufficient to do away with the fear in which the red men were held by us [and] there was trembling and fear that we were going to be captured. . . . Coming to a swale . . . we saw three Indians on horseback approach. . . . It was with magnificent terror that we kept on slowly towards these Indians whose faces remained immobile and solemn with no indication of friendliness. . . . I gave one wild yell, the Scotch cap full of currants was dropped, and I made a wild dash to get by—and did—whereupon there was a peal of laughter from the three Indians. They say Indians never laugh, but I learned differently.

For the most part, Mormon belief in the Book of Mormon meant that the prevailing Mormon attitude was closer to that of the Spanish padres, the French Jesuits, and the Ursuline sisters than the Methodists, Protestants, and Baptists of the eastern United States. Then, too, Mormons had a goal, if not a passion, to redeem the American natives. The main story concerns a family of four (eventually six) brothers with their parents who left Jerusalem in 600 B.C. and were guided to the New World. The brothers eventually divided into two rival parties: the righteous Nephites and the wicked Lamanites. This latter group rejected God, degenerated into idolatry and savagery, was cursed with a darker skin by God, and by A.D. 420 had succeeded in destroying the more civilized Nephites. Their descendants, Mormons believe, are the American Indians.

Although Joseph Smith's maternal grandfather had been an Indian fighter, prior to the Mormon exodus west, the Saints had no sustained relations with Indians. Between 1825 and 1846, the U.S. government practiced an Indian removal program for the purpose of driving all eastern Indians west of the Mississippi River, a policy strengthened in 1830 when Congress passed the Removal Bill. The Sauk and Fox, for example, had been driven from Illinois into Iowa by the cruel Black Hawk War of 1832.

Immediately after the publication of the Book of Mormon in 1830, Joseph Smith sent Mormon missionaries out to proselytize some Catteraugus in New York, the Wyandotte in Ohio, and some Shawnee and Delaware west of the Missouri River near Independence, Missouri. Although these efforts were unsuccessful, they set a foundation of seeing American Indians as potential Christians and as fellow members of the house of Israel. In 1841 Chief Keokuk accompanied by Kiskukosh, Appenoose, and about 100 other chiefs and males of the Sauk and Fox crossed the Mississippi from Iowa and visited Joseph Smith in Nauvoo.

During the Nauvoo period of Mormon history (1839–46), several important gestures of inclusiveness were extended to some Indians. In 1845 Joseph Herring, a Shawnee, and Lewis Dana, an Oneida, were ordained to the highest, or Melchizedek, Priesthood. Lewis Dana was sealed to Mary Gont in the Nauvoo Temple, but Herring, who was too fond of drinking, was excommunicated in Winter Quarters on January 18, 1847, and disappears from the record. Lewis Dana came west with the pioneers. Although such incidents were rare and not always successful, they conclusively demonstrate the potential equality of red men with white men. William Carey, an African American, married Lucy Stanton, but they probably did not marry in the temple.

In general, the Saints and Indians had a good relationship during trail days, and there was mutual respect and cooperation most of the time.

In Iowa

The pioneers met few Indians as they traversed Iowa in 1846. After they reached Potawatomi lands at Mt. Pisgah, Indians occasionally visited, but these encounters were undramatic. (This tribal name has three accepted spellings—not to mention the many phonetic varieties produced by white diarists; today, however, many county and land records use "Pottawattamie" for official documents and maps.) On June 8, the Mormons passed the Potawatomi settlement on the Nishnabotna River, their first sustained contacts with natives. The Indians were curious and friendly and asked to trade for whiskey. The Saints met Chief Pied Riche, called "the Clerk" by the French because of his education. The chief, who had been driven from his ancestral lands in Michigan by the Indian removal policy of the 1830s, felt some kinship with the Mormons. He was also a polygamist. The chief's welcome must have calmed the Saints' anxiety and were the friendliest words they had heard or would hear for a long time: "So we have both suffered. We must keep one another, and the Great Spirit will keep us both. You are now free to cut and use all the wood you wish. You can make your improvements and live on any part of our actual land not occupied by us. Because one suffers and does not deserve it, is no reason he should suffer always. I say, we may live to see all right yet. However, if we do not, our children will."

Pitts's Brass Band played, and others were "escorted" to the bridge. Indians swam in the water while the Mormons built bridges in the Council Bluffs area. Hosea Stout wrote on June 30, 1846: "The Indians followed us today for several miles and in fact they thronged around us all the time we were building the bridge & at times [came] in droves to the camp but they were very civil friendly & good natured and done none of us any injury while we were here."

Parley P. Pratt may well have owed his life to some Indian boys. Hosea Stout continued his record on June 30: "In an attempt to cross [the river] Br Pratt & mule came very near being drowned. He floated to shore and was so much exhausted that he could not get out. After resting awhile, he attempted it again and came near being drowned the second time. I believe he was finally assisted over by some indians boys, not however until they were satisfied that they [Mormons] were 'Good Mormonee' as they call us." In fact, several journals record that "Are you good Mormonee?" was a key question.

Ira Hatch's family had a lot of exposure to the Natives and vice versa. Ira, who was a young boy in Iowa and Nebraska, later recalled: "We didn't cross the Missouri River as some did, but stopped at Bonary Lake as the forage for our animals was better there. Father, having been raised among the [I]ndians in New Hampshire and New York, spoke their language, as did my older brothers. They obtained permission to build a cabin and farm out among the Indians. We raised some wheat and potatoes here in the summer of 1846."

Ira's brothers, Meltiah and Orin, joined the Mormon Battalion that July and mingled with various tribes on their way west. Ira recalled his brothers' stories: "Many were the nights I remember sitting before the fire, listening to tales. . . . They had met many friends among the Indian tribes along the way. As both of my brothers spoke several Indian dialects, they had conversed with the Apache, Pima, Maricope, and Yuma Indians."

Brigham Young reveals an interesting bit of merchandising procedure soon after they arrived at Council Bluffs in 1846: "Elder [Willard] Richards and I . . . visited the Indian agent for the Potawatomi and traders, and priced their goods which they were willing to sell us at fifty percent lower than to the natives. We purchased several articles and returned." Young received permission to settle in the greater Council Bluffs area after the departure of the Mormon Battalion.

The Indian agent, Robert B. Mitchell, invited Pitts's Brass Band and the young Mormons to spend the day at Point aux Poules. Helen Mar Kimball Whitney was thrilled at the chance to get dressed up again: "This was delightful, especially to the young people. . . . This was the first time that our chests had been disturbed or opened since packing them in Nauvoo [and] it was delightful to once more . . . bring out the pretty bonnets, laces, ribbons, parasols and kid shoes, etc., that had been packed away, and to think we were again to attend a ball. And I . . . think we astonished the good folks at the Point to see so many well dressed and merry hearted boys and girls."

Helen later accepted an invitation from Chief Riche's daughter, Fanny, "with one or two others." Since the wagons back to the Mormon camp had left after their visit, Fanny "urged me to stop the night, which invitation I accepted. . . . Though dressed in her native costume she looked neat, and kept the house tidy, and could cook equal to the white women. . . . [She] showed her taste and skill in braiding my hair in broad plats, after the latest French style, and put it up a la mode, and after dinner accompanied me to camp."

Across the river at what became Winter Quarters, the Mormons were in close contact with the Oto and Omaha. The latter were a small tribe of only about 1,500, well known for their consistent friendliness to whites. The Oto, on the other hand, were considered thieves by both Indians and whites. They numbered about a thousand. Both tribes were basically farmers living in permanent earthen lodge villages. Chief Big Elk and the Omahas agreed that the Saints could settle among them. The Indians might benefit from their expertise and what the Saints would leave behind when they vacated the area. Also they saw an alliance that might help protect them against the warlike Sioux, who frequently raided Omaha villages. Oliver B. Huntington wrote that both tribes "quarreled over who would use abandoned Winter Quarters" in 1848 when the Mormons left for Zion, or moved across the river.

An early history of Council Bluff notes: "Inasmuch as neither the records of the Indian Office nor those of the Mormon Church disclose serious difficulty among them, it may be assumed that they dwelled together in harmony and brotherly love." Actually, there was some disharmony because of cattle thefts and constant tribal struggles near the camp. A few battles took place within hearing distance of Winter Quarters, but the Saints did not want to incur hostility with any tribe, so they said little about the problems to the agent.

The Winter Quarters Saints got a friendly visit from William Carey, who claimed to be an Indian but who "most of the persons believed him to be a descendant of Ham"—meaning African American. Wilford Woodruff mentioned him on February 26, 1847, and several other times. Originally "from New orleans" he had been baptized in

Nauvoo by Orson Hyde. Woodruff called him "an eccentric character. He was the most perfect natural musician I ever saw on a flute, fife, sauce pan, ratler, [rattle] whistle &c. He married Br. Stanton's daughter [Lucy] for a wife." On February 27, Woodruff was visiting Brigham Young when "the flutier Br. Carey came in ... & made the most music on several instruments of any man I ever herd." He eventually left Winter Quarters with a small group of disaffected Mormons to "start his own church."

Bathsheba Smith considered one Potamatomi a "stately looking man." Sarah Leavitt thought the Potamatomi chief "very helpful." Mary Ellen Kimball considered some Potamatomis the "best looking and most clean" she had seen. "They really looked nice in their costumes of skins, ornamented with beads."

In contrast, the characteristic scent of the skin-wearing Indians alarmed the livestock. John Clark wrote: "Two hundred Potamatomi indians ... crossed ... on their way to the buffalo range. On coming down the street the scent, or wild odor from the band ... made every horse & mule in their way brake and leave for the commons below."

On the Trail

According to historian John Unruh Jr., "Little scholarly attention has been given to the relationships between the emigrants and the Indians." In fact, travelers seldom acknowledged the help they received from Native Americans. Oregonians were greatly indebted to the Nez Perce and other tribes, who willingly traded salmon, vegetables, and buffalo for white goods. The handcart companies also received help from compassionate Indians. Indians provided route information, acted as guides, traded, carried mail, cut and carried grass for the livestock, and chopped wood for fires. They also gave rides to stranded foot travelers, identified edible plants, helped transport livestock and wagons across rivers, returned lost cattle, sold fish, horses, vegetables, and clothing to immigrants, and rendered assistance to lost pioneers.

In addition to the tribes already mentioned, Mormons headed west also encountered Pawnee, Sioux, Arapaho, Cheyenne, Shoshone (or Snakes), Crow, Ute, and Paiute tribes. Because of their religious beliefs, they seldom experienced difficulties since they treated

Indians with more friendship and less hostility than other western travelers. Furthermore, Mormons traveled in large companies and restrained their consumption of game, grass, and wood. They routinely gave Indians presents of salt, sugar, clothing, whiskey, tobacco, and trinkets, but most California/Oregon-bound companies did the same thing. When the Saints settled in the Great Basin, preempting Indian lands, they experienced the same type of Indian troubles as other settlers. There were intermittent conflicts for about twenty years—some horse and cattle stealing from 1849 through the Black Hawk War of the 1860s. A marked exception was that the smaller companies returning to Winter Quarters in the late summer and fall of 1847 experienced stolen cattle and ambushes.

Jane Grover recorded a potentially hostile encounter with Indians, presumably in 1846, that was published in Edward Tullidge's *The Women of Mormondom*:

> One morning we thought we would go gather gooseberries. Father [Nathan] Tanner . . . harnessed a span of horses to a light wagon and, with two sisters by the name of Lyman [we went] to pick berries. . . . We reached the woods and told [him] to rest himself while we picked. . . . Suddenly we heard shouts [and] saw Father Tanner . . . running his team around [then] we saw Indians gathering around the wagon, whooping and yelling. . . . We walked forward [and] got into the wagon to start when four of the Indians took hold of the wagon wheels . . . and another came to take me out of the wagon. I wanted to run for assistance. He [Tanner] said, "No poor child: it is too late." I told him they should not take me alive. His face was as white as a sheet. The Indians had commenced to strip him, had taken his watch [and] were trying to pull me out. . . . I began silently to appeal to my Heavenly Father [and] I arose with great power [and] talked to those Indians in their own language. They let go the horses and wagon. . . . The little girl and Father Tanner looked on in amazement. They returned all they had taken [and] we hastened home.

A significant raid by Pawnees occurred in 1851. Orson Hyde wrote: "Near one branch of Loup Fork we were assaulted by 300 Pawnee Indians and robbed of between 700 and 1000 dollars." It was later reported that the goods, including provisions and guns, were all recovered by soldiers at Fort Kearny.

According to Merrill Mattes, a historian of the Oregon Trail, outbreaks of violence occurred along the Oregon Trail, on the south side of the Platte River, especially in 1863–64. Sioux and Cheyenne were "killing, burning, raping, and kidnapping" ranchers, supply station operators, and others along the Little Blue River," which was west of Lincoln, Nebraska, and south of the Platte. Mattes saw this violence as part vengeance for the Sioux whom whites massacred at Ash Hollow, Nebraska, in 1854 and for the Cheyenne, massacred at Sand Creek, Colorado, in 1864.

A false alarm prompted a sarcastic account by William Chandless, en route to the Valley in 1855. He was concerned about his train of forty freight wagons, loaded with goods to sell to the Saints. On the afternoon of September 11, 1855, "We had an alarm of Indians coming over the Bluffs on our side. . . . [The] wagons formed closely in battle corral; great bustle and animation; caps and cartridges served out; my revolver a good deal admired. . . . I offered to bet that our men caused more casualties among us than among the Indians, or than the Indians among us. . . . After waiting the best part of an hour, the supposed Sioux turned out to be a troop of Calvary scouring the country: so much for a cheap telescope."

Indian Customs

Among Mormon records are keen observations of Indian culture and customs, including Indian skill with the bow and arrow. Frederick Piercy, a young artist on the trail on June 17, 1853, commented with admiration on an Indian sharpshooter: "I asked one of the young men to give me a specimen of his skill in shooting with the bow. He fixed a small cracker on a stick which he stuck in the ground, and standing about 12 yards from it, aimed 2 or 3 times but did not hit it. A still younger one, seeing his want of skill, impatiently took his place, and split the cracker with the first arrow."

Other pioneers described the entertainment of Indian "serenades" and demonstrations of horse racing. In 1850, Martha Spence Heywood recorded that her company stopped near Fort Laramie to visit the nearby Indian camp. She considered them "clean and handsome, the children very pretty and good for wild children." In one tent she saw some "Indians and squaws looking quite stylish and gay. . . . The children were very handsome and smart looking." In another tent she was told to "Sue a Ochi." She finally realized "its significance, meaning to depart. I afterwards learned they were, what is vulgarly termed, 'sparking.'"

Thomas Bullock described Indian burial customs in June 1847: "Passed 4 bodies of Indians tied up in Skins and fastened to the trees; this being a preferable manner of disposing of the dead, to burying them in the ground for the Wolves to dig them up again and devour them."

On July 31, 1850, Mary Ann Weston Maughan noted: "An old Indian had died of the small pox, the Indians left a little boy with the corpse; we saw a kind of platform made by driving 4 stakes into the ground and covering it over with sticks [and] was covered with a buffalo robe. . . . The little boy was standing by its side close by with a dog hung up by the neck and a wigwam made of boughs."

Frederick A. Cooper of the George Rowley Company of 1859 commented, at Devil's Gate, "They had just had a great battle between two tribes. The victorious tribe was parading around with scalps suspended on sticks which they held high in the air. . . . They invited [us] to visit their camp that night to witness them torture to death their prisoners, however, we respectfully declined."

Sometimes Indians would show the Mormons certificates from other groups praising their good conduct. Thomas Bullock noted such a transaction on May 25, 1847:

> The Indians were in and round the Camp from Sunrise to the time of Starting, going about just as their curiosity led them, some to get bread & other things, some trading moccasins, Blankets, Horses &c. One of the Chiefs "Wash te he" was very pressing for a written paper, when I wrote the following:
>
> This is to certify that Wash te ha of the Dacotah tribe of Indians, with Wash te cha the principle Chief and thirty other men, women and children, visited our Camp . . . behaved themselves civilly and peaceable, we gave them bread. They were very friendly to us, and the best behaved Indians we have yet seen.
>
> W. Richards
> Thomas Bullock–Scribe

Pioneers were unaware of the significance of many Native beliefs, especially their abhorrence at wantonly wasting natural resources. The western tribes hunted buffalo—their main staple, because the meat could be dried and used all winter. It was a proverb along the trail that the Indians used all parts of the buffalo "except the voice." They wore the teeth, hoofs, and horns as ornaments, made warm robes from the skin, and ate just about everything else.

Indian Kindness

Matthew Caldwell, marching in Arizona with the Mormon Battalion, owed his life to the kindness of some Pimas in 1846:

> [W]e found where some buffaloes had been, and, so thirsty were we that we actually drank from the buffalo drippings, not even noticing that they were literally full of wrigglers. I was so sick; I was compelled to crawl under a grease wood. . . . The captain of the guards saw me [and] I told him I could go no further. "That's too bad. . . . If you get better, come on in." In a short time an old Indian came over to me [and] noticing I was much swollen, he began rubbing me with the hill, [sic] of his hand. More Indians came [and] picked up my knapsack and handed them to one of the other Indians. . . . I finally found they wanted me to help in getting myself on the horse. When he caught up with my company, he put me down with them. This happened on the 24th day of December. On Christmas day the Indians brought us watermelons which were enjoyed very much.

John D. T. McAllister noted in 1851 that "West of devil's gate met some who were friendly. . . . A steer and a cow went off with them and they drove them both back again to the camp."

Sarah Ann Ludlum, a member of the Willie's Handcart Company in 1856, was pleased when the first Indians they met "came to our carts and pushed them into camp for us. . . . [T]hey left camp and soon returned with fresh buffalo meat which they traded for clothing and salt."

Two women in handcart companies had incredible good luck along the trail. In 1856, a Sister Redde was missing from the Willie Handcart Company. Levi Savage recorded: "Some men rode back along the trail looking for her, finding only her tracks and those of some Indians." They assumed she had been kidnapped and returned to camp; but another search party found her unharmed thirty-six hours later.

Elizabeth Watson, traveling with the George Rowley Handcart Company in 1859, turned up missing on August 2. After a day, they gave up the search and moved on. They were amazed and delighted to find her on August 15 waiting for them at a trading post west of Independence Rock. She had been given food and directions by the Indians, nearly killed by anti-Mormons, and finally brought by a kind traveler to the camp after spending three horrible nights alone.

George Staples, age fourteen, had a rare adventure, in about 1850. Sent separately from his family with a company of Saints, he developed mountain fever and was not expected to live. They left him with a fur trader who in turn gave him to a Sioux woman. He was taken to Salt Lake two years later, much to the sorrow of his Sioux family, who had been very good to him. "The woman who had mothered him wept bitterly." Traveling on the trail a few years later, George was happily reunited with his Sioux family.

Robert Campbell, heading to Zion in 1849, was impressed when he heard about a Sioux who killed a white man because his "friend died of cholera." The tribe held a meeting about this warrior's act of misplaced revenge, and "his own nation killed him a few hours after."

Mormon Kindness

Sarah Maria Mousley shared lemonade with an Indian guest in 1857:

> An incident connected with the Indians I will here relate as they have been very friendly to us. We returned the compliment in the same manner. They called at our table for refreshment and I was making lemonade which I offered to one who had watched the process and whom I had handed a chair. He seated himself with great dignity and took in his hand the cup I offered but would not touch the drink until I would drink with him. I began to drink from another cup but he handed his to me as much as to say drink from this. I took it, drank and returned it. He drank and said "good squaw" with many gestures of satisfaction.

Six-year-old Mary Ann Hafen of Switzerland left for Zion on July 6, 1860, walking next to their handcart with their milk cow hitched in front. In Mary Ann's autobiography, she preserved an unusual experience with Indians: "One day a group of Indians came riding up on horses. Their jingley trinkets, dragging poles, and strange appearance frightened the cow and set her chasing off with the cart and children. We were afraid that the children might be killed, but the cow fell into a deep gully and the cart turned upside down. Although the children were under the trunk and bedding they were unhurt." They did not hitch the cow to their cart again, but let three Danish boys use the cow. They took turns with the cow a week, and then they would help her father pull their cart a week, which permitted her mother, who was suffering from swollen feet, to rest in the cart. Although the Indians didn't deliberately cause any problems, what happened as a result worked out to be a blessing for the Hafens.

Sarah Sutton, Oregon-bound in 1854, commented: "These roads are infested with thieves and rouges [sic] watching for good oppertunity to take Emegrant cattle and horses. The indians are far better than whites in any estimation." Other pioneers likewise believed that many cattle thieves were really white men dressed like Indians.

Indian Agents

An unpleasant piece of history is the role that Indian agents of the U.S. government played in heightening fears, spreading rumors, and causing genuine trouble. One agent was so determined to push the Saints out from their settlement at Genoa, Nebraska, that he set fire to nearby fields in 1858. Ann Ward, who was then a child, later recorded:

> [We] were astounded by the information that the Pawnee Indians had selected the Genoa settlement as their reservation. The Indian agent had previously indoctrinated them that they should locate within the city boundaries of Genoa. The Indians showed a higher sense of right than the agent. They stated that they were willing to move ten miles further west, and be neighbors, and admitted that the agent said he could not restrain the Indians from coming and taking possession of the homes.... He even hinted they might ravish the women.... The agent continued to harass the Saints [and] suddenly a fire came sweeping over the prairie.... Only four or five homes escaped the blaze....

Grain stacks and houses were on fire [and] it was started willfully at a point between the agent's house.

Jean Rio Baker, who was a great admirer of western scenery on her journey in 1851, was enchanted by this scene:

> We saw a little army [of Indians]. The government agent was with them in a buggy and sitting between his knees was the daughter of the chief, a pretty little creature about three years old who seemed to be quite pleased at our appearance. [They are] going to a great council of various tribes to endeavor to settle their differences and bury the toma-hawk. They made a great appearance, all on horseback and very gaily dressed, some with lances, others with guns or bows and arrows. . . . The men passed on one side of us, the women and children on the other, but all of them well mounted. Their clothing was beautifully trimmed with small beads. Altogether it was quite an imposing procession.

Eroticism in White/Indian Relations

About a dozen well-documented accounts exist of Indians at-tempting to trade for Mormon women. Somewhere in Nebraska in 1849, Caroline Barnes Crosby met a band of "splendidly dressed" Sioux warriors who "offered my husband a young squaw for me, and wanted to buy our children." Crosby declined, tactfully but forcefully.

In 1852 sixteen-year-old Mary Field (Garner) attracted the atten-tion of some Indian men with her long red curls: "A Chief took a special fancy to me . . . and offered many ponnies [sic] but Mother refused. . . . We were all very worried for fear he would steal me so Mother decided to hide me [and] took our feather beds and placed them over two boxes and I crawled under there . . . [but] he followed the train for several days . . . [and] even felt the feather bed I was under."

Since these Indians apparently made their offers in good faith, it seems dangerously irresponsible for some white men to have joked about selling women. In 1856 Priscilla Merriman Evans, a convert from Wales, recorded: "My husband in a joking way told an Indian who ad-mired me, that he would trade me for a pony. He thought no more about it, but the next day here came the Indian with the pony and it was no joke with him. Never was I so frightened in all my life. . . . There was no place to hide and we did not know what to do. The captain was called and they had some difficulty in settling with the Indian without trouble."

Some Mormon males, displaying little sense, played dangerous frontier jokes on the Indians. To be the bravest one in the group, one man "in fun" said he would trade his wife for a horse. The Indian was serious, and it nearly led to a hazardous encounter. Even more astounding is a story about a stepmother who, "in a joking manner" offered her stepdaughter to an Indian. He saw no humor in the affair and followed the train for days during which time the girl was kept out of sight. I doubt that this joke endeared the stepmother to that girl.

F. W. Blake wrote in 1861: "Two Indians met our train yesterday. They were mounted on ponies. One of them, enraptured I suppose, with the sight of the girls offered to barter his pony away for one of them. He wanted one with dark hair. Poor chap he was doomed to disappointment, he might have struck a bargain with some poor henpecked fellow." No cases are known of actual trades, but these stories, building on the body of captivity narratives, would have lost none of their thrilling terrors in the retelling.

Only one recorded incident of a Mormon man attempting to acquire an Indian wife has been preserved. In 1846–47, John Lowe Butler wrote: "Thomas Emmett traded a horse for a squaw" even though he had a white wife. The Indian wife was not allowed to leave the reservation at "running waters," making the liaison a brief one. His white wife's reaction is not recorded.

Sixteen-year-old Mary Jane Chambers, en route to Oregon in 1845 with her family, fetched a prime offer according to her brother, Andrew: "Indian chiefs offered father fifty horses and a hundred blankets for her; they didn't care whether the girl was willing. . . . [T]his was their custom. . . . This scared Mary Jane, and she didn't want to show herself when the Indians were around."

Not to be outdone, a group of Indian women offered "many ponies" for some handsome men they saw on the Oregon Trail, according to John Unruh Jr. In a dramatic switch, one seventeen-year-old boy, John McWilliams, rushing to the gold mines in 1849 claimed that a Nez Perce chief offered him "one hundred horses if he would marry the chief's daughter." John decided it was because he "looked half-Indian with his long black hair and no beard," but the offer failed to tempt him. I have found no similar accounts of offers for any Mormon males.

Although the cultural presumption was always that Indians would find white women attractive, while properly brought up white women would be repelled by "savages," an interesting counter-narrative was printed in the *Aurora [Ohio] Guardian* on November 16, 1854:

> The *Columbus Fact* states that recently a band of Indians gave a performance in Somerset, Ohio, and that two girls, sisters, were so captivated by the dance and the whoop of the sons of Nature that they asked permission to accompany them, which being gallantly granted, they proceeded as far as Putnam, where they were overtaken by the mother of the girls, a spry widow who called on the police to aid her in recovering her "wild going" daughters. But after a little private interview with the chief, the mother discharged the police and made a third "willing heart" to follow the Indian men to their western camp.

Indian Hostilities

White people brought disease and death to Indians, who died by the thousands from cholera, smallpox, and measles. The Indians could not understand why the settlers recovered from such diseases, and they did not, and that is rumored to be the reason they massacred Marcus and Narcissa Whitman, their adopted children, and others in 1847. They thought a curse had been put on them, blamed whites for ruining their hunting grounds, and feared—not without cause—that their whole way of life was being destroyed.

The Indians were told that their lifestyle was wicked and did not please the Lord. Most everything they held dear was criticized. The salvation of "the heathen" was the main object of the missionaries. According to historian Julie Roy Jeffrey, one headline screamed: "Six hundred millions of Heathens, . . . miserable, and perishing in sin . . . [need] immediate help."

Too many white travelers were ready to avenge the least alleged Indian atrocity, and too many Indians stole cattle and provisions from destitute emigrants. Patience was not one of the virtues the pioneers took west, and tempers on the trail often flared over trivial matters.

At least ten Mormon accounts of kidnapping or attempted kidnappings by Indians seem well documented. In 1860 some Sioux "stole a Danish maid, 35 years old, who was behind the wagon train driving an old lame cow." Seized by one warrior, she fought him fiercely and kept throwing herself from the horse, significantly slowing her captor. Men from her wagon train rescued her, unhurt but terribly frightened.

Sara Alexander's memoirs recount an 1859 incident "that happened to one of the companies. . . . Two young girls wandered off . . . when five Indians sprang from some bushes and carried one of them off. The other being further behind was saved. . . . The train stopped over several days hoping to rescue her, but they had to move on and she was lost to them forever." Alexander does not identify either woman by name. At least one account exists of an attempt to kidnap a child. In 1848, not far from Fort Laramie, an old Indian stole a little boy by putting him under a blanket and riding away, but the Mormon men gave chase, overtook him, and rescued the boy. The Indian passed it off as a joke, saying "I just kidding."

Some companies lost significant livestock to Indian raids, especially horses. When Brigham Young's company was returning from the Salt Lake Valley in the summer of 1847, his son-in-law, Edmund Ellsworth, reported: "At Strawberry Creek we met and camped with the group returning to Winter Quarters for their families. That night the Indians stole fifty-two head of our horses. The loss greatly distressed the co. which was on the return to WQ." This was not the only attempt to steal horses from the companies returning to Winter Quarters.

The Indians also stole food and property. They frequently visited pioneer camps along the trail, begging for food and other items, and often not passing up opportunities to pilfer. From the Indian point of view, however, such items represented an honorable toll exacted for passing through their territory and killing their game.

Jacob Weatherby was killed by Omahas near the Elk Horn in 1847. Hosea Stout, police chief at Winter Quarters, tried to enlist the help of the Indian agent Robert B. Mitchell in finding the killer or killers; but Mitchell had no jurisdiction over the Omahas, and Major John Miller, agent over the Omahas, was absent. Mitchell warned the Mormons against vigilante action. One unnamed Mormon was killed in 1849. Nineteen-year-old Christian Jensen was headed east to serve a mission on June 7, 1867, when his small train was attacked near Sulphur Spring Station.

In 1856, Territorial secretary Almon Whiting Babbitt and three members of his small party were ambushed. Babbitt had invited one or two of the hand carters to travel with him as he had a light wagon and light load. A Sister Williams with a small baby asked to go. Another woman, a Sister Margetts and her baby, were offered a ride, and in some accounts her name is included. There is yet another account but these are the same major events in any version; three fresh graves were evident. One woman was supposedly killed along with the baby and one woman captured. Babbitt was also killed.

As might be expected, non-fatal injuries were more common. In May 1848, Howard Egan Sr. was wounded when some Pawnees tried to steal cattle from the company on the Elkhorn River. During the chase, Egan was shot in the hand and dropped his gun. He managed to swim across the Elkhorn River before collapsing. Some men brought him to camp. His son, Howard Jr.,

> saw two men holding Father up and leading him towards our wagon from the ferry. His arms were hanging down and his chin was on his breast. I heard the men say that the Indians had shot him through the wrist . . . . [At Fort Bridger there were many] Indians . . . dressed in buckskin clothes, and more dogs than you could shake a stick at. It was here that Father traded for the same pistol he had held in his hands and dropped when shot, in the fight at the Horn River. It had passed from Indian to Indian and arrived at Fort Bridger long before we did.

This "believe it or not" event became a legend among trail stories. It likely was augmented over the years, but many miracle-like stories did occur and those who viewed the scenery and watched the buffalo roam would find it hard not to believe the gun story and anything else having to do with getting to Zion.

Chapter 10

Interactions with African Americans

While we were preparing our supper, a farmer . . . accompanied by a Negro came up and offered to assist us in repairing our wagon. Setting at once to work, in about two hours all was right again. . . . Our Negro visitor remained with us and shared our supper [and] proved himself a very intelligent man. —Jean Rio Griffiths Baker, May 1851

Elijah Abel, "a man of great knowledge," was baptized into the Mormon Church in 1832, only two years after it was organized when total membership was about a thousand. Abel made history; he was one of the first blacks to join the Church whose baptismal date is known and the first to be ordained an elder (1836). He gathered with the other Saints to Nauvoo and was ordained a seventy in 1841. He served as the sexton in both Nauvoo and Winter Quarters, earning $1.50 for each grave he dug. He filled a mission to Canada and Ohio in 1883 at age seventy-three and died two weeks after returning in 1884 "in full faith."

Although blacks became converts, apparently only one other man was ordained to the priesthood until President Spencer W. Kimball changed the course of Mormon history by stating, in an announcement dated June 8, 1978, "that the long-promised day has come when every faithful, worthy man in the Church may receive the holy priesthood, with power to exercise its divine authority, and enjoy with his loved ones every blessing that flows therefrom, including the blessings of the temple. Accordingly, all worthy male members of the Church may be ordained to the priesthood without regard for race or color."

During Joseph Smith's Lifetime

During Joseph Smith's lifetime, Church leaders were more tolerant and sympathetic to blacks. When Parley P. Pratt was asked to preach a sermon on July 4, 1832, aboard a boat en route to western Missouri, he "complied, on condition that . . . all classes, black or white, should have the privilege of assembling in the cabin to hear the discourse. This was readily complied with and very soon a large assembly was convened and in waiting, consisting of ladies and gentlemen, lawyers, merchants, farmers, servants, waiters and colored gentlemen."

In the winter of 1838–39 when the Saints were being driven out of Missouri, the Absalom Free family struggled across the state on foot, suffering from frozen feet. Unable to travel, they knocked on many doors before they found a friendly welcome. According to *Women of Mormondom*:

> At every house on the route the exiles called, soliciting permission to shelter and care for the disabled men; but at every place they were turned away, until at last at eleven o'clock at night they were graciously permitted to occupy some negro quarters. . . . The party stopped and occupied the negro quarters, nursing the men during the night, and so far restored them that they were enable to go on the next day.
>
> A message went out from the mob that stated: "No d–d Mormon should stop among white folks!" Some of the complaints from citizens of Missouri were based on the knowledge that the Mormon Church opposed slavery.

William Marsden reported that, in New York City in 1841, he "stopped with Brother Oliver Brusons, a colored man of the African race three weeks." His use of "brother" suggests that Brusons was a member of the Church.

In August of 1842, Orson Hyde asked Joseph Smith: "What is the situation of the Negro?"

Joseph answered: "They come into the world slaves, mentally and physically. Change their situation with the whites and they would be like them. They have souls and are subjects of salvation. Go into

Cincinnati or any city, and find an educated negro, ... in his carriage. He has risen by the power of his mind to his exalted state of respectability. Slaves in Washington are more refined than the president. ...

Hyde then commented: "Put them on the [same] level and they will rise above me...?"

"If I raised you to be my equal and then attempt to oppress you would you not be indignant and try to rise above me? ...."

Another example of Joseph's nontraditional view was the warm reception he gave to a group of free black converts from Connecticut in 1843. Jane Manning, a free black born in 1822, was

> fully convinced that it was the true gospel. ... We started ... by canal to Buffalo, New York. We were to go to Columbus, Ohio before our fares were to be collected, but they insisted on having the money at Buffalo and would not take us farther. So we left the boat and started on foot ... over eight hundred miles. We walked until our shoes were worn out, and our feet ... cracked open and bled until you could see the whole print of our feet with blood on the ground. We stopped and united in prayer to ... ask God ... to heal our feet. Our prayers were answered ... forthwith.

Joseph Smith was touched by Jane's story and said: "God bless you. You are among friends; now you will be protected."

The others soon found work and boarding in town, but Jane was unable to find employment. Seeing her in tears, Joseph comforted her and went to get Emma. According to Jane's record, he assured her: "You have a home right here if you want it. ... We dry up all tears here." She stayed with the Smiths and helped with the household chores. Jane's brother, Isaac Manning, also stayed with the Smiths. Jane soon married Isaac James, another black member of the Church. After Joseph's death, they emigrated to Utah.

When Joseph became a candidate for president of the United States in January of 1844, one of the planks in his presidential platform read: "Break off the shackles from ... the black man, and hire him to labor like other human beings; for an hour of virtuous liberty on earth is worth a whole eternity of bondage."

The Saints had memories of music by African Americans while in Nauvoo. Among Helen Mar Kimball's descriptions of Nauvoo was that "oft in the stilly night" waking from our slumbers we would hear delicious strains of music wafted by the breeze over our quiet city from some steamer passing up or down the river, as they were frequently accompanied by minstrels, sometimes colored people and their music was perfectly enchanting—"Behold how brightly breaks the morning" ... and "Home, Sweet Home," and in many Ethiopian airs they excelled ... [and] will no doubt remind many beside myself of their most charming serenades .... Negro melodies are always sweet, and there is something most exquisite in the sound of music from the water.

On the Trail

This sympathetic attitude changed after about 1847 under instructions from Brigham Young. While blacks could, and did, become members of the Church, black men could not be ordained into the Mormon priesthood, receive their temple endowments, nor marry white women. (In contrast, Joseph Smith had encouraged some Mormon men in the early 1830s to marry Indian women and, in this manner, fulfill the Book of Mormon prophecy that the Indians would become "white and delightsome.") In fact, Brigham Young told a high council meeting at Winter Quarters on December 3, 1847: "Mulattos are like mules, they can't have children."

In 1846 in Iowa, Hosea Stout took in a young black man named Peter Manning, a relative of Jane Manning James. Stout recorded on June 19: "This morning I ... was overtaken by a black boy named Peter Manning who wanted to drive a team for someone who would take him to the Bluffs and I took him in. This was a great relief to me as I was unable to see to the cattle and horses and do what was necessary on the journey for I was very feeble. ... We came to the creek [and I] put up here & then [the] boy went back with [a] borrowed harness. I found Peter a great help to me."

A few slave owners freed their slaves when they joined the Church, but many brought them on to Utah. In 1846, "three colored slaves" traveled with the Amasa Lyman family on the trail to Zion. Lyman was a New Englander, so it is not clear if Lyman actually owned them or if they were servants.

The company of Mississippi Saints, en route to Winter Quarters in January 1847, included more than three dozen blacks. John

Brown, who was in charge of that company, recorded deaths from the cold climate:

> We purchased our wagons and teams etc. at St. Louis . . . . It finally turned cold and we had a very severe time of it. The negros suffered most. My boy, whose name was Henry took cold and finally the winter fever set in which caused his death on the road. I buried him in Andrew County, at the lower end of the round Prairie, eight miles north of Savannah, Missouri. We reached the Bluffs a few days before the Pioneers started and while I was lying here, Bankhead's negro died with the winter fever. It was the severest trip I had undertaken. I took two wagons, the two black boys that survived the trip, David Powell and Matthew Ivory, and joined the Pioneer camp.

Other black men who accompanied their owners to Utah were Hark Lay, Green Flake, and Oscar Crosby, who went with the pioneers. On the trail, most served as teamsters, herders, or cooks. Green Flake, also a Mormon, crossed the plains with Brigham Young's vanguard company of 1847 as a teamster, driving the wagon that Brigham Young used. It belonged to James M. Flake; and according to historical records, it is in the LDS Church History Museum today. Green built a cabin and had a garden ready when the Flake family arrived in 1848.

Also in 1847, at least two free families crossed the plains with the companies. Jane Manning James, her husband Isaac, and their children arrived in the valley in September as did Elijah Abel and his family. Isaac Manning, Jane's brother, was another 1847 pioneer. They traveled in the Ira Eldredge Company.

In the much larger pioneer groups of 1848, at least thirty-eight more blacks crossed the plains. Among this number were the thirty-four blacks who accompanied the Mississippi Saints. Agnes Love Flake's personal slave, thirteen-year-old Lizzy, took care of the two young Flake boys, herded cattle, and cooked.

John and George Bankhead brought about a dozen blacks to Zion in 1848. They remained slaves until the end of the Civil War and then were freed. John Bankhead helped them get settled on a homestead in Utah.

Several Mormon families owed their successful journey to Zion and even their lives to their faithful slaves. Mary Lee Bland was born to a wealthy family in Kentucky in 1817 who disowned her when she joined the Church and married William Ewell in about 1844. She kept "Mammy Chloe" as her maid. In Nauvoo, Mary Lee and William had two children and were in Iowa in 1846 when the Mormon Battalion was mustered. William enlisted, and their third child was born a few months later. William died after being reunited with Mary Lee and the family at Winter Quarters. Mary Lee and Mammy Chloe got the family, which now included a fourth child, to Utah in 1849. "Mammy Chloe taught me to spin and weave materials for our clothes, carpets for the floor, and she taught me to weave straw hats," recalled Mary Lee. ". . . [T]hus we made our living . . . until my sons were old enough to earn and make a home for us."

One all-purpose domestic, Charlotte, who belonged to the Williams W. Camp family, did some life-saving preparations for the trek, which included extracting the sugar from cane syrup. She also made crackers and packed them in barrels. It was on the trail in 1850, however, that Charlotte proved indispensable. Probably along the Platte River, "Charlotte was . . . washing white blankets and other articles. Some children were playing nearby along the river when a part of the bank caved in, taking the children with it. Charlotte was a good swimmer [and] jumped into the river and rescued several youngsters including the Camp children. She held them by their heels and rolled them over an old barrel. . . . She loved the children. . . . She was their first teacher and taught them to be polite."

Joseph Lee Robinson married a wealthy widow, Susan McCord Burton, in January 1846 as his first plural wife. She freed her slaves, but "Faithful John" begged to remain in her service. "We traveled west through Iowa," recorded Robinson. "One boy took the measles . . . . Also the faithful negro servant [John] of my second wife, became a cripple. He drove one of the teams and so it made it harder on me for awhile. He was a member of the Church." Robinson's memoirs record just how faithful John was. Robinson sent John ahead to the Salt Lake Valley with the second company in June 1847 "with some seed, grain and provisions, to raise something for us to come to." By the time the Robinsons reached Utah, John had "fine potato, corn and wheat crops ready to harvest." In fact, Robinson praised his excellent farming, since John got "close to a bushel of potatoes from each hill," assuring the Robinsons of good vegetables for the first few months of 1848. Jesse N. Smith, a family friend, commented: "There is no white man better than Faithful John."

Faithful John settled in Parowan on January 13, 1851, where he lived for the rest of his life. He reportedly helped construct the striking Old Rock Church. Descendants of the Robinson family erected a headstone in April 2006 that reads: "Faithful John Burton 1797-1865. Greater love hath no man . . . ." The other side is inscribed: "First African-American Parowan" citizen. It is also engraved with a wagon and oxen.

Occasionally the Mormons met African Americans on the trail. In 1846, at Winter Quarters, Logan Fontenella, a black man who had been raised by Indians, served as an interpreter to Chief Big Elk and the Mormons. Fontenella also worked at Fort Kearny as an interpreter.

The California gold rush brought at least a thousand blacks west by 1850 and some four thousand by 1860. But only one black '49er, Alvin A. Coffey, is known to have left an account of his journey. In 1849, Missourian J. Watt Gibson, in an encounter reported by Merrill Mattes, noted that Gibson "caught up with his runaway Negro who '[made] a contract with him to drive his team and work one year in California, after which he is to have his freedom.'" Blacks were also in western military units and traveled the Oregon and California trails. A traveler with the Goodell Company of 1854, bound for Oregon, noted: "The darkies had a dance." Helen Carpenter, a young bride in 1857, traveled with "a seventeen-year-old black boy Henry," whom her husband bought for $25 from Henry's father, who specified that Henry should receive six months schooling.

Twenty-year-old Amanda Gardner Johnson accompanied her owners to Oregon in 1853. Although she was offered her freedom before she left Liberty, Missouri, she refused, explaining in 1922 when she was almost ninety:

> [My owner] asked me if I wanted to be given my freedom and stay where I had been raised, and where all my people lived, but I was afraid to accept my liberty, much as I would have liked to stay there [Liberty]. . . . [They did not think] we had morals or souls. I was afraid to accept my liberty, so I came to Oregon with my owners. . . . When I think back nearly 70 years to our trip across the plains I can see herds of shaggy-shouldered buffaloes, slender-legged antelopes,

Indians, sagebrush, graves by the roadside, dust and high water and the campfire of buffalo chips over which I cooked the meals.

Jean Rio Baker spent much time commenting in her diary about her relations with African Americans along the trail. In May 1851 when Jean's wagon train was traveling through Iowa, her family received a visit from a black man who "amused us very much by his description of some Indian wars . . . in which he had been engaged. . . . We conversed until 12 o'clock (midnight). . . . He had been a slave from birth, but was free in everything but name and [managed] a large farm."

In 1852, just west of the Missouri River in Nebraska, pioneer George Bowering, acting as clerk to the Council Point Emigrating Company, observed that "three Indians came up to the one [wagon] the colored man was with and wanted him to let them have something and when they found that he would not give them anything they put for [a colloquialism for "went toward"] the one [wagon] behind, the colored man seeing this also put for the other and it is supposed that if it had not been for him they would have robbed [William] McKee."

Bowering also witnessed a rare baptism on the Green River in 1852. He recorded the details: "Isaiah Banderburge, a colored man was baptized for the remission of sins and confirmed under the hands of Elders Tidwell and Telemachus Rogers."

In 1867, on the Overland Trail, a black man was credited with saving "Mr. Allen's horses" during some trouble with Indians. In an 1843 company bound for Oregon, Peter H. Burnett sent his "negro girl" "to the river after a bucket of water the river was running high as the wind was blowing hard, it was supposed she threw her bucket as a wave came up. And it took her in as she never was seen again." Despite evidence that blacks were present in Mormon companies on the trail, they remain shadowy figures. Thomas Bullock names Green Flake in the vanguard company, but he is the only one to do so. Other references seem almost accidental: "our colored man," "two black boys," a "negro man," "darkies," a "negro called Old Frank," "Dick, a black man," a "colored man of the African race," and "Peter the black boy." Other journals mention their tasks as teamsters, breaking steers, working on steamboats, and even their baptisms.

European Converts' Observations

Slavery had been outlawed in England since 1772 but Thomas Fisher, who sailed from Liverpool in 1854, recorded that Sister Jane Hunter from the London Conference was not allowed to sail with the company after the medical inspection "on the grounds of her being a coloured woman of the Negro race. It appears that [in] New Orleans, the capital of the state of Louisiana, colored persons emigrating there are liable of being kidnapped on the plea of being runaway slaves."

European converts who gathered with the Saints by the New Orleans route were shocked and indignant to encounter it there. For example, in 1851, Jean Rio Griffiths Baker praised New Orleans warmly but noted:

> The only thing which detracts from its beauty is the sight of hundreds of Negroes working in the sun. Oh slavery, how I hate thee. [Jane also attended an auction for female slaves, which she described:] It is a large hall, well lighted, with seats all round on which were girls of every shade of colour, from ten or twelve to thirty years of age and to my utter astonishment they were singing as merrily as larks. I expressed my surprise to Mrs. Blime and she said "Though I am English and detest the very idea of slavery, yet I do believe that many of the slaves here have ten times the comfort of many of the labourers in our own country with not half the labor. I have been thirteen years in this country and although I have never owned a slave, or intend to do so, still I do not look upon slavery with the horror that I once did. There are hundreds of slaves here who would [not] accept their freedom if it was offered to them. For the reason they would then have no protection, as the laws afford little or none to people of color." I could not help thinking that my friend's feelings had become somewhat blunted, if not hardened by long residence in slave states.

Jean Rio Baker continued: "I was shown a gent of color who is . . . a managing clerk in one of the largest stores. He pays his master 500 dollars, his salary is $1000. He is married to a free woman [and] they live in a very handsome house which is the property of the wife as a slave is not allowed to possess real estate. They keep a carriage and 4 servants and this is by no means a singular case." In visiting an exclusive area of New Orleans, she was surprised that the white elites dress their slaves even more expensively. "I saw slave girls following their mistresses in the streets, clad in frocks of embroidered silk or satin, and elegantly worked muslin trousers either blue or scarlet. Morocco walking shoes, and white silk stockings, with a French head-dress. . . . Jewelry glitters on their dusky fingers (which are plainly seen through their lace gloves), and in their ears. Their only business seems to be to follow the ladies who own them and carry their reticule."

A convert from Scotland, Richard Bee, recorded a grimmer experience at a St. Louis auction where "many Negro slaves were placed on public exhibit and bartered off to the highest bidder, no consideration being made to the family ties, but separated at the will of the auctionist [sic] and purchaser, in spite of the protests and cries of the unfortunate victims. Parents from their children, husbands and wives separated, brother and sister parted, perchance never to see each other again; their pleading made no impression on their less than human trafficers of human beings. Sellers, buyers, spectators alike only scoffed and laughed at their entreaties.

British artist Frederick Piercy traveling with an 1853 Mormon company was both intrigued and shocked:

> I saw and conversed with . . . a thinker and, as might be expected, [he] entertained the most infidel and radical notions. . . . His arguments in favour of negro-slavery were certainly of a candid description. He said that it was natural throughout creation for the strong and powerful in mind and body to enslave those inferior to them; that it was upon this principle that animals were subdued by men, removed from their natural sphere, made to plough, and were afterwards consigned to the slaughter-house; and that if the principle held good with respect to horses, oxen, &c., it was equally so with reference to negros who were truly inferior animals to white men. I questioned his assertion as to their inferiority, which he met by saying that it was only because I had not lived among them. . . . I certainly saw no evidence of constitutional inferiority in them, either mentally or physically. Indeed, the wonder is, considering their degraded state, that they are found so intelligent.

Piercy continued his observations during his April 1853 visit to New Orleans and later to Memphis, noting with appreciation:

I cannot refrain, here, from paying a tribute to the mirthfulness of negros. Their hearty laughter makes the old Mississippi ring again. Laughing is no slight matter with a real negro, and considering the exertion attendant upon one of their performances, it is a wonder that ... they ever venture upon another. Where there is a negro there is sure to be fun, joking and jollity. They have almost invariably a keen sense of the ridiculous, and an enjoyment of it not to be eradicated by slavery. They are generally very ready-witted, and full of words. Like their betters they delight in authority, and from what I have heard, I conclude they are the most merciless of task-masters. While in [Memphis] I was quite amused in listening to two rival negro-teamsters quarreling. It ended in the smartest of them gaining the victory by saying to the other. "Ugh! Ugh! You poor skunk, you'll be for sale soon, and then I'll buy you." ... I ... witnessed the intense love the negros have for finery and gay colours. Ebony Apollos and sable Venuses promenaded the streets, draped in colours which reminded me of exotic flowers.

Piercy also observed the range of skin colors denoting mixed heritage. He even commented "that a slight existence of African blood in European veins was, in the case of females, the cause of a most attractive and charming kind of loveliness." Less poetic writers like Richard Burton wrote that he saw in an 1860 Mormon company "an exceedingly plain middle aged and full blooded negro woman."

Rasmus Nielsen, a Danish pioneer passing through New Orleans in 1854, described "black slaves at work, thirty to fifty in a gang. On the steam ship are six blacks. They do the heaviest work. They buy them here for $25.00 each."

James Moyle, an English convert who traveled to New Orleans in 1854, attended an auction there. "It was revolting to my feelings to see the men, women, and children that we saw there sold like cattle or horses, and although they had a black skin they were human beings."

Emma Higbee, born in 1836, remembered those slave auctions, probably witnessed in St. Louis because she was born in Missouri. "We saw children taken from their parents and given to rough traders. The storms at sea did not seem nearly so terrible as that auction sale with human lives and happiness at stake."

I found "nigger" used only once in a statement made in 1864 by a St. Louis native who was "waited on by niggers." English converts usually used "negros" or "darkies," as in "The crew was all darkies and not very sociable." "Sons of Africa" was another euphemism. Jean Rio Baker in 1851 commented that "the poor despised sons of Africa, too, have a little church to pray and praise the Lord in, but it is only lately that their masters have allowed them this privilege."

Blacks in Utah

The 1850 census of Utah enumerates only twenty-six slaves. This could mean that some blacks really were servants, not slaves, and that some had been freed. Kate B. Carter published the first information about blacks in Utah in 1965. It includes Apostle Orson Hyde's article about the Church's position on slavery, published in the *Millennial Star* on February 15, 1851:

> We feel it our duty to define our position in relation to the subject of slavery. There are several men in the Valley . . . who have their slaves with them. There is no law in Utah to authorize slavery, neither any to prohibit it. If the slave is disposed to leave his master, none are allowed to interfere between the master and the slave. All the slaves that are there appear to be perfectly contented and satisfied. . . . Our counsel to all our ministers in the North and in the South is: to avoid contention upon this subject, and to oppose no institution which the laws of the country authorize; but to labour to bring men into the church . . . and then teach them to do right, and honor their God and His creatures.

Jane Manning James and her family traveled to Iowa in 1846. Near Council Bluffs, midwife Patty Sessions wrote on June 10: "Put black Jane to bed with a son." This baby is considered to be the first freeborn black in that state. Two years later on May 8, 1848, Patty Sessions "put black Jane [Manning James] to bed with a daughter born 10 2h A.M." Two years later, Jane gave birth in Utah, giving her a claim to also be the mother of the first free black baby in Utah. However, some records give that claim to Dan Bankhead Freeman, who belonged to John Bankhead, pioneer of 1848. Dan Freeman appeared not to be a "free man," so he could not have been the father to the first free black baby. When Jane died in 1908, Joseph F. Smith, a counselor in the First Presidency, spoke at her funeral.

One black man was among the rescuers of Willie and Martin handcart companies in November of 1856. According to Daniel W.

Jones, Tom Bankhead, who went to Utah in 1848 with several other Bankhead slaves, was among those who braved the cold. Two other Bankhead "boys" acted as down-and-back teamsters in the early 1860s.

During the Reformation of 1857, John Brown of Mississippi consecrated his property, livestock, and supplies to the Church, including an "African Servant Girl" valued at a thousand dollars. She was the single most valuable item in an estate valued at more than $3,000. It is not clear who accepted her on behalf of the Church or what happened to her.

Utah records have at least one instance of a slave transaction. On September 7, 1859, Thomas S. Williams sold "Dan, a negro boy," age twenty-six, for "the sum of eight hundred dollars" to Wm. H. Hooper. Until 1858, Dan, born in Tennessee, had belonged to Williams Camp.

Also in 1859, famous newspaperman Horace Greeley visited Utah and interviewed Brigham Young, among other topics, on "the position of your Church with respect to Slavery?"

Young replied succinctly: "We consider it of divine institution, and not to be abolished until the curse pronounced on Ham shall have been removed from his descendants."

California became a free state in 1850, but Utah remained a slave territory until forced to grant slaves within its border freedom by Lincoln's Emancipation Proclamation on January 1, 1863. Mormons usually called their slaves "servants," a euphemism more compatible with the New England background of most of them. Blacks who went to California with Mormon masters were freed when they got there.

According to Kate Carter's research, Samuel Chambers, "a large mulatto with straight white hair, joined the church and 'his family traveled to Utah in 1870 with a group of colored Latter-day Saint converts.'" Samuel bought some land in Salt Lake City and planted fruit trees and a vegetable garden. He built two homes, prospered, shared his bounty with others, "and became the largest tithe payer in Wilford Ward."

Charles H. Rowan, a black man, drove a team for the Lyman/Rich group, which traveled to San Bernardino in 1851. Charles later married Lizzie Flake, who was with the Agnes Love Flake family in the Amasa Lyman company. This marriage of Lizzie and Charles produced a daughter, Alice, who is thought to be the first black in America to teach in a school (in California) for white children.

In 1936, Amasa M. Lyman Jr., in his reminiscences, wrote: "I knew all three of those negro servants [actually slaves].... Hark Lay belonged to William Lay. Hark was always hard to manage. He died in California. William Crosby went to California and took ... Oscar Crosby.... James M. Flake, who owned Green Flake, was killed in California.... After the slaves were freed, Green Flake lived at Union Fort, Salt Lake Country, but died in Idaho. His death got big headlines in Salt Lake City." Richard Van Wagoner and Steven Walker add some fascinating details. When the widowed Agnes Flake moved to California in 1851, she gave her slave, Green Flake, to the Church as tithing. Brigham Young kept Flake for a year, Flake served Heber C. Kimball for a second year, and he was then given his freedom.

Blacks all over the world are now members of the Church. The Prophet Joseph Smith would be pleased at this success because he was their friend when few whites showed any interest in their welfare.

Jane Manning James was faithful to the end, but apparently many blacks who went to Utah did not stay very long. The promises of California called across the mountains, and they left to search for other wealth and opportunities.

They also helped to make the mountains sing while in Zion.

Chapter 11

Disease, Accidents, Death, and Burials

I can see my mother's face as she sat looking at [her sick son]. Her eyes looked so dead that I was afraid. She didn't sit long, however, for my mother was never one to cry. When it was time to move out, mother had her family ready to go. She put her invalid son in the cart with her baby, and we joined the train. Our mother was a strong woman, and she would see us through anything. —Sarah James, 1856 Willie Handcart Company

According to historians, about 500,000 people migrated westward between 1841 and 1868, and about 10 percent of them died—an estimated 20,000 of those en route to Oregon or California. (During urban cholera epidemics, a death rate of 10 percent or more was not uncommon.) Over one-half of those trail deaths were infants and small children. The Saints began their march into Iowa in February 1846 when it was too early. Many in the famous Donner-Reed party died in the Sierras on their journey to California because they arrived too late to get across the mountains. Some of the most dramatic death scenes in trail history occurred in 1846 when the push westward began in earnest. Writer Bernard DeVoto called 1846, *The Year of Decision*. Deaths were caused by many common and predictable events, as well as the strange and exotic. Likewise, the medical treatment of that period ranged from the common sense and commonplace to the bizarre and ineffectual. About 7,000 Latter-day Saints died on the trail west between 1846 and 1869.

Among the nightmarish moments of trail life were deaths from disease, freak accidents, being crushed by heavy animals and wagon wheels, drowning, freezing temperatures, starvation, exhaustion, lightning, heat, dehydration, and stampedes. Many children became instant orphans on the trail when both parents died. The Saints, except for the last two handcart companies of 1856, had fewer deaths than Oregon-bound pioneers, but they also had shorter distances to travel. Some adults lost all of their children to either disease or accidents.

Public fears to the contrary, Indians were not a leading cause of trail deaths. An exception was 1854, a year of serious Indian uprisings. Thomas Sutherland recorded near Fort Laramie: "We traveled 8 miles to Bordeax Station. . . . At this place the Indians killed the 29 soldiers with their officer, they are buried close by the road. I have visited the grave and some of the men's heads are not even covered. It was the settlers that buried them, as the remainder of the soldiers could not leave the fort. . . . There was also a man's face lying on the bank with the teeth firm in the jaw bone and the flesh appeared recently taken off. Several military gloves were lying on the grass close by."

But such events accounted for only a small minority of trail deaths. John Unruh Jr. estimated that nine out of ten deaths were caused by disease, and only 4 percent by Indians. More Mormons were killed by lightning than by Indians. Luke W. Gallup wrote: "Several men killed by lightning," in 1850. In 1853, Richard L. Jones noted that two men were killed by lightning. One traveler was injured and one was killed by a lightning strike in the first handcart company in 1856, according to Archer Walters.

While the Mormon experience in deaths and diseases was typical of others, they differed from other immigrants in at least three ways: they relied more on faith healing, they were better organized, and they generally had more women and children. Unruh notes: "Mormons . . . whose passages to Salt Lake City were invariably better organized and included a higher percentage of females succumbed less frequently to disease on their north side of the Platte River trails."

Still, ailments on the trail and aboard ship ran a wide gamut. Immigrants on the trail complained of headaches, piles, mumps, asthma, bloody flux, infections, tuberculosis (often called consumption or phthisis), inflammation of the bowels, measles, smallpox, scurvy, cancer, cholera, boils, blisters, scrofula, sore eyes, erysipelas, all sorts of gastrointestinal problems, neuralgia, arthritis, rheumatism, the itch, sunburn, frostbite, aching teeth, inflammation of the lungs, and a host of fevers—typhoid, scarlet, "mountain," puerperal, and malaria (*mal aria*, Italian for bad air). Adding their ounces of misery were mosquitoes, gnats, chiggers, lice, and fleas.

In the greater Council Bluffs area in the summer and fall of 1846, midwife Patty Sessions, a practical nurse and midwife, was one of many who fell desperately ill. On September 2, she described her situation:

> I have been very sick [and] have not wrote any since the 7 of August to day.... Brs Brigham and Heber laid hands on me. Sister young gave me some tonic on Wednesday that seemed to reach my disease. The Doctor said I had the inflamation [sic] in the stomach and it would be a miricle [sic] if I got well. I felt calm and composed told them where my garments were and all things necessary for my burial.

Weather

Weather was also a frequent cause of sickness and death. Immigrants, constantly exposed to the vicissitudes of the weather, wrote about that subject more than anything else in the more than 1,000 trail accounts studied. Some consist of little more than weather reports and distances traveled. Temperatures could range from at least 12 degrees below zero to more than 110 above. In Iowa and Nebraska, sudden storms were not infrequent. Immigrants suffered from exposure to heat, mud, wind, rain, cold, sleet, snow, hail, tornadoes, and blizzards.

Across Iowa the enemies were rain and mud, which, though bothersome, were not insurmountable. This weather held up the wagons for a long time, however. George Bean wrote with candor about Iowa conditions in 1846. "It rained incessantly for two weeks, much suffering prevailed. A great deal of grumbling, and in some cases almost open rebellion was indulged in. Many of us were obliged to lie on the ground and . . . get soaking wet almost every night."

On the high plains during hot months, weather was a terrible adversary and storms could generate strong winds and tornadoes. Fires were blown out, tents flipped over, clothing and bedding were soaked, and animals stampeded, terrified by the crackling lightning and booming thunder. Wind-driven dust and sand could blind and choke immigrants. During cold months, blizzards caused snow drifts twenty feet deep. Deep snow could halt companies for weeks, water froze solid in buckets, and a few pioneers froze to death. Rivers and streams rose during torrential downpours, washing out the few bridges and making fords dangerous to cross. People, animals, and supplies were lost, and wagons were overturned.

Some travelers who wandered from camp and became lost or disoriented were never found. A few were found dead, their bodies partly eaten by wild animals. One aged woman in a handcart company near Green River disappeared. At Fort Bridger, the company learned that some soldiers had discovered her body, partly eaten by wolves, and buried her. One of the soldiers had a piece of the woman's dress, which confirmed her identity.

Wind and dust were responsible for much discomfort. Mormons were fortunate to avoid what Sarah Sutton, en route to Oregon, described July 31, 1854. "We have not seen any rain for two months, nor do we expect to see any. . . . We are nearly smother'd [sic] and covered with ashy dust . . . and the sage . . . looks like it would set on fire without help."

C.C.A. Christiansen, a Mormon convert from Denmark, complained in 1857: "Our faces were gray from the dust, which sometimes prevented us from seeing the vanguard, our noses with the skin hanging in patches, especially on those who had as much nose as I have; and almost every lower lip covered with a piece of cloth or paper because of its chapped condition, which made it difficult to speak, and particularly to smile or laugh. Many used goggles and veils to keep the dust and sand from blinding and choking them."

Accidents with Firearms

Most immigrant companies were traveling armories and many gun-related accidents took place. Revolvers, rifles, shotguns, and gunpowder injuries were common. Pioneer men felt it necessary to be armed for hunting and defense. Among the most popular arms of trail days were Sharps, Spencer, and Winchester rifles and the Colt revolver. Some companies even brought small cannons. Too many men were inexperienced with firearms, resulting in a plethora of accidents.

Two fatal but accidental shootings of women happened within two days of each other in the 1855 Richard Ballantine Company. Mary Ann Ford Simmons wrote: "When we were about two day's journey from Ft. Laramie, a sister was making her bed in the wagon when a gun close by was accidently discharged and shot her arm off. She ran out into the camp with her arm hanging by a piece of flesh. She was taken back to Ft Laramie but died on the way. A day or two later a young man was playing with a gun and accidently shot a young girl in the leg. She too was sent back to Fort Laramie but died on the way."

Many of these weapons were of poor quality and lacked safety devices. Loaded rifles and shotguns were routinely left in wagons for immediate use and too often inflicted injuries or deaths through jostling or by being quickly snatched up by the muzzle. One man was shot though the wrist, another though the knee. Another shot the end of his thumb off. A wise rule of the trail was: "Always look to your gun, but never let your gun look at you." John Cook stooped to untie a rope at Winter Quarters in 1848. His pistol fell to the ground butt first and fired a bullet through his neck. He died in less than three minutes.

Sometimes improperly cared for weapons broke when fired. On rare occasions, kegs of gunpowder would explode. Jean Rio Baker wrote in 1851: "Saw a returning merchant train from Salt Lake. They had one of their wagons take fire and when two of their men tried to extinguish it, their gun powder exploded and killed them both."

Contamination and Infection

Unsanitary conditions prevailed at the camp grounds, causing many illnesses and deaths from infection. Wounds large and small were common and became easily infected. The many animals that accompanied the migration contributed to the unsanitary conditions. Emigrants lived day and night for months in close proximity to animals and were affected by their noise, smells, droppings, urine, and hair. Dung, for example, is a notorious place for the breeding of germs, especially those causing lockjaw. The vector of disease that could be interrupted by washing hands and utensils was not understood, so dirty hands helped spread disease. Food was prepared and eaten under circumstances that also spread disease.

Cholera

Cholera, a bacterial infection of the small intestine caused by human waste's contamination of food or drinking water, was the most lethal of all diseases. A water-borne disease, it reached the New World before 1832, and had started to accompany trains westward by 1842. It attacks suddenly and violently, causing severe diarrhea and vomiting that can lead to dehydration and death within hours, if left untreated. It is the discharge of body fluids, including extreme dysentery and vomiting, that causes the alarming spread of the disease throughout a whole camp very quickly. The best treatment, little known during trail days, was simply replacing the lost fluid.

Harriet Utley Carter watched five in her family die in Winter Quarters from "black measles," including her mother. On the trail in 1852, her father contacted cholera. She recalled:

> How terrible it was, so cold and damp. . . . Mother was sick before my sister died but she kept up and helped take care of the children. It seemed like every family around us was having the same kind of trouble. We couldn't get any help and there were very few doctors. They seemed helpless with such a terrible epidemic. . . . [Father] was so sad and discouraged [but] decided to start west for Utah in 1852. Father contacted the disease (cholera) and when he was very bad, I got in bed with him and said if he had to die I wanted to die too. He died and was buried there. The people burned all our clothes and bedding.

Immigrants in sailing vessels were especially vulnerable. In 1849, forty-five passengers on the *Berlin* died of cholera; fifteen were children. Lucena Parsons was in a company in 1850 that buried twelve children. Nine died from cholera, and three from being crushed by wagon wheels. Five of those children were in one family. Lucena wrote on June 25, 1849: "This morning the mother of the 5 children that have died was taken sick and died at evening." A total of nine from one family died of cholera in that company.

A brother and sister, Henry and Louisa Williams, shared a single grave in 1850 near Heber Springs. John Steele recorded the scene of mourning: "This morning Henry and Louisa Williams, the two stricken with cholera yesterday . . . were buried. The young lady died about midnight, and her brother lingered until dawn. A deep, wide grave was prepared, in which the bodies were laid, coffinless, to mingle with the clay. The parents and another son . . . gazed upon the scene in silent . . . grief."

Some trail companies estimated that, of the numbers who died, two-thirds were from cholera. One diarist said that bodies "lay in rows of 50 or more." Warren Foote saw a repulsive scene in 1850: "Beds and bedding are strewed about with the stains of the cholera vomit upon them." Such contaminated bedding was usually burned or discarded.

Louise Graehl of Geneva, Switzerland, traveled as far as the Mormon camp west of Independence in 1854 where her little daughter died "while playing with some dolls." They had real walnut wood for her coffin. In a touching gesture, little Louise "was carried to her resting place by 6 young ladies" in camp.

In that same camp was Jean Frederick Loba, age eight, who recalled: "In the evening, Mr. Stoudemann . . . called for the elders of the church for a blessing. . . . But the next day he passed away. . . . Impressed with the solemnity and the sadness which brooded over us all, we [boys] pledged each other not to surrender . . . but hardly had we made a vow, when the youngest of the Stroudemann boys . . . was gone. And so this entire family, with the exception of the eldest son, Charles, was stricken and buried at Pleasant Grove [Kansas]."

Oregon-bound in 1853, Marilla R. Washburn records her mother's pioneer remedy: "My brother and I took the cholera. Mother gave us all the hot whiskey she could pour down us and put flannel cloths soaked in whiskey, as hot as we could bear, on our stomachs. This cured us."

In 1850, Martha Spence Heywood wrote: "I started [from St. Louis] on the night of 2nd of May in the steamer *Mary* with about 240 Mormons. Cholera broke out. . . . We lost 58 by death and remains were buried on the banks as we came along." Martha "used the knowledge I gained on my trip from St. Louis" to treat "a child of Brother Barney's . . . and she recovered rapidly." Martha does not elaborate on her successful treatment.

Mary Ann Stearns [Winters] wrote in 1852: "Mother's remedy consisted of charcoal and molasses, laudanum and paregoric, camphor and a little cayenne pepper with as much raw flour as charcoal and it proved to be a good remedy, for all who took it recovered except Brother Robinson. Mother's health had improved greatly–she was gaining strength every day."

Other treatments for cholera included brandy and loaf sugar, a concoction made of charcoal and molasses, camphor, cayenne pepper and flour, as well as the standbys of laudanum and paregoric. Tar and pitch were sometimes burned around wagons and camps to disperse the "poisonous particles" in the atmosphere.

Inattention to digging and using latrines at campsites caused cholera to spread, and many companies tried to avoid the most contaminated places. Amelia Stewart Knight, six months pregnant and Oregon bound in 1853, had a thoughtful husband who drove a mile or two away from the unpleasant camps. If it was hot, the flies and other insects were even worse. Amelia wrote July 4: "It has been very warm today. Thermometer up to 110. I never saw mosquitoes as bad as they are here. Chat [her son] has been sick all day with fever, partly caused by mosquito bites." The constant movement of companies, however, did improve general conditions simply by removing people from accumulated human and animal waste.

Trail accounts do not contain instructions for properly preparing and covering latrines. If they existed, it seems unlikely that their use was enforced. Women's long skirts, often dragged through mud and manure, were worn day and night in many cases. Toddlers exploring campsites were particularly enticed by germ-laden deposits, and unsupervised older children also found fatal attractions.

Samuel Gifford from Pennsylvania insisted that his immigrant companions avoid standing water and boil river water before using it for cooking or drinking. The discoveries of Lister and Pasteur lay in the future, but boiling killed the visible vermin and "wigglers" in river water, with the invisible but real benefit of purifying the water. Only five died of cholera in his company in 1850. Although the Word of Wisdom forbade tea and coffee, most Mormons routinely drank these beverages on the trail, doubtless saving many lives.

Accidental Deaths

Lettie Henderson, age six, died en route to Oregon in 1846 after drinking a bottle of laudanum that hung on a nail in the family wagon. Many women died under the wheels of wagons or feet of oxen. Thomas Bullock, approaching the Poor Camp on October 30, 1846, recorded: "[We] ascended a very steep hill. As soon as brother Gabbutt's Wagon had ascended the hill, his Wife Sarah Cabbutt [sic] [while attempting to get out of the way,] laid hold of a [churn] dasher which being cracked, gave way, and she fell against the Oxen, which so startled them, they started off at a full run. She fell to the ground and the wheels of the Wagon passed over her loins or kidneys. . . . She exclaimed 'oh, dear, I am dying.' She lingered until 5 minutes to 1 and breathed her last."

Six-year-old Robert R. Gardner was the first death related to the crushing wagon wheels during the exodus from Winter Quarters in 1847. According to James Smithies, Robert fell under the wheels near Ayers Natural Bridge in eastern Wyoming, died August 18, and was buried "on the west side of the Black Hills exact [sic] half a mile from the Bank of the Platte river."

On June 15, 1848, six-year-old Lucretia Cox slipped between the feet of the oxen, some of which weighed 1,000 pounds, and the wheels rolled over her tiny body. "She gave two gasps and expired," wrote Wm. Thompson, clerk of the Heber C. Kimball camp. After this incident, Kimball sharply admonished the mothers to take better care of their children. "It is better to tie up children in the wagons then bury them," he said.

Other young fatalities include a boy who got tangled in a horse rope and was dragged to death. An infant in a handcart company was smothered when its mother laid on it. Jane Walters, born to a "Sister Walters," in the Hunt Wagon Company in 1856, died four weeks after her mother was killed by a stampede. One child "was killed by heat." A little girl in a Mormon company in 1852 was crushed when a wagon tipped over and a large box of tools fell on her. One witness commented that "her cheeks were [still] red," after she had been dead for two days.

Several accounts describe how women were run over because they were hampered by their clothing. Even though the oxen's plodding gait covered only two miles per hour, there was no way of quickly stopping them and the damage was done in a matter of seconds. The very slowness of the oxen tempted people to get in and out of wagons on the move. Limbs and ribs were bruised and crushed, bones broken, internal organs crushed, and flesh torn.

A "Mississippi Saint," Harriet Crow, climbed up on the wagon tongue to get a drink of water out of the slow-moving wagon in 1847. She fell and was run over but was not seriously injured. Ellen Kinsley fell under the front wheel in 1851 and was killed. Sometimes wagons were overturned by bolting animals, careless driving, soft banks giving way, deep ruts, holes, and ravines. The weight of the wagon, the softness of the earth, and other factors determined the seriousness of an accident.

The many draft animals themselves were also a source of accidents. People were gored, stepped on, kicked, thrown from horses, or fell off them. Sometimes animals fell on their riders or those leading them. A bad-tempered animal would bite. In 1847, Wilford Woodruff was bitten to the bone through three thicknesses of clothing, one of which was buckskin. In 1850, Woodruff's horse ran away with his wagon while his daughter was inside. She did not suffer serious injuries.

The foreign immigrants took greater risks since many of them had no experience with draft animals. According to John Powell in 1856, one Danish brother foolishly thought "he could control his oxen by tying a rope around their horns. The oxen, not used to such treatment, bolted, dragging him under his own wagon crushing him to death." In 1857, a "Sister Brown" with heart trouble died of fright when she saw her husband kicked by one of his oxen. He was unhurt, but the scare killed her.

The prolonged hardships of the trails often brought out the worst in human nature; and too often, trivial matters became of great consequence. Stressed-out immigrants erupted into violence over imagined or petty wrongs—animals, food, supplies, work assignments, guard duty, and waiting for others. There were fist, gun, and knife fights. Dr. Samuel Matthias Ayers tersely wrote in 1850: "A man shot a youth who crept in with his daughter." Frontier justice validated a man's defense of his family.

Medical Treatment

Since the Mormons considered themselves to be modern children of Israel, led by modern prophets, they tended to rely a great deal on faith and administrations by Church leaders to heal the sick. Rebaptism for health was a practice that began in the Nauvoo Temple and continued well into the twentieth century.

Sixtus E. Johnson wrote on August 4, 1861: "Sister Batey was baptized for her health . . . and died Aug. 9 of inflamation of the lungs." Those called upon to nurse the sick combined their knowledge with the fervent exercise of faith in hopes of helping their patients, resulting sometimes in recoveries so dramatic that they have survived in family lore.

Parley P. Pratt administered to his little son "who was lifeless" in 1847 on the Mormon Trail. The child recovered. Ten-year-old David C. Hess was bitten by a rattlesnake in their little cabin in Iowa in 1847. He lay near death for months but recovered after an administration from the elders.

Amputations were sometimes the only way to save a life, but they were not risk free. At least two travelers on the Oregon Trail died from shock when crude amputations of shattered limbs were attempted by knives and carpenter saws, with red-hot wagon bolts as cauterizers. Edwin Bryant witnessed an unsuccessful amputation on seven-year-old Enoch Garrison's mangled leg in 1846 and wrote: "I saw the procession of the little boy to his final resting place and it produced sadness and depression." Ephraim Hanks sterilized his hunting knife in the fire and amputated the frozen limbs of Martin handcart members, washing the wounds with castile soap after the skin and bones were removed. Even frostbite was a painful ailment, and a variety of remedies had only limited success.

Trained physicians were rare. The role of skilled midwives like Patty Bartlett Sessions has already been mentioned. Almost any one, when called on, "did a little doctoring." Thomas L. Kane, who fell ill in Council Bluffs in July of 1846, sent for Dr. H. I. W. Edes of Fort Leavenworth, about 150 miles away. Thomas survived and, presumably, paid the doctor his fee of $200, but the details of his treatment have not survived. In 1846 a "Dr. Sprague," probably a homeopathic physician, treated patients on the Missouri River. A "hydropathist" wrapped her patients in wet sheets. Military posts such as Fort Kearney and Fort Laramie offered at least what the army considered military treatment, although in 1852, the Fort Kearney hospital was filled with cholera patients who overflowed into a nearby tent.

Willard Richards was always called "Dr. Richards," but his training consisted of a six-week course in Thomsonian herbalism. Thomas Bullock, traveling with the Pioneer Camp of 1847, wrote on May 31: "Dr. Richards . . . removed me into his Wagon and administered Composition Tea. . . . In the evening Dr. administered a Lobelia Emetic and attended me through the operation." Another "botanical doctor" was Priddy Meeks who went west in 1847.

Thomsonianism was relatively safe, compared to the "heroic" treatment of depletionism, which was rapidly becoming outmoded. This form of treatment was based on the ancient notion that all diseases had their origin in an imbalance in one or more of the cardinal humors (blood, phlegm, black bile, and yellow bile). Typical treatments were copious blood letting and emetics, designed to "cleanse" the body by purging and then "restore" lost heat by having the patient take hot baths, eat cayenne pepper and ginger, and drink medicine made from bayberries, sumac, and red raspberries. Although many journals mention receiving this medical treatment, I found no references to the equally popular "blistering" or "cupping." Chloroform was discovered in 1831 and in general use by 1845, but it is not mentioned in Mormon trail accounts.

In early July of 1847 when Brigham Young and several others suffered mountain fever, William Clayton recorded: "Many of the brethren have gone down sick within past three days & a number more this even[ing]. They generally begin with headache, succeeded by violent fever & some go delirous [sic] for a while. Bro. Fowler . . . is raving. I am satisfied diluted spirits is good in this disease after breaking up the fever."

Immigrant medications were varied, imaginative, and often unusual. Common drugs were Epson salts, calomel (an emetic), morphia and laudanum (derived from opium), tincture of camphor, Ayer's Pain Killers, Dover's Powders, balsams, lobelia, quinine, and Warburg's Drops. Stomach pumps were sometimes used. Pioneers also used flour of brimstone in honey for piles, and chokecherries or brandy for diarrhea. Wounds were often treated with camphor or a homemade liniment compounded of red pepper, whiskey, and laudanum. Elm bark was considered a sovereign antiseptic. Dysentery was treated with brandy. Composition tea, a gruel sometimes made with boiled milk and flour, was a remedy for bowel complaints and general ailments. Tea was a universal panacea, especially mixed with lobelia or cayenne pepper— recommended for almost any ailment, especially cramps and chills. Two parts saltpeter and one part sweet nitre, mixed with water, was used to paint the esophagus as a remedy for diphtheria. Brewer's yeast in water was given to those with smallpox. Dry flour was often applied to the inflamed limbs of those suffering from erysipelas. A bag of hot salt was used for chest pains.

Mormons also relied on asafetida, a strong-smelling gum rosin, the odor of which was thought to repel disease. In 1852, Mary Ann Stearns recorded that an Oregon-bound woman begged Mary Ann's mother for the asafetida bags the children had used in Council Bluffs when smallpox struck. Mary Ann was struck by "the effect it had on her. 'Oh, I am so glad to get it and will pay you anything you ask.' Mother told her she was welcome to it. . . . In a little while she came over [with] a basin of beans."

A reliable standby was medicinal alcohol. Heber C. Kimball kept a jug of brandy; and his adopted son, Peter O. Hansen, recorded: "He consecrated it and asked God that it might preserve us from the cold." Whiskey sweetened with sugar was used to revive the exhausted, and whiskey was also believed to cure snakebite.

Folk wisdom also decreed that tobacco had its medicinal merits for sick cattle and making poultices, especially for snakebite. Some believed smoking a pipe cleared the head and was good for toothache. Snuff and chewing tobacco were thought useful in keeping the mouth and lips from drying out.

Dental problems were nearly always treated with extraction, generally done with ordinary nippers, pliers, or pincers. Some, like Lorenzo Young, "drew" their own ulcerated teeth. William Clayton, traveling west in 1847, had Luke Johnson pull an aching tooth for him. Johnson "got half the original tooth, the balance being left in the jaw. He lanced the gum . . . and jerked it out. . . . [The] operation did not take more than one minute." (See Chapter 3.)

The standard procedure for extracting Indian arrows was to position the wounded man with his back against a wagon wheel. Someone with blacksmith pincers positioned himself in front of him and pulled. If the point did not break off, there was good chance for recovery.

Aboard Ship

Some European Saints were vaccinated for smallpox before going aboard ship. In 1850 one company was treated en route for smallpox. Sometimes they were quarantined on board ship before debarking and kept in a medical building at the dock. Medicine chests were common items of shipboard equipment. The bottles were usually numbered with directions for their use found on the inside of the chest's cover.

About 90 percent of those on board ships who died were small children, representing a dramatic increase in the death rate for foreign Mormon emigrant children. All seven of the deaths in the second emigration from England in 1840 were youngsters. Some of those who later died on the Atlantic Ocean were sick with consumption when they began their journey. Others died from dehydration due to seasickness, or they contacted cholera, measles, smallpox, whooping cough, or other diseases. Riverboats and trains also claimed their victims en route to the jumping-off places to the Far West on the Missouri River.

Some corpses were sewn into shrouds and tipped overboard. Others were buried along the riverbank. Riverboats often carried coffins for just such reasons. June Wood Danvers tells one colorful story of Mormons traveling upriver in 1849:

> The captain was a brutal, unaccommodating, and a very, extremely harsh man. . . . He weighted corpses and dumped them overboard. One LDS died and George Wood, his brother, got permission to make the burial on shore and hired a Negro to help dig a trench. Before the burial was completed the captain sailed off, leaving the burial party stranded on shore. . . . [Joseph Walker also on board found some rope and threatened to hang the captain, saying:] "We have tried persuasion to see if there is any humanity in your worthless carcass. See this rope. If you don't go back to those people, I'll hang you from your own cross beam and I'll have plenty of help to do so."

The captain reversed course.

Perhaps two of the most unusual narratives involving death occurred in 1855. Two of that year's travelers were already dead at the commencement of their journey. A young and inexperienced teamster, Isaiah Moses Coombs, was hired as an independent teamster at Mormon Grove, near Atchison, Kansas. In his cargo was Albert Gregory, a Latter-day Saint missionary, who had died at Mormon Grove and was being returned to his family in Utah in a metal coffin. Coombs wrote: "A light wagon was selected for this purpose and two yoke of young half-broken cattle were purchased to draw the [wagon]. This wagon and team with Bro. Gregory's body and effects were placed in my care." The trip got off to a chilling start when the untrained oxen ran away with the wagon and the body. Coombs managed to fulfill his assignment, however, and delivered the body to Utah.

In 1855, Oregon-bound William Keil hauled his dead son, William Jr., from Missouri in a lead-lined coffin filled with alcohol to preserve the body, in a wagon drawn by four mules. Young William, who had died of malaria before he could see Oregon, was laid to rest twenty miles from the ocean in what became Washington.

Drownings

In 1864, thirty-three immigrants died in St. Joseph, Missouri and were buried in the St. Joseph Cemetery. English convert "Sister Shelly" attempted to draw a bucket of water from the river en route to St. Louis from New Orleans. The force of the current drew her into the river where she floated for a moment and then sank to rise no more. The engines stopped immediately and a boat was sent in search of her, but it failed to find her body. In 1851, Jean Rio Baker recorded that a man fell overboard traveling upriver to St. Louis: "The boat stopped instantly and every effort was made to save him, but to no avail. As he sank he threw his pocket book which was picked up by one of the men and given to the Clerk in order to be restored to the relatives of the deceased."

Far out on the plains, John H. Gundlach traveling to California in 1850, "saw a man viewing the chasm at Devil's Gate slip over the edge, swept away by the river." On May 26, 1848, "a lively little boy" named Henry Beer drowned when about 100 wagons were ferried over to join the Mormons at the Elk Horn River staging ground. It was the first tragedy for those who left for the trek west that year. "We all turned out and searched 'til the body was found. A coffin was made . . . of a solid log of wood. . . . The body was kept in the wagon until we reached camp at the Liberty Pole," John Pulsipher wrote.

High water took a toll on the stock and also on the young men trying to swim the animals across. One diarist wrote that "fifteen men drowned from getting cramp" while swimming cattle over. Another diarist on the Oregon Trail recorded a report of "said to be 40 drowned." Quicksand on the Platte could be deadly. Richard Bee, while driving cattle across the Loup River in Nebraska, was caught in quicksand. The fact he was driving cattle saved him, for he grabbed the tail of an ox, who pulled him to safety.

In 1854 Marie Guild pulled her brother from a whirlpool in which he nearly drowned. His journey had been so arduous that, instead of thanking his brave sister, he asked, "Why did you not let me sleep, instead of causing me such great agony. Death is easy to a drowning person [compared] to the suffering to be brought to life again." One teenager, "the main support of a crippled mother," was "caught in the current and carried out of sight" in the Platte River in 1868.

The worst water-borne disaster of the Mormon migration occurred near Lexington, Missouri, on the Missouri River in 1852. The *Saluda* exploded that spring, wounding and killing "about 100" of those aboard. (See also Chapter 14.) The river was full of floating masses of ice, causing the steamboat to creep along. The captain, anxious to make up time, overheated the engines. Most passengers were still in bed when the accident occurred. William C. Dunbar, who lost his wife and two children, gave this sorrowful narrative:

> I am of the opinion that I was blown into the river by the explosion. . . . As soon as I regained consciousness and began to open my eyes, I looked around and saw the mangled form of a child lying close by me. Recognizing its clothing I soon made the startling discovery that it was my own dear baby boy, whom I, a short time before, had seen in its mothers arms. . . . I attempted to rise . . . but found myself unable to do so. . . . Owing to the injuries my back had sustained, I was unable to move for several days. . . . I do not attach any great blame to the Elders who chartered the *Saluda*; it was perhaps nothing but an over-anxiety to get the Saints away from St. Louis, where so many of those who had previously stopped, had apostatized and never went to the Valley.

Henry Ballard, a returning missionary, was "stunned and thrown back" by the explosion. "After recovering . . . I returned to the boat to look for my baggage but could find nothing. Two shepherd dogs that I had brought with me from England had been entirely blown away." The Mormon casualties were buried in the Lexington Cemetery.

Five emigrants died in a shipwreck in the Pacific in 1855. Mormon teenagers Agnes and Alexander Anderson were aboard the *Julia Ann* en route from Australia to San Francisco, when the ship wrecked on a small coral reef island in the Society Islands in the Pacific.

> They were awakened about midnight with a loud noise and then mad confusion as water rushed into the rooms. Passengers clung to ropes and the deck rail trying to keep out of the ocean. Agnes found herself on the reef, but heard her mother yelling: "Agnes, Agnes" and jumped back into the water to try to go to her family. Men held her back: It was dark and cold as "the bashing from the waves" dashed

about. The pounding proved too much for two youngsters, Mary Humphries and ten-year-old Marion Anderson. Both were washed off the poop deck into the foaming surf . . . .Two women and a baby also died. Agnes and five of her family survived the wreck.

One little boy drowned in 1855 on board the *Charles Buck* when he "got entangled in the ropes of the ships . . . and was thrown overboard." In 1855, two emigrants fell overboard, and in 1862, "two young girls were drowned" in a creek in Echo Canyon in the Ansel Harmon Company. In 1865 a little boy traveling by boat on the Missouri River was frightened by the animals nearby, got up from bed, and fell through a trap door and drowned. The door had accidentally been left open.

Funerals and Burials

At Winter Quarters, the death rate was so high and burials so slow that some people noted the constant passage of "funeral wagons." Personal accounts report agonized mothers trying to keep flies away from their dead children as decomposition set in. An estimated six hundred died in the greater Winter Quarters area. The sexton, at $1.50 per grave, earned more than most men.

When the Saints set out on the trail west, funerals and burials were often hurried affairs, becoming briefer and more perfunctory the farther west the company traveled. In some cases, corpses were not buried at all but were found in tents or beside the trail. According to Thomas Griggs, in 1861 one sister was buried immediately, without even changing her clothes.

In a particularly ruthless example, a handcart company rescued a Mormon family on the Green River on September 11, 1860. According to the journal of Danish emigrant Carl Field, their original company had left them behind "on account of two very sick children." Eleven days later, "the fourteen-year-old daughter . . . died, and was buried."

Some travelers told gruesome stories about graves being dug before the sick were dead and about dumping the dying into graves while they were still alive. In 1848, Helen Mar Kimball Whitney gave birth to a son on August 26. Five days later, the baby died. Helen was so near death from the complicated delivery that the camp laid over a day and she kissed her loved ones farewell, expecting to join her baby. Her father, Heber C. Kimball, announced that she would not die and administered to her. She immediately began improving. He then had the baby exhumed to assure Helen it was really dead.

In the nineteenth century, premature burial was a real fear, given the possibility of mistaking a coma for death—hence the practice of wakes and sitting up with the dead. According to Merrill Mattes, some companies kept graves open for some time to see if the deceased would revive—an obvious luxury that was soon squeezed out by time constraints. In the East and more settled communities, sometimes people were buried with a bell-pull, a wire running up from the casket to a bell on the surface so the revived could signal for help.

In 1859 sixteen-year-old Fanny Fry Simons was almost buried alive after she had been rendered senseless by a handcart rolling over her. She records, "When I came to myself, my grave was two feet deep and I was in a tent. The sisters had sewed me up to the waist in my blanket ready for burial." In 1862, Ebenezer Farnes, who was not present when his father was buried, insisted on returning to the grave. "My intentions," he said, "were to dig up the grave and see if he was dead when they buried him, as one of the men who helped to put him away told me that he did not think father was dead, as his shoulders were warm with sweat." He found the grave but did not record whether he exhumed the body.

The weather impacted burials, especially the handcart companies. During desperate days when the ground was frozen, the dead were placed in snow banks. In the case of overnight deaths, a preferred place for a grave was where a campfire had been the night before, thawing ground frost.

Coffins were luxuries. Some rough coffins were improvised from packing cases, dry goods boxes, wagon boards, hollowed-out cottonwood logs, or sheathed in pieces of bark. Many others were wrapped only in blankets, sheets, or burlap bags. One account reports a burial in a soldered sheet-metal coffin.

Some graves were marked by flat stones, boards, buffalo skulls, even by carving on a nearby tree. Inscriptions in ordinary black lead pencil would last for many years where there was little rain. In one instance, an engraved wagon tire served as fifty-year-old Rebecca Winters's headstone when she died of cholera on August 15, 1850, near Scotts Bluffs. Her daughters, fourteen-year-old Rebecca and eight-year-old Helen Melissa, huddled together in grief as they watched a family friend carve Rebecca's name and age on the rim of an extra wagon wheel and half-bury it upright as a headstone. Hers was one of the best-known of the estimated 7,000 Mormon trail-side graves. Fifty years later in 1899, surveyors for the Burlington Railroad discovered the grave, the iron tire rim having resisted time's ravages. The considerate surveyors backed up and surveyed around the site. When they notified Mormon officials in Salt Lake City, Rebecca was identified as the grandmother of Augusta Winters Grant, a wife of Apostle Heber J. Grant. In 1922, after Grant was president of the Mormon Church, he chartered a special train and a party traveled to the site for commemoration ceremonies and the erection of a suitable monument.

Sometimes, fearing desecration of the grave, the survivors took strenuous measures to obliterate all traces of a burial to discourage wild animals (and sometimes Indians and other whites) from digging up the corpses. This was done by driving the loose cattle and wagons over the site, building fires on the location, and covering the grave with cacti.

Numerous travelers engaged in the melancholy pastime of counting graves. One 1852 immigrant noted 175 graves between Winter Quarters and Fort Laramie. In 1850 Shadrach Roundy counted 142 graves during the month of July alone. In 1850 another traveler enumerated 500 fresh graves along the south side of the Platte. The curious wore footpaths back and forth to the main trail to view these and read the markers, if any.

Conclusion

Although trials and arduous labor still faced the pioneers who arrived in the Salt Lake Valley, psychologically and physically, the most grueling part of the ordeal seemed to be over. There was a general improvement in health and a rejoicing in births instead of long lists of the dead. John Taylor enthused to Orson Spencer in 1848, then serving a mission in England: "In proof of the health of the place, [Salt Lake Valley] there have been about 15 graves dug. . . . To balance this, in one row of eight houses adjoining, in one week there was seven births . . . and the brethren suppose there will be 120 births in the twelve months."

Death was no rare visitor along the western trail. Causes of death ranged from ordinary measles to freak accidents to murder. Certainly it was a rare company that did not experience some danger, disease, or death; yet the rewards of reaching their goal, for most immigrant families, was worth the risks. One of the conventions of the pioneer spirit, in fact, was to claim that difficult and tragic experiences along the trail and in the first years of settling the raw frontier country only made the survivors stronger. It is a legacy that their descendants have been proud to pass on.

Instead of focusing on the gruesome and the hazards, they concentrated on distinctive memories of the trail west: the magnificent sunrise at Chimney Rock, the multi-colored sky on top of Independence Rock at sunset, "bathing" in the Platte River, participating in a buffalo hunt, or sampling a fresh antelope steak. Scenic wonders were a lifelong memory for those who climbed Chimney Rock or Independence Rock and left their signature behind or listened to the splash and roar of the water against the rocks at Devil's Gate. Others marveled at the "romantic scenery," traded with the Indians, picked wild flowers, ate "Sweetwater ice cream," caught a trout or catfish, climbed the majestic Rocky Mountains, viewed the smogless heavens at South Pass, or beheld the beautiful Utah Valley from Big Mountain. They were home.

Chapter 12

The Dark Side

The wind is blowing a heavy gale; it seems as though the very heavens would come down to earth! The tent is penned down or it would be carried away. The elements are in great commotion, and my mind is dark and dismal! I think, "what if we have to wander forty years in the wilderness as the children of Israel did!" —Louisa Barnes Pratt, 1846

Even the dark side of immigration provides a window of understanding about what some 75,000 Mormons endured to make Zion a place of beauty and refuge. From the beginning of the great trek in 1846—"from civilization to sundown" (an expression used by many early pioneers), the potential for serious social problems existed among Mormon immigrants, yet this darker side of the journey to Zion receives little emphasis. Nauvoo had a chief of police because one was needed. That same need existed in Winter Quarters. The Saints' apprehension about violence was not confined only to armed mobs and outsiders.

Trail accounts record dozens of incidents of selfishness, pettiness, quarreling, fighting, and disaffection. What does this pattern indicate, and how can it be put into proper perspective? Modern affection for and veneration of the pioneers have cherished, enshrined, and promoted their achievement, but it was the achievement of human beings. Being a Saint was the hard part.

An important part of keeping perspective is acknowledging that common decency was the norm on the immigrant trails between 1831 and 1869, from New York to California. There are thousands of accounts of help for the poor, the orphans, widows, the sick, and the occasional retarded pioneer. These stories of heroism and compassion are thrilling. Mormon trail accounts are often rather prosaic, routine, bare-bone records with few flights of interest and fewer of literary merit. Their observations were often recorded late at night while fighting off fatigue, hunger, cold, sickness, and discouragement. They might not be typical but those thoughts are the ones that mattered enough to write down.

Such stories are as likely to involve women as men. Aaron Jackson, in the Martin Company, sank down in the middle of a stream on a sandbar, too weak to continue. His sister-in-law, Mary Horrocks Leavitt, waded to his assistance until he was rescued, then helped her sister Elizabeth pull their handcart to shore. Maria Normington, age thirty-six, also traveling in the Martin Handcart Company, rushed to help a fellow Latter-day Saint mired in the water because he had been promised a safe journey and she didn't want the promise broken. Mary Pearce, an 1855 pioneer, rescued a little boy found nearly naked and starving. She took him into her wagon, used her own clothing to make him something to wear, and cared for him until they got to the Valley. These acts of kindness were not rare and were also repeated by women en route to Oregon or California.

Young heroes like David P. Kimball, George W. Grant, Stephen W. Taylor, and C. A. Huntington, all age eighteen, earned their place in Church history by traveling to the Sweetwater in October 1856 where they carried dozens of weak handcart pioneers across the icy water. The men who brought food, clothing, and teams to help rescue the handcart pioneers endured stark, life-threatening conditions. This near-miraculous rescue theme dominates Mormon history, but it is also a major theme for the entire Overland Trail experience, as the Donner/Reed tragedy also shows. Some men pulled their handcarts with their last ounce of energy, then gave their tiny morsel of food to their children, and died of exhaustion and starvation.

Patience Loader, also in the Martin Handcart Company, wrote that she was shocked at the profane language of the young men who rescued them in 1856, even as she sang their praises for their heroic deeds. The darker side is not as faith-promoting, but Mormon pioneers represented a sort of Hegelian dialectic in human affairs.

Many of the immigrant Saints showed their vulnerability as did their leaders.

The Mormon migration was a family, not an individual, affair; but crossing the plains with its attendant rigors, fears, and sacrifices too often tore the fabric of family life to shreds, and families cracked under the pressure. One contemporary observer, John Chislette, noted that the hardships of the trail "destroyed all romance." John Jaques, traveling in the Martin Handcart Company, agreed: "[The] fatigues of the journey [caused] the manliness of tall, healthy, strong, men [to] gradually disappear, until they would grow fretful, peevish, childish, and puerile, acting sometimes as if they were scarcely accountable beings."

The experience of the last two handcart companies of 1856—the Willie and Martin companies—was hardly typical since more than 150 died in those two companies alone. They functioned under exceptionally brutal conditions; but almost every pioneer company suffered more or less from inadequate food.

Oregon and California Pioneers

A helpful context for evaluating the darker side of Mormon travelers is to look at parallel accounts of non-Mormons. Travelers en route to Oregon or California were notorious for quarreling and fighting. Peter H. Burnett discovered in a few days in 1843 that it was hell trying to "lead 293 free spirits." He served as captain of that large group of Missourians heading for Oregon for just a week before resigning because of "10,000 little vexations." Burnett wrote: "In these struggles, the worst traits of human nature were displayed, and there was no remedy but patient endurance." Historian Lloyd W. Coffman wrote: "The biggest obstacle they had to overcome was how to get along with each other." The Oregon Trail folks even quarreled about keeping or not keeping the Sabbath.

Missionary Mary Richardson Walker, a new bride, wrote a candid diary as she traveled to Oregon in 1838 with seven other missionaries. On April 25, she wrote: "Rested well on my ground bedstead and should feel much better if Mr. W[alker, her new husband]. would only treat me with more cordiality. It is so hard to please him

I almost despair of ever being able. If I stir it is forwardness, if I am still, it is inactivity."

At one time a lamb was attacked by a wolf; and two of the missionaries, Elkanah Walker and Asa Smith, killed the injured animal without consulting the other two couples, who became angry. Mary would not cook it until everyone mellowed which took about two days. Asa Smith wrote May 7: "I think we shall lose all of our piety before we cross the mountains."

There were murderers in many companies. Young pioneers John Steele and Abigail Scott wrote about murders in their companies in 1850 and 1852. In 1852, John Clark from Virginia noted that a man who killed his driver was "tried & hung on our old waggon at midnight."

Benjamin Bonney traveling to California in 1845 when he was seven, vividly recalled the brutal behavior of a Texan named Sam Kinney:

> When he [Sam Kinney] saw this Indian ... he called to the driver ... to stop the oxen. My father said ... "what are you going to do with the Indian?" Kinney said, "Where I come from we have slaves, and I am going to capture that Indian and take him with me as my slave .... I generally have my way. Any man that crosses me regrets it. I have had to kill two or three men already because they did not want me to have my way, so if you want trouble, you know how to git it." Kinney was an individualist and would not obey the train rules, but was such a desperate man, and apparently held life so lightly, that no one wanted to cross him. Kinney jumped off his mule and struck the Indian over the head ... [and knocked him down] and got his handcuffs and dragged him to the back, fastened a rope around his neck, and told his wife to hand him his blacksnake whip ... then he told his wife to drive on.

The rest of the story is too brutal to repeat, but the Indian finally escaped.

The rush for gold increased to a frenzy by 1852, and tales multiplied of weaker members of companies who were left behind at places like Fort Laramie or simply abandoned at trail side. "Dying men were abandoned" and "men on the plains have less feeling for one another than dumb brutes," was mentioned in several Oregon accounts. Gilbert Cole, en route to California in 1852, noted that one man was nearly hanged for "abandoning his wife and children."

A woman abandoned at Fort Laramie that same year managed to walk to South Pass, only to find that no company would let her join them. Many children suffered on all trails because of the rush of the adults to get to their destinations. However, some pioneers thought the presence of women and children was a good thing. Margaret Haun, en route to California in 1849, commented: "Our caravan had a good many women and children.... They exerted a good influence, as the men did not take such risks [and] more attention was paid to cleanliness and sanitation . . . and the meals were more regular and better cooked."

It is also important to point out that many rescue parties were sent out from the coast every year to take food and water to the destitute pioneers trying to reach the golden state and Oregon.

Selfishness and Immaturity

Abusive language, marital bickering, selfishness, sponging, excessive harshness, and other manifestations of selfishness and human weakness appear in many trail accounts. William Clayton described how his company, returning to Winter Quarters the fall of 1847 from the Salt Lake Valley, acted without Brigham Young along to maintain discipline. On October 8 he wrote: "Many hard speeches have passed among the brethren, such as damned hypocrites, damned liars, mutineers etc. And most of those who started ahead are ordered to travel in the rear....This savage . . . conduct was one thing which induced some to leave and undertake to go through alone and more peaceably, and it will still leave feelings of revenge . . . which will require some time to cover up."

According to Eliza R. Snow, leaders of the second company of Saints to leave Winter Quarters in 1847 also quarreled, complained, and acted immature.

Given the shared religious values of the Mormon pioneers, departures from Christian behavior into selfishness, whining, and violence may have seemed even more shocking by contrast to the expectations. It may even suggest that journal-keepers took the time and effort to record more negative things than positive. William Atkins, traveling with George Rowley's handcart company in 1859, recorded the conduct of two Mormons and their wives who joined the company in Genoa, Nebraska Territory. "They had several cows which they milked every night and sold it to the others and in this way soon acquired what little the saints had plus various articles of jewelry." Atkins noted that one of the men later was executed for murder and the second died a few years later.

One 1867 LDS group from Denmark, stranded with no food when they arrived at the North Platte Camp, suffered several deaths from various causes. The unnamed man in charge of the provisions spent the money reserved for food on a bankruptcy sale. He sent them no message. Their wagons and teams arrived, but they still had no food. A wealthy Dane, also unnamed, stepped forth to contribute money for food to help the destitute. Johanna Kirsten Larsen wrote: "Brother [Brigham] Young [Jr.] and another man left the same night for the east and returned on the third day with provisions which were distributed according to numbers in each family. Captain [Leonard] Rice ordered all to pack up and hook on to the wagons. . . . It did seem good to get into fresh air and obtain a drink of fresh water."

Water was sometimes at a premium on the trail, leading to reports of selfishness. When Robert Gardner asked another fellow member for a cup of coffee for his sick wife, the man refused. Once, according to Lars Christensen, when water was scarce, one "hoggish man" took water from a child who was bringing it to his mother. Going more than the extra mile was Mary Powell, age twelve in 1856. She walked and ran "ten miles extra" to the Platte River to get her mother a drink of water.

By the 1860s, a few stations had water available for sale. In 1862, Amelia Eliza Slade wrote that her family "was oblidged to buy our drinking water at twenty-five cents per keg." (Many forty-niners had to buy water along the last part of the trail to California, paying as much as $1.00 per glass).

The Danish company who were stranded without food at their Nebraska camp in 1867 later learned a song by Eliza R. Snow, probably by request, warning Mormon immigrants against holding unrealistic expectations of Zion. A missionary with this Danish company, suggested they sing this song:

Think not when you gather to Zion
Your trials and troubles are through
That nothing but comfort and pleasure
Are awaiting in Zion for you.
No, no, 'tis designed as a furnace
All substance, all textures to try
To burn all the wood, hay, and stubble;
The good from the dross purify.

Johanna Kirsten Larsen got the message. "I think he had a purpose in suggesting the song," she recorded "At least it gave us food for thought and study."

Not all Saints were willing to take the message of the song to heart. Bickering and squabbling erupted over animals, their feed, food, supplies, work assignments, guard duty, waiting for others, and providing for others. There was much conflict about whose turn it was to perform a routine task such as fetching wood or water and searching for stray cattle. Brigham Young complained that his pioneer camp of 1847 was constantly "jawing over loose cattle."

On July 9, 1848, in present day Nebraska, Oliver B. Huntington recorded that a man blamed his wife when the wagon turned over, particularly because the accident revealed his hidden barrel of wine: "That night he quarreled with his wife and whipped [her]. The guard about 11 o'clock saw it and when the hour came to cry, he loudly cried '11 o'clock, all is well and Gates is quarreling with his wife like hell.'"

Incidentally, there were occasional references to drinking a glass of wine but only a few to men who had over-indulged. The Mormon Battalion soldiers, however, were an exception, indulging in drinking on several occasions.

There are many examples of abusive languages, of fist, gun and knife fights, and attacks. (There were at least two fights in the pioneer company of 1847.) Mormon men did not always keep agreements, and Saints hardly felt the necessity of putting any agreement into writing. This subsequently led to troubles such as stealing, milking other people's cows, killing other people's pigs, and also shady business deals and agreements.

In a mixed handcart company in 1859, the English captain in one unit of ten was incredibly petty in his complaints about the

Scandinavians: They washed their hands in the wrong place, their smoke bothered him, and they blew their noses too close to camp.

The Saints controlled such bickering with preaching, group prayers, and camp courts. Violators who were not sufficiently repentant were scolded, disfellowshipped, excommunicated, whipped, and occasionally expelled from the company—a particularly severe punishment once they were beyond settled areas. (See "Discipline" in Chapter 5.)

Physical Violence

Mormon trail history includes at least one murder. Elias Smith wrote September 22, 1851, near the border of Utah and Wyoming:

> Near where we camped there was a grave made a day or two before ... purporting to be that of James Monroe. He was with [a] train taking thro a large quantity of goods to the Lake .... [Sept. 24] Before we started this morning two men came by from the Valley after the body of James Monroe. He was shot by Howard Egan, who came from the Valley and met him where we saw his grave and shot him with a pistol for some interference with his family during his absence in the gold mines of California.

Monroe had had an affair with Egan's wife, resulting in her pregnancy, and Egan had meted out "mountain justice." George A. Smith successfully defended Egan in court.

Desperate Reactions to Suffering

In addition to the alleged cannibalism to which the Donner/Reed party was reduced, hunger caused others to react in desperate ways. In 1859, a starving handcart company was camped on the Big Sandy River in Wyoming at a mail station. Several mountain men rode up, full of whiskey, and announced: "We want to get a wife, who wants to marry?" William Atkins recorded: "To our great surprise, two of our young women stepped out and said they would marry the men.... So there were two weddings celebrated that day in the mountains."

Insanity and delirium were also responses to hunger. In 1856 Patience Loader awakened to find that William Whittaker, who had already eaten the flesh off his own fingers, was gnawing at her hand. The poor man died shortly afterwards and was buried at Willow Springs in present Wyoming. Another woman in the same company, Elizabeth Horrocks Jackson, later wrote about a night of terror:

> About the 25th of October, my husband . . . tried to eat, but failed. He had not the strength to swallow. I put him to bed [and] he seemed to rest easy and fell asleep. About 9 o'clock, I retired. The weather was bitter. I listened to hear if my husband breathed he lay so still. I could not hear him. I became alarmed. I put my hand on his body when to my horror I discovered that my worst fears were confirmed. My husband was dead . . . rigid in the arms of death. It was a bitter freezing night, and the elements had sealed up his mortal frame . . . and there was no alternative but to remain alone by the side of the corpse until morning.

Elizabeth's sister Mary Horrocks had helped her take care of the family, but Mary fell ill after her brother-in-law's death. According to Elizabeth, "So severe was her affliction that she became deranged in her mind, and for several days she ate nothing but hard frozen snow."

Abandoned Members

William Empey was disappointed in a group of Danish converts in 1854 in St. Louis. After the group took a river boat to Council Bluffs, he discovered they had left behind a sick family who could not help themselves—a woman and three children. One child was dead, one was dying. There is the possibility that they were innocently forgotten, but Empey had to solve this problem as best he could.

According to Samuel Openshaw, a 1856 handcart company discovered an abandoned or lost man who walked with crutches. Fortunately someone from his company came back for him. Openshaw also recorded on August 14: "We found Robert Thirkman. He had stopped behind from Haven Company last Saturday night and [had been] cut off from the church. We took him along with us."

In 1860, Oscar Stoddard, captain of the last company to travel by handcart, recorded: "One Swedish girl was left by her parents with Brother Myers at Bear River. A sister, left by some former company was taken up at Wood River and brought to the Valley, and a family named Cherrington, whom we found at Green River, who had had much sickness and had lost three children by death and another sick unto death, but they were so anxious to come to the Valley that we took them in and brought them along. The sick daughter died in East Canyon."

Stealing

Stealing was a problem, though not a major one, among the Saints, and usually involved food when rations were short. Some thefts were imaginative if not bizarre. One man stole a cow's hoof, and one little boy figured out how to eat the inside of a cake without its being noticed. John Bond stayed away from a night meeting in 1856 on the trail so he could indulge in some dumplings one of the women in camp had made and had hidden under her wagon.

Several men were caught stealing horses. According to John D. Lee, William Meeks "stole the horse and wagon that Brigham Young left in his care in the Valley in 1847." He was driving it when they encountered the Young party heading to Zion in 1848. Needless to say, Young was not amused.

Levi Jackman wrote in early 1848 in the Salt Lake Valley: "The most of the people were desirous to do right and were and did all they could to help the poor and needy. . . . I had expected that we had left the thieves behind, but in this I was disappointed for we found that they were in this place too. As fast as they were detected, they were dealt with according to law."

For every person who stole or lost something, many others restored those items to their travel mates and fellow Mormons. Saints came to the aid of Thomas Grover in February 1846, when his oxen and wagons were lost by the carelessness of a young man who reportedly spit tobacco juice in the eyes of his oxen while crossing the Mississippi River. Others contributed replacements for the lost items so Grover could continue the journey.

Selfishness and Harshness

Mosiah Hancock was annoyed in 1848 when the older men in his company gave so little help to his mother whose husband was away with the Mormon Battalion. Many did not wish to help the poor, the crippled, and the widowed, perhaps because they were barely surviving themselves. One Swedish convert, Mary Soffe, claimed that of the thirty dollars her husband paid in advance, she and the children received but one loaf of bread.

In 1856 Jesse Haven had trouble with his handcart and reported that 100 other carts passed him by without stopping to assist him. In 1860 Ann Prior Jarvis was offended when one brutish man in a handcart company rode in the wagon and let women, some of whom were carrying children, walk.

At times, especially in the handcart companies, harshness seemed excessive. Company captains had overwhelming responsibilities and near-impossible assignments. On occasion, however, they clearly exceeded their authority. Heber McBride in the Martin Handcart Company was not complimentary about his leaders:

> The captains of the companies were worse than brutes. . . . They took a great deal of satisfaction in showing their authority over the people and making them obey orders or keeping back their rations. One night when we came into camp it was after dark and had been raining very, very hard through the day and there was no wood to be got and mother was very sick. We thought she was going to die and we gathered a few sunflower stalks and wet buffalo chips and had just got a little fire started when all hands were ordered to attend prayers. And because we did not go to prayers Daniel Tyler came and kicked our fire all out and spilled the water that we were trying to get warm to make a little tea for mother.

At the end of the day, many older pioneers would drop in their tracks and go to sleep, only to be awakened later by a call for prayer. According to John W. Southwell, "Then that accursed bugle would blow the call for prayers. . . . I have heard the order given, 'pull them out and compel them to attend prayer.'" Sometimes a mother gave birth while the wagon was jostling along because the leader would not wait, or she did not want to hold up the camp.

Sexual Misbehavior

John Edwin Banks left some terse comments in 1849 en route to California about "large companies bursting into fragments" over human misbehavior. One woman had an affair with a fellow traveler; her lover shot her husband and "the villians are at large." Banks also noted that one train from Illinois had a murderer who "will be hung tomorrow at Pacific Springs."

In Nebraska in 1860, Robert Stoney recorded the trial of an adulterous couple that involved what we would see as a double standard:

> We had a council meeting when Brother Slater and Sister Webb, who were summoned to attend, appeared to answer the charge of adultery. They denied the charge, but proof was found that they had slept together. It was agreed that they be excommunicated from the church on the account of their lies. I cut the woman off freely, but the man, I felt a thrill run through me when I raised my hand against him. I asked the Lord at night respecting it, and I felt an influence coming over me, and I was afraid and arose. I have asked since, and I intend to ask him again and again until I know.

Although seldom noted in trail accounts, prostitution was practiced on the trails, especially near military installations, such as Fort Laramie and Fort Kearney. "Hog Ranches" catered to soldiers, freighters, and emigrants. These establishments also flourished at outfitting stations and jumping-off places. Sometimes "lewd women" plied their trade right on the trails. One woman, known as Salt Lake Kate, was considered the toughest female on the road. Prostitution, along with gambling and drinking was part of the westering movement. At times even Indians were involved. In 1859 poverty-stricken Pawnee women at Genoa offered themselves for as little as a piece of bread.

More serious, however, were a few illicit sex matters among the faithful. Some early Mormons could be quite candid and blunt about such matters. According to Hosea Stout, the chief of police in Nauvoo and Iowa, on May 6, 1846, during the long layover in Garden Grove, Iowa, a "young man was caught in bed with a certain girl in camp and a lot of boys upset the wagon putting them to an uncommon nonpluss and disappointment." The next morning the girl believing that a certain boy instigated the affair "threw a cup of hot coffee on his face and eyes . . . and almost scalded his eyes out. Her bed partner was said to have denied the faith and went off whineing to Missouri."

During the subsequent stay at Winter Quarters, it became the duty and obligation of Stout "to enforce obedience to the Law of

God or to punish transgressors for the breech of the same." When it became known that several of the young men were out late at night with some girls, Stout knew exactly what to do. He gave some of them eighteen lashes.

Wilford Woodruff wrote that, in 1846 at Winter Quarters, a "wicked man" led some young women "into folly evil & wickedness. Three young men consorted with them and each received thirty blows on the back with a Hickory goad." This seems to be the same incident, except the number of blows is different, but Stout's account is correct because he was the one administering the punishment.

According to Stout, on November 28, 1847, William W. Phelps was accused of adultery for improperly entering into polygamy. He was given the opportunity of being rebaptized or being cut off from the Church. A month later Milo Andrus was tried for living with a woman unlawfully. That same month, according to "Minutes of Council of Twelve and Seventies, December 9, 1847," John D. Lee was tried for "vulgarity with women," during which it was alleged that he was too amorous with his wives one entire night. Nine days later, Heber C. Kimball said, "I prophesy good concerning John D. Lee he will yet raise and do good." (Lee was later executed for being the leader of the Mountain Meadows Massacre.)

On February 26, 1848, the matter of Benjamin Jones and Rosana Cox living together unlawfully came up. Jones "preferred [charges] by himself" and was penitent, so Brigham Young forgave and married them.

On March 11, 1848, as recorded by Stout, Benjamin Covey was convicted of "sleeping with a girl less then twelve years of age." The hearing revealed he had also defiled two girls about the same age. He was excommunicated "with the understanding that his wives and children were under no more obligations to him."

In 1850, near Scott's Bluff, Angelina Farley hardly knew how to report lewd behavior. "Mother and I was witness to a scene very discreditable to W.E. and L.P. which if known could ruin her entirely. . . . Oh my God, what are we! Are we to be left to the rule of satan." Again, significant of the existence of a double standard, Angelina noted that only the woman would be ruined if the incident became known.

In 1850 a gullible Mormon picked up an "abandoned wife" at Fort Kearney. It was subsequently learned that she was a "woman of bad character," so the Mormons left her at Fort Laramie where, no doubt, she could find "work." When Zebulon Jacobs returned home from his mission in England in 1867, he noted a young sister traveling with them and wrote: "If she is not married she ought to be and that pretty soon."

Some marriages could not stand the strain of the trail. In 1854, Hans Hoth watched his wife become enamored of a fellow emigrant. He divorced her when they got to Salt Lake. In 1856 a married woman with the Martin Handcart Company was accused of spending two nights in the woods with a Gentile; she was excommunicated from the Church and not permitted to continue west with the camp. This action may actually have saved her life, for so many of that company perished in Wyoming snows.

Sometimes the improprieties were complicated to the extreme, and company leaders had their ingenuity and fairness taxed to the limit. In 1855 a Sister Harrison, in the Seth M. Blair immigrant company, claimed that J. A. York "wanted her to be a wife to him during this journey, but not to be married to him." When York was called before the camp council, he proclaimed his innocence. Careful questioning revealed that Sister Harrison had courted York and "had it in her mind to get him for a husband." She claimed to have had a dream that "York's real wife would die and that she would succeed her." She begged for forgiveness, and the matter was dropped.

The Urge to Quit

Accounts of the Mormon trail also include reports of those who dropped out after setting out or, after reaching the Salt Lake Valley, reconsidered their commitment and left both Mormonism and Utah. Some of the journals and autobiographies may have been edited by family members who tried to protect the family name. But of the accounts I have found, more than 70 percent, by my estimate, pertain to the 1850s. There are at least two good reasons for this concentration: The '50s covered a full decade, including eight of the nine handcart companies. Also, polygamy was publicly announced in 1852 and caused much disillusionment among Saints in the East and Europe. According to historian Sandra Myers, this 1852 announcement "increased both the volume and the intensity of anti-Mormon literature in travelers' accounts." Church leaders ignored the bad publicity, dismissing the disaffection among members as evidence of their apostasy.

John A. Ahmanson reported that the "announcement of polygamy had a demoralizing effect on the Church" in Denmark. He helped bring some of the Saints to America in 1856, but his experience in the Willie Handcart Company was probably also influential in his decision to leave Utah in 1857 with a large group of "apostates."

Leaving Mormonism was an agonizing decision. Many of these disillusioned members had already left their kinfolk. Some had been disowned by their families. And in practical terms, the emigrants from Europe were in an alien world in America, sometimes unable to speak English, and with little chance of physical survival if they left their traveling company. By the time they reached the jumping-off point (Florence, Nebraska, for the handcart companies), their chances of success had dwindled were they to turn back alone. These were a special class of the "up-rooted" not treated in Oscar Handlin's classic study of immigrants in an alien world. Florence and Council Bluffs were havens to disenchanted Mormons who left Salt Lake City, as they were the first large communities they reached.

In Council Bluffs in 1853, some disaffected Scandinavians were excommunicated and settled in the area, giving Iowa and eastern Nebraska their earliest Scandinavian settlers. By 1856 there were many quitters and apostates in the greater Omaha area, and their presence may have been one reason why the Martin and Willie handcart companies made their decision to start so tragically late that season. An English convert, Benjamin Platte, noted in his autobiography that, even though Apostle Franklin D. Richards advised them to lay over that season, "there were some apostates there, or Josephites and we did not want to stay [with them], and we declared we would go through or die trying."

In 1862, according to Oluf C. Larsen, "Omaha seemed to be a resting place for the weary and discontented coming from Europe and from the east as well as for the apostates. . . . The faint hearted were easily deceived and captured by them. Several of this class left the camp and stayed behind." A year later, Mary Charlotte Soffe was offered a job by some apostates in Omaha who warned her she would die crossing the plains. Mary's mother wanted to accept the offer, but Mary would have none of it and pushed on. In 1870, Jesse N. Smith noted that Omaha "was thronged . . . with apostates and backsliders from Utah who preached and declaimed diligently to induce some to stop, but most went on west to see for themselves."

Mary Powell, age twelve, wrote that her father was urged to stay as he was a stone mason. He was paid "eight dollars per day" to work while camped in Florence in 1856, and offered eighty acres of land and help with a house if he would stay.

Mormons, who were surprised that such people existed, might have recorded some of their experiences for the negative novelty of it. Orthodox Mormons characterized these backsliders with negative terms: "evil," "gizzards," "devilish," "those who went out among the Gentiles," "the Devil's crew of apostate Mormons," and a more gentle—"some were very sly."

Samuel Openshaw saw many "cunning" apostates in 1856. "Some looked upon us as if we were deceived; others who were old apostates came with all the subtlety of the devil, and all the cunning they have gained by their own experience, trying to turn the Saints to the right hand or to the left . . . but few or none adhered to their advice."

A second important group consisted of those who reached the Salt Lake Valley but then decided they could no longer affiliate with the Saints. Such escapes required courage, emotional stability, and means sufficient to make the journey. Brigham Young made a chilling comment on March 27, 1853, that he would not "allow apostates to flourish in the Valley, I will unsheath my bowie knife, and conquer or die." In 1848 when a group of "16 souls . . . became dissatisfied with the country themselves & Neighbours & left the valley on the 18th of May. Eventually they met Young en route to the Valley, who gave them a severe scolding, then, according to John D. Lee, gave them some flour, and sent letters back east with them. Young later consistently expressed exasperation at those who received help from the Perpetual Emigrating Fund, only to abandon the faith without repaying their debt. Lee referred to this company of back-trailers, also in 1848, as a "Poisnous contaminous influence."

F. W. Blake disaffiliated from the Church soon after he arrived in 1861. He refused a mission call and "went forth in Zions Street ever afterwards an unbeliever in the pretentions of Brigham Young, & an apostate to the doctrines of Mormonism."

A particularly detailed account is the 1859 record of Thomas McIntyre, a Scottish convert, who met five groups of go-backs numbering about a hundred former Mormons altogether. On July 18 he noted, "We met six wagons of apostate Mormons from Salt Lake City finding fault with everything and everybody." On July 20, he added, "There surely must be a stream of apostate Mormons from the Valley." Only three days later, "we met eleven wagons of apostates from Utah. They find no particular fault with the valley. They seem to have done remarkably well as they seemed to show from their display of fine stock they had along with them." His most telling comment, however, was made July 29, and, being a true son of Scotland, he was probably properly offended. On that day they met "three wagons of malcontents from Salt Lake City. Of course 'everything is wrong in Salt Lake City. Mormonism in England is quite another thing.'" Here the operative word is "malcontent," not "apostate"; and the phrase "Mormonism in England is quite another thing," suggests that not all go-backs were apostates. Some were merely disillusioned.

McIntyre continued, "Our folks are always very fond of interviews [with] strangers, especially those from Salt Lake City. One of our Scotch sisters asked them if there were any of their country folks with them. 'No,' said one bristling up, 'Scotsmen and Irishmen will do anything for Mormonism, but noble sons and daughters of England will not be trampled on.' They believed Mormonism was true, but their authorities were acting unrighteously and the Lord would soon come out of his hiding place and scourge them. They had gone to the valley with handcarts, as we were doing, and were returning with a very fine outfit, a very good evidence of their prosperity there."

As the Mormon reports of go-backs cannot be considered particularly objective, neither can those of the go-backs who naturally justified their behavior. Historian John Unruh concluded that "go-backs were notorious rumor spreaders" who "tended to magnify incidents of trouble and hardship."

Vindictiveness toward Missourians

On occasion, some Saints took grim comfort in finding the headboards of Missourians they suspected of having participated in persecuting Mormons during the 1830s. Some were pleased when they found such graves desecrated by wolves. On October 7, 1849, for example, William Appleby, walking along in western Nebraska or eastern Wyoming, saw the grave and headboard of a "gold digger," one E. Dodd from Galatin County, Missouri. "The wolves," Appleby noted, "had completely disinterred him. The pantaloons and shirt in which he had been buried lay strewn around the grave. His under jaw lay in the bottom of the grave with the teeth all completed and one of his ribs on the surface of the ground nearby were the only remains of him discernible." Appleby believed that this was the same Dodd who had been a prominent participant in the Haun's Mill massacre in Missouri in 1838 and considered such desecration as "righteous retribution."

Apostle George A. Smith also saw this grave and preached a trailside sermon referring to his prophecy that "wild beasts should pick the old mobocrat, Dr. Dodd's bones." Some Mormons actually released their pent-up anger on the bones of deceased Missourians. In 1850, near Scotts Bluffs, N. W. Whipple found some graves of Missourians that had been dug up by wolves. Their bones lay around bleaching in the wilderness. To Whipple, this was the fulfillment of some of the prophecies of Joseph Smith regarding those who had murdered and plundered the Saints in Missouri. Whipple found the names of the deceased on the headboards of their graves, and he noted, "I had the satisfaction of kicking their skulls about and trampling upon their ribs and other bones that the wolves had left bare." Since the wolves scattered the bones, some could have been from other graves.

Conclusion

Of course, Mormon historians have tended to downplay the dark side of the Mormon immigrant experience, but Mormons were like most westering peoples—good and bad, indifferent and human. However, the camps of the Saints were more orderly, and they observed a stricter routine, especially in keeping up their religious activities. They were usually traveling with family and friends, and concerned with their safety. Obedience to leaders was not a part of trail life in the typical camps. Although traveling Oregon companies tended to elect their own officers and draw up lists of their own rules, they also felt free to break those rules, if provoked, and to deny the authority of their officers. These camps had fierce individuals.

The darker side of the western trek is also a part of trail history. The puzzle is how they maintained as much dignity and kindness as they did under the situations which they were forced to travel. The real heroes of the trail were the handcarters. Their bravery, endurance, and suffering were not surpassed in any other experience in trail history. The second company under Daniel D. McArthur got his ultimate praise in his report to the Church authorities: "Peace prevailed. . . . I must say that a better set of Saints to labor with I never saw."

Some of the handcarters proclaimed that they would not have taken an easier way to Zion, even if it had been available, but these declarations came later when the experiences had dimmed, and life in Zion was much better than in the old country.

The trail was not simply a stage for heroic and noble deeds in the face of suffering inflicted by harsh conditions. Likewise, the Bible is full of terrible actions by otherwise noble men and women.

Chapter 13

Unsung Heros

When we started, we had eighteen team of oxen and not one of them reached the Valley. They didn't seem to be able to stand the trip as well as we did. When they were worn out and about ready to die, the men would kill them and we would sit up all night watching for a little piece of meat. —*Sarah Hancock Beesley, 1859 Handcart Pioneer*

As we herald the humans who survived the trek west and applaud their accomplishments, we often forget that they would have all been back in the East, or still at the camp ground, or even in the old country, but for the strength, patience, and docility of the four-footed creatures who pulled the wagons. Even the handcart pioneers would have been hard pressed to get to Zion without the supply wagons that accompanied them, carrying the bulk of the food, and those too ill to walk.

Brigham Young's 1848 company brought 1,275 oxen, 184 loose cattle, 19 mules, 699 cows, 411 sheep, 141 pigs, 605 chickens, 37 cats, 82 dogs, 3 goats, 10 geese, two hives of bees, and 8 doves. Rachel Emma Woolley's father brought along a pregnant sow. When she was in labor, they put her in the buggy that Rachel was driving, but all of the piglets died.

The westward movement was accompanied by running arguments over the relative merits of draft animals: especially oxen, horses, and mules. Oxen (castrated bulls), were preferred, horses were used by wealthier pioneers, mules were tolerated, and cows were a last resort. Sometimes families used mixed teams, or were forced to use what they had. Lucy Henderson and her family hitched up six calves on the final approach to Oregon in 1846 "and they brought us through." In 1859, Charley True's family made it all the way to California with a small ox "Blackie" and a cow "Starry," hitched up to their wagon. Charley said his team caused a few chuckles among those watching their arrival, but their feat was more than many a grand carriage and horse team accomplished.

Oxen

Oxen were durable, had more strength and stamina, did not balk at mud or quicksand, were patient and easy to keep and drive, and had no complicated harness—just yokes. Indians did not care to eat them, so oxen were seldom stolen. They could, however, be eaten in an emergency by immigrants. They were also relatively cheap. In 1846 oxen went for about $20.00 a head, in 1847 $22.50, and in 1855, $35.00. Ten years later, the price had risen dramatically for teams, wagons, and yokes; oxen were about $75 a head. In 1865 Peter Olaf Holmgren paid "$226 for a wagon, and $144 for a pair of bullocks and yoke."

A great advantage was their docility. Even children, could and did (with a little help, especially during the morning yoking up) drive oxen, thus transporting themselves and their possessions successfully all the way to the Valley of the Great Salt Lake. Oxen made a vast difference in the success of the march to Zion in 1847–48 because so many men were elsewhere. Boys as young as seven drove oxen on occasion. Twelve-year-old girls were often at the side of oxen with whip in hand.

Harriet Decker Hanks, whose husband died on the trek through Iowa, started for Zion on June 13, 1847: "One hundred persons of which myself and baby were [numbered], left our Winter quarters to cross the plains. . . . I was given the honorable position of driving an ox team. . . . I drove my oxen through the day--milked 5 cows at night and morning—Baked the bread for fifteen persons eleven of them men—done everything that came to me to do but yoke my oxen. . . . I drew the line at that request. . . . My weight at that time was 80 pounds." Emeline Grover Rich, a young plural wife, said that nine out of ten drivers in their 1847 company were women.

The disadvantage with oxen was that they were the slowest of the draft animals, averaging about two or three miles an hour. Shoeing was difficult, but necessary for oxen. Horses or mules could balance on three legs while the blacksmith was working on the fourth, but an ox lacks that balance. There are only two ways to shoe an ox: hoist it in a special harness which few immigrants carried along, or dig a shallow trench and then (try to) turn the animal upside down in it.

On June 6, 1850, Robert Chalmers explains another procedure in his diary: "One of our oxen had worn his feet through. In such a case we skin a piece off the first [dead] ox we find and put a moccasin on which will last 4 or 5 days. Dead oxen or horses we found every day we camped." This method is mentioned more frequently by travelers bound for Oregon or California than by Mormons. Oxen also had the inclination to run off and join buffalo herds.

Because of the yoke, if an ox collapsed or died in the yoke, the other one was frequently injured, or even killed, his neck twisted by the yoke as the other animal fell.

A favored way of breaking oxen to the yoke was to hitch a pair up and have them drag heavy logs around the camp. Mormons from European cities who had little acquaintance with draft animals had a frustrating time learning to yoke up their oxen. Many of the immigrants could not speak English, so the instructions were not always clear to them. To make matters worse, the men often learned with unbroken animals—a formidable task even for the experienced. At the various jumping-off places for the Far West they were given cram courses on "ox-teamology" which consisted mainly of walking along the left side of the lead ox with a whip, prod, or goad, urging the team on and guiding them. It was therefore much simpler than handling the reins of horses or mules. Oxen are always driven from the left side.

F. F. Christensen, who crossed the plains in 1857, wrote: "The oxen were not trained to pull wagons & knew nothing about gee & haw and less about our Danish talk. We had to tie long ropes to the heads of the leader oxen to prevent them from taking their own course."

Bathsheba Smith left a comment about the Welsh. "The Welsh did not know anything about driving oxen. It was very amusing to see them yoke their cattle. Two would have an animal by the horns, one by the tail, one or two others would do their best to put on the yoke while the apparently astonished ox, not at all enlightened by the guttural sound of the Welsh twang, seemed perfectly at a loss what to do, or to know what was wanted of him."

Joseph Curtis passed on the following delightful memory.

> Now I will tell you about the Sircuse [circus] we had the first few days on the plains. Our captain told us to be up Early in the morning for to get ready to start in good time. After breakfast was over we got our cattle together and tried to yoke them up. I can assure you that this was quite a task for us and after we got them hitched up to the wagon we started out. Now come the Sircuse and it was a good one. The Capt. was a watching us and telling us what to do. He told us to take the whip; and use it and say "whoa Duke," "gee Brandy" and so on. Now the fun commenced. Then we went after them pretty lively and when the cattle went "gee" too much we would run to the off sides and yelling at them we "hawed" them and bunted them with the stock of the whip. Then they would go "haw" too much and we was a puffing and sweating and if you was there to look on you would say it was a great Sircuse. This was a great experience and a tuff one and by the time we got half way across the plains we could drive an ox team as well as you can enny day.

One company of Danes who had previous experience with Danish oxen, driven in harness, tried to hitch up American oxen Danish fashion in 1857. F. F. Christensen reported, "The frightened animals struck out in a wild run, refusing to be guided by the reins. They crossed ditches in their frenzy, strewing parts of the wagons by the wayside. An experienced teamster with a cracking whip finally stopped them, and the Danes hastily concluded to adopt the New World yoke."

Cows

When a cow went into heat, Loren Hastings, traveling in 1847, noted it with a circumlocution: "One old cow, not being very virtuous and less modest, has produced some excitement among the oxen and bulls."

Sometimes cows would snatch up a piece of clothing from a bush. Artist Frederick Piercy wrote in 1853: "I washed my silk hand-kerchief one day in the Platte River and put it on the grass to dry. One of the young girls in camp said: 'There's a critter a eaten some-thing.' Sure enough. . . . I saw the bright red corners of my best silk handkerchief vanish into a cow's throat. I learned it was no uncom-mon thing for these animals to appropriate such delicate morsels."

Thomas Memmott, in camp at Florence in 1862 wrote: "An old cow got into the food, ate a loaf of bread and six cakes; part of the July 24 feast."

Calves born along the trail were too weak to follow along. Sometimes the owner would give the calf to a farmer or rancher along the trail, but care had to be taken or the cow would break away and return to her calf, causing "considerable trouble." The harsh solution to this problem was to kill the calf and hang its hide on the wagon, whereupon the cow would follow the skin. This is what Thomas Cropper did in 1854, and Welborn Beeson wrote in his trail diary in May 1853: "Oceole had a calf tonight. I shot it because it could not travel." Beeson was en route to Oregon and had barely started on his journey.

If ox-teams gave out, cows were often pressed into service. James Willie, captain of one of the two ill-fated late handcart companies in 1856, reported on September 3 that "more than one-half of our cattle stampeded." These oxen had been drawing the accompany-ing wagons that carried the food. "We were under the necessity of yoking some wild Arkansas cows and traveling the best we could," Willie observed.

Horses

Horses were expensive, running up to $150 a head. They were faster than oxen and seldom ran off, but they had less stamina on the trail, required expensive and complicated harnesses, could not forage as well, and were often stolen.

Helen Mar Kimball Whitney left a memorable portrait of her-self on her white pony in 1846, wearing a dark green riding habit made of merino, a very soft, silky, wool from merino sheep:

I had a very long riding habit of dark green merino which father had brought me from the east; I had worn it but a few times when we learned we were to leave for Mexico. . . . I wore it through the winter, and it was still a good dress, being a strong material. . . . I was separated from my dear mother by an almost impassable road of mud. . . . One morning I undertook the disagreeable and perilous journey on the back of a little white [pony] and by the by, she had carried me over the Mississippi the last time that I crossed it to Sugar Creek, accompanied by Horace [her husband] on his pony.

There were some extra exciting activities in some companies. Wilford Woodruff described how Ephraim Hanks captured a wild mare—"the fastest & most beautiful Animal of the Horse kind I ever saw"—on September 6, 1850. "He run by the side of Her on a small bay Horse flung a larriett over her Head flung himself from his Horse onto the ground. The wild Horse drew him half a mile over the sage plains untill she was stopped by being choaked down. She then tried to bite, kick & strike him but he fought her by whiping her with a rope until he conquerd Her and led Her in triumph into camp."

One fortunate young lady from St. Louis had the rare pleasure of riding her horse on the trail to California. Elizabeth Keegan, age twelve, wrote back home to siblings her impressions of the journey in 1852. "I rode through on horseback and I had a fine opportunity to see and examine everything of note along the way."

Mules

In some ways mules, which cost around $50 and up, were much like horses but had more endurance. They were used for years on the Santa Fe Trail, could withstand heat, poor forage, and poor shelter better than a horse, and were less likely to drink bad water. In fact, some mules died because they did not know how to drink from a bucket or refused to do so. On occasion pioneers mixed other ingredients, such as coffee, to get them to drink brackish water.

They were fast and strong. Indians usually did not try to steal them. Mules were also ornery, most likely to bolt for home, and were difficult to train. So they were both a curse and a blessing. In 1853, artist Frederick Piercy commented: "Elder [John A.] Miller early taught me that the only way to manage a mule was to administer a dose of strangulation, the consequences was they acknowledged my authority and I harnessed them immediately. . . . We passed over sand bluffs which were decidedly the worst we had encountered and had to double team all our wagons. The mules were brave little fellows to pull."

Mary Pugh Scott, traveling to Utah in 1848 with two sister wives and three small children, was assigned a team to drive. Mary was dubious when she began the journey. "Here we . . . have been raised in luxury, . . . bravely trying to drive a Mule Team across the plains, holding our Babies. We take turns driving. You can just imagine we three women climbing in and out over wagon wheels to cook on the camp fire and wash clothes."

One of the best descriptions of breaking mules to the harness was left by George Winslow, en route to the gold fields in 1849. He wrote to his wife: "We have bought forty mules, which cost us $50 apiece. . . . We engaged some Mexicans to break the mules. To harness them they tied their fore-legs together and threw them down. The fellows then got on them and wrung their ears which is the tenderest [part]. By that time they were docile enough to take the harness. The animals in many respects resemble sheep; they are very timid, and when frightened will kick like thunder."

Donkeys are seldom mentioned in trail journals. Helen Mar Whitney said she rode a "hinny," by which she may have meant a "jenny," the female offspring of a male horse and a female donkey. Mules are the offspring of a mare and male donkey. The wagon trains included a few ponies, but they were usually the children's pets and made no real contribution to the gathering to Zion.

Mired-In Teams

The overland trail along the North Platte River had been utilized by a few horse teams by 1847 when the Saints first pulled out to find Zion. Three years before the pioneer trek began, the Stevens-Murphy Company, a group from Missouri assembled at Council Bluffs, determined to get themselves to California by wagons. It was a nightmare experience at the beginning of a journey of two thousand miles. The cattle suffered trying to cross swollen creeks and rivers. The risks for humans trying to reach the promised land were great, but even worse for animals and pets. Sometimes a journey that began in tragedy ended the same way. Moses Shallenberger, a young member of that party, recorded this incident in 1844: "The wagons crossed [the Missouri River] in a rude flat-boat, and we intended to swim the cattle . . . but some were stuck in the sand, which had been tramped by them untill it was as tenacious as quicksand. When the water receded, a few of the mired cattle were dug out with pick and spade, but others were fastened so securely and deep, they were abandoned."

When the Mormons began their exodus across Iowa in early 1846, the mud was horrendous. On June 12, not far from the Missouri River, Brigham Young's history noted: The east bank of a small stream became "very miry, some forty or fifty cattle had to be pulled out of the mire which prevented building a bridge." Leonora Cannon Taylor, who was near the area in a bad storm, wrote: "The storm continued with great violence. Several large Tress [sic] fell near br. Young's tent. One [tree] fell on a Cow, one on a Mule, one on a Donkey, yet none of them were killed."

Caring for Animals

The death, injury, or loss to Indian raiders of draft animals was a serious problem crossing the plains. Brigham Young's company, returning to Winter Quarters in the late summer of 1847, lost about fifty horses one night when they failed to post guard. Several attempts to get them all back failed, but they did recover a few. The losses slowed Young, Kimball, and the others down to a slow, hungry return.

The pioneers also found abandoned or runaway animals. On August 25, 1854, Robert Campbell "found a very excellent pony with bridle and saddle and some meat and provisions tied on its back. It probably belonged to some Calif emigrant." Less than a month later on September 16 near Fort Laramie, Campbell "found an ox at the creek. Two more oxen turned up at their campground on October 5. And in the same company on October 8, "Bro Fisher had to leave an ox behind that gave out, but he found another on the way."

Even animals that were too weak to continue could make a contribution. In 1862, William Wood Sr. "came across a stranded played-out cow. The poor brute had been left to perish. She had just the power to wink her eyes. I butchered her very quickly. . . . She was almost a skeleton. We had been on half rations and thought it a Godsend."

Well-organized companies never permitted animals to be harshly treated. William Appleby relates that a Welshman and Englishman in a Mormon company beat and shouted at their cattle in 1849. They were bought before the camp council, severely reprimanded, and assigned extra guard duty. They made a confession, asked forgiveness, promised to do better, and were restored to fellowship.

Young people were pressed into service along the trail to keep the animals from drinking too much of the brackish water, especially along the dangerous arid areas. Susan Noble, age fifteen, had that chore in 1847. "My, how we boys and girls worked to keep the cows and sheep from drinking too large a dose of this brackish water. The weather was so hot, and the animals increased in their thirst by the salty country that, in spite of our poundings and pleading, they would gorge themselves upon the morbific, soapbubbly stuff and then almost immediately became sick."

Animals were at times driven too long, and the wagons were sometimes too heavy; but such cases usually arose out of ignorance or necessity, not because of brutality. Lucy Henderson recalled how her parents prepared to cross a desert stretch in 1846, en route to Oregon: "We filled every keg and dish with water so the cattle should have water as well as ourselves. We had no grain or hay, so Mother baked up a lot of bread to feed them. When we had crossed the desert the cattle smelled water, and ran as hard as they could [with us] nearly bouncing out. We could not stop them."

In 1847, George W. Bean clashed with another teamster: "[The man] was angered . . . and he began to reek vengeance upon my oxen. I leaped to the rescue of my faithful friends and fairly shouted: 'You can beat me if you like, but not my oxen.' He lashed away at them again and I cracked him over the head with the butt of my ox-whip." The man demanded that George be court-martialed for assault and battery. George "worried for days about the court-martial, but my prayers were answered." Martha Spence Heywood related an anecdote about finding an abandoned steer and healing it with care and love. It was "so weak from the 'scours' [dysentery] that the men rejected him, but Sister Butterfield thought she could cure him and drove him along . . . and turns [sic] out to be a better animal than the one she lost."

How to treat ailing animals produced much folklore. Heber C. Kimball's company brought with them a Delaware Indian who had a good reputation as an animal doctor. Animals suffered from the biblical scourge of murraine, hollow horn, bloating, alkali water, and exhaustion. A popular remedy was feeding sick cattle linseed oil mixed with tobacco; if the oil was not available, bacon slices would work. They were also given salt or tartaric acid dissolved in warm water. In 1847 John Ensign Hill drilled holes in the horns of his sick ox, took a syringe and forced red pepper tea into them, then he tried to get some tobacco down the animal by rolling it up into meat balls. The animal did not survive.

Brigham Young's account of crossing Iowa in 1846 included a spiritual approach:

> At Indian creek one of [Wm Hall's] horses sickened with bloating and colic. [He] laid hands on him and he recovered [but] went . . . two miles when he was again attacked more violently. Reuben Strong said he believed there was breath in him yet. . . . [They] laid hands on the horse and commanded the unclean and foul spirits of every name and nature to depart and go to the Gentiles at Warsaw and trouble the Saints no more, when the horse rolled twice over in great distress, sprang to his feet, squealed, vomited and purged, and the next morning was harnessed . . . and performed his part as usual."

On March 22, 1846, Brigham had another incident with his horse and tried doctoring with an unusual method. "[My] horse was bitten on the nose by a rattlesnake. I cut the snake into pieces and applied them to the wound. They drew out the poison, leaving the horse uninjured."

Heber C. Kimball had a similar injury to his horse but tried laying on of hands instead. He said that it was "just as proper to lay hands on a horse or an ox and administer to them in the name of the Lord and of as much utility as it is to a human being, both being creatures of His creation, both consequently have a claim to his attention." He practiced what he preached. Horace Whitney recorded in 1846 that, when one of Heber's horses was bitten by a rattlesnake, "he laid his hands on the part affected and rebuked the sickness occasioned by the poison in the name of the Lord which prayer was almost immediately answered."

On March 6, 1846, Patty Sessions wrote laconically in her journal: "Our horse was sick last night but they laid hands on him and he is better today." Peter Neilsen recalled: "When cattle became sullen or tired, [we] went secretly among them and blessed them and they immediately would move on showing that the Spirit of the Lord can subdue and make bidable the ox as well as man." I have not heard of any other group of pioneers who practiced such healing on their animals.

The most famous blessing of an ox is the story that Joseph F. Smith told about his mother, Mary Fielding Smith, the widow of Hyrum Smith. In 1848, along a peculiarly desolate stretch of the trail west of present Casper, Wyoming, one of her oxen laid down in its yoke. Although her son and a brother were in the same company and although she was then a plural wife of Heber C. Kimball, she was generally in charge of getting her own wagon west. At her request, they blessed her ox; it recovered, gained its feet, and made it into the valley. Sister Smith was given a fresh team and wagon to help get into the valley, however.

Stampedes

The most dreaded trail disaster was a stampede, since the frightened oxen were almost impossible to control. Israel Barlow witnessed a scary runaway stampede. "Several hundred of our frightened oxen, cows, and steers raced away at full gallop bellowing into the darkness with the men on horses after them. . . . The terrors of a stampede are not soon forgotten." Sarah Maria Mousley left a dramatic account from 1857 in her memoirs.

> I was called to witness the most terrific of all scenes, a stampede on the plain. The cattle started almost together and, Oh, my father, my heart sickens as I recall the scene and my soul is grieved in memory of the painful occurrence. I beheld men thrown, women leaping from

their wagons, children screaming as team after team ran on in wild confusion dashing headlong on the wild prairie without power to impede their progress. In the wild scene of apparent death God gave me presence of mind sufficient to remain in my wagon which I did and alone, except the unseen guardian . . . shielded me from the shafts of the destroyer. . . . [After the stampede] I alighted from my wagon only to witness the most terrific of all scenes my sisters . . . were badly injured. In their fright they jumped from the wagon [and] some of the cattle had steped [sic] in our dear Willie's face and [she] was streaming with blood and crying for help.

Most wagons had no brakes; those that did were of little help. Horses and mules had reins, but oxen had only chains and yokes. Almost anything could cause a stampede: the smell of Indians, a barking dog, and sudden unexpected movement by a person. Benjamin Bonney, a young lad on the trail in 1845, noted the reactions of oxen when meeting their wild cousins. "When oxen smell buffalo they go crazy. They want to join them. . . . They stop and paw and bellow as if they smelt fresh blood." Peter O. Hansen remarked in 1848 that one stampede began because a pioneer wearing a white shirt walked by "the corral by moonlight," and another stampede was caused by a man "wearing a red shirt." James Armistead reported in 1853: "We had a stampede caused by a dog fight. It was a fearful sight to witness, 150 head of cattle rushing headlong and madly confused, men halooing, women and children screaming, dogs barking and oxen bellowing and running in all direction in a whirling mass." The dangers were real to both humans and livestock. William Freshwater saw "cattle yoked together one dragged the other to death" during a stampede in 1862.

The main way of dealing with a stampede was to let the animals run, although a useful variation was to make them veer inward until they were running in a circle and began simply milling. In 1856, a herd of buffalo stampeded past a wagon train but a bold and unnamed grandmother "stood at the head of the oxen holding an umbrella before the eyes of the lead oxen so they could not see what was going on."

Animal Deaths

Richard L. Riech, who researched the question of animal mortality on the trail in 1991, estimates that there were eighteen dead oxen for every human death. Comments about dead animals along the trail were frequent. One emigrant, bound for California, wrote that the Humboldt River on the California Trail, was "not good at best, but at this time is unwholesome from the great number of dead animals lying in it. You will see 20 and 30 dead animals in two or three miles."

Teenager Sallie Hester, en route to California in 1849 witnessed some horrid scenes as they crossed the infamous forty-mile desert before reaching the Sierras: "The weary journey last night, the mooing of the cattle for water, their exhausted condition, the cry of 'Another ox down,' the stopping of the train to unyoke the poor dying brute, to let him follow at will or stop by the wayside and die, the weary, weary tramp of men and beasts, worn out with heat and famished for water, will never be erased from my memory."

By 1850, one pioneer described this desert as studded by "one dead creature every twenty feet." Another one writing in the same year claimed that he could have "stepped from one dead animal to the next." Riech wrote that "abandoned, prostrate cattle were often run over by emigrant wagons before they died." The stench in this desert was over-powering, and the heat added to the misery of the dying animals. Vultures would often swoop down and "peck out the eyes of an animal not yet dead," or wolves and buzzards would begin to eat the still-living beasts. Gruesomely, along this same stretch of desert, leeches on the draft animals' throats and stomachs drained enough blood that the animal was fatally weakened.

John T. Gridley, also traveling to California in 1850, recorded with pardonable pride: "All horses with which [we] left home (Illinois) reached California, much reduced."

Some starving pioneers en route to Oregon and California lived off their cattle during the last few weeks on the trail: "The only food they had was their animals, and men became so famished that they cut meat from the mules and horses which had perished from hunger and thirst." Some members of the Mormon Battalion, bound for Winter Quarters in December 1847, traveled for several days without food, according to fifteen-year-old William B. Pace. The company finally "agreed to make a supper out of Old Jack. . . . Shortly after they returned with a part of old Jack Dressed & ready for to be confiscated into a repast for some ten or twelve half starved Mormon Soldiers. . . . Some stood off and would not partake while others pitched into it like as many ravenous wolves devouring their Prey."

These dead animals were a blessing at times to travelers. Kirsten Ericksen Benson, walking in the 1857 Christiansen Handcart Company, remembered that her shoes were worn out by August. "We had to get raw hide from the dead cattle along the road and make shoes for ourselves so as to be able to pull."

Helen Stewart, en route to Oregon in 1853, described the Platte River as a death-trap for animals when the river had high water. It was "four miles wide, and sand bottom" as well. She relates an anecdote that is hard to believe: A man had "a drove of sheep and he put in thirty thousand and he got out five thousand." Lorenzo Dow Young started for the Valley in 1850 with a flock of 500 sheep, but lost 127 of them in various situations on the journey.

Pets on the Trail

Most of the children wanted to bring their pets, but trail life was hard on them. Most dogs and cats had to be left behind. Joseph Fish remembered a scene of sadness in 1846 as the ferry pulled away from Nauvoo: "As we slowly left the Illinois shore my sister Anna Marie, and I looked back and there we saw our favorite dog Prince standing on the bank, too old to attempt to swim the river. He had been our [long] companion and to leave him thus brought the tears to my eyes." Pets did accompany the 1848 Heber C. Kimball Company. They included seventeen cats and fifty-two dogs.

Six years earlier, the 1842 Oregon Company led by Dr. Elijah White started out with twenty-two dogs; but being misinformed that dogs became rabid "in crossing the mountains," the company held a meeting in Kansas and took a vote. A two-thirds majority voted to kill all twenty-two dogs. "This action did not at all accord with the feelings of the ladies," recorded White.

James Clyman, heading east along the California Trail in 1846, sadly reported that his dog Lucky rushed into the boiling water at

Brady's Hot Springs and was scalded to death. At least two other dogs died at the same spot.

Near Independence Rock, John Steele, traveling to the gold mines in 1850, wrote: "We passed an abandoned wagon. It looked like a splendid outfit . . . and under the wagon lay a faithful watch dog, dying at his post. When we touched any article, he showed his teeth. . . . I doubt whether he was able to stand, but he would not be coaxed, and we [had] not the heart to shoot him, so we left him to his fate."

Virginia Reed, of the Donner-Reed party, owed her life to her dog, Cash. In a letter to a cousin, she captured the trial of an icy night in 1846 even before they reached the Sierras: "Pa caried Thomos [her brother] and all the rest of us walked, we got to Donner [The others in the company], and thay were all a sleep. We laid down on the ground [and] spred one shawl down, and we laid down on it and spred another over us, and then put the dogs on top. It was the couldes [coldest] night you most ever saw, the wind blew and if it haden bin for the dogs we would have Frozen." Two months later when they were starving, Cash again saved their lives when they killed and ate him.

A few dogs did get to their destination. Charley True, bound for California in 1859, would "not think of leaving my dog Prince. He traveled along week after week and month after month." He stayed in the wagon the last half of the journey, however.

We will never know how many of the eighty-two dogs in the Brigham Young camp or the fifty-two dogs with Heber C. Kimball's company in 1848 made it all the way to the Valley. Some of them must have died, but their burials were not noted. No doubt Young and Kimball did not want the dogs along, but tearful pleas from children moved them to allow their inclusion on the trail to Zion. Pets were an important luxury, perhaps the only one that most children needed. They were a part of the past that was connected to love instead of pain. Many of the children had haunting memories of life in Nauvoo, Winter Quarters, or Council Bluffs; and pets could comfort children still mourning for lost family members.

Martha Spence Heywood certainly recognized the relationship between success on the trail and caring for their animals in her 1850 account. "A journey like this will teach a person to place a higher value on the animals appropriated to the service of man," she summarized. If animals could talk, we would have a different perspective of trail history. Not many pioneers appreciated their four-legged companions. If all those travelers had the same sensitive concern that Martha showed, I believe there would have been fewer than eighteen animal deaths for every human.

Chapter 14

Saints by Sea

Considering all things . . . the little world [on board ship] be-
haved itself remarkably well. . . . The weather was charming [and]
the most unimpressionable must have been affected by the glorious
rising and setting of the sun, by the beauty and vastness of the ocean,
and by the power of the winds. —Frederick Piercy, 1853

The tall, white sails of the *George W. Bourne* caught a gentle
breeze and the winds, now a little warmer, lifted the scarf of a petite,
well-dressed, dark-haired woman who stood by the rail on February
14, 1851. The golden setting sun and full-moon sky fought for her
attention as she enjoyed the scene. Jean Rio Griffiths Baker and
eleven other family members were en route to Zion to gather with
the Saints. She looked sophisticated and wealthy compared to most
of the other Saints on board. She had a literary style (heavy squalls
evoked "the bellowing of a thousand wild bulls") that revealed her
love of words and of music:

> I can hardly describe the beauty of this night. The moon nearly
> at full with a deep blue sky studded with stars, the reflection of which
> makes the sea appear like an immense sheet of diamonds. . . . Well I
> have seen the mighty deep in its anger, with our ship nearly on her
> beam ends, and I have seen it, as now under the cloudless sky, and
> scarcely a ripple on the surface, and I know not which to admire most.
> . . . I feel most powerfully the force of those words, "The Mighty God,"
> which Handel has so beautifully expressed in one of his Chronicles.

Jean Rio Griffiths Baker and thousands of converts like her began their journey an ocean away from the American continent, a cir-

cumstance that prolonged their travel by months and the expense by hundreds of dollars. In 1840, Apostles Brigham Young and Heber C. Kimball obeyed Joseph Smith's call to present a more forceful declaration of the gathering to prospective converts in England (D&C 45). Converts heard of the necessity of gathering at the same time they heard of the need for baptism. Elders fervently quoted Matthew 19:29: "And every one that has forsaken houses, or brethren, or sisters, or father, or mother, or wife, or children or lands, for my name's sake, shall receive an hundredfold, and shall inherit everlasting life."

In 1843, nineteen-year-old Priscilla Mogridge of Widbrook, England had no doubt of her course of action:

> It was a great trial for a young maiden to forsake all for the gospel—father, mother, brothers and sisters—and to leave my childhood home and native land [but] the saints were already leaving [the] fatherland, in obedience to the doctrine of gathering, which was preached at this time with great plainness by the elders as an imperative command of God. We looked upon the gathering as necessary to our salvation.... Young as I was and alone of all my family in the faith, I was called to take up my cross and lay my earthly all upon the altar.

Most early converts from Europe spent an average of fifty-four days at sea, then had to continue by rail and river to the campground, followed by an additional three or four months on the trail. All of the LDS passenger ships but three between 1841 and 1855 landed at New Orleans. The early ships did not provide much except passage. In March 1840, Brigham Young and Heber C. Kimball "paid $18 each for a steerage passage, furnished our own provisions and bedding and paid the cook $1 each for cooking.... The brethren in New York furnished us with an ample supply of provisions [and] the sisters made us ticks and filled them with straw for beds and ... straw for pillows."

The agents who booked the ships were supposed to supply enough food for the passengers, and the passengers cooked it themselves; but the corruption and suffering caused by lack of drinking water and decent food was so scandalous that the British Parliament enacted the Passengers' Act (1854) that stipulated: "Every emigration agent ... should supply the passengers with seventy days provisions." They included oatmeal, rice, wheat flour, and sea biscuits, tea, sugar, salt and "three quarts of water daily." Substitutions included potatoes, or split peas, pork, beef, preserved meat, or dried salt fish. This act also stipulated that any ship carrying over 100 adults had to have a steward to hand out the provisions, and another steward to cook the provisions. The ships carrying 500 passengers had to include a "medical seaman."

Jean Rio Griffiths Baker, thanks to her affluent circumstances, had considerable privileges: "Our general custom is to sit on the deck and take our meals on our laps; each family has their own department in front of their berths, and can have their meals without being intruded on by the others. We can cook our food in any way we please and can amuse ourselves in any way we like, go to bed and get up when we choose; indeed, we are under no restraint whatever." She left a detailed account of her travels from Liverpool to the Valley of the Great Salt Lake in 1851.

> January 4, 1851: Left Liverpool
> March 20: Arrived New Orleans.
> March 23: Left on Steamboat for St. Louis
> March 29: Arrived St. Louis
> April 9: Left St. Louis on steamboat.
> April 19: Arrived at Alexandria, Missouri
> April 22: Left Alexandria by wagons and oxen
> July 2: Arrived Kanesville (Council Bluffs)
> July 7: Began trek to Zion
> September 29: Arrived in Valley of Great Salt Lake.

Total days on water, 73; total days on trail 155; 71 of them from Alexandria to Council Bluffs.

She arrived thankful, cheerful, and awed at the "majestic" scenery, but with only one yoke of her original eight yoke of oxen.

Jean's journey took almost nine months. By 1880, steamships greatly decreased the amount of time spent traveling to eleven days from England to New York; the Saints could then arrive in Ogden by rail and reach Salt Lake City a day later.

The last Church-sponsored ship, the *Constitution*, with Captain William Hatten, sailed on June 24, 1868. There was not a single death among its 457 Saints, who united in their appreciation to the captain for his hospitality. He allowed a July 24 celebration and was generous in supplying food, two kindnesses that kept morale high. It was following the *Emerald Isle* with 876 Saints, which had sailed a few days earlier. In contrast, the passengers were ill treated, thirty-seven died, and many others sickened from contaminated drinking water. Perhaps fittingly, it came in nine days after the *Constitution*. Both were voyages to remember—and forget.

The Role of Church Agents

The unpaid LDS emigration agents were one of the greatest advantages experienced by the Saints who came by sea. These devoted and hard-working men secured passage, provisions, and protection from thieves and short-change artists. By avoiding middlemen, they passed the savings on to the poor. This arrangement received favorable press in England, and the *Morning Advertiser* reported on June 2, 1854:

> I heard a rather remarkable examination before a committee of the House of Commons. The witness was no other than the supreme authority in England of the Mormonites (Samuel W. Richards,) and the subject upon which he was giving information was the mode in which the emigration . . . is conducted. . . . He gave himself no airs . . . and at the close of his examination he received the thanks of the committee. . . . There is one thing which, in the opinion of the Emigration Committee . . . they (LDS) can do, viz., teach Christian shipowners how to send poor people decently, cheaply and healthfully across the Atlantic.

The *Edinburgh Review* of January 1856 wrote with admiration: "The ordinary emigrant is exposed to all the chances and misadventure . . . of a heterogeneous, childish, mannerless crowd during the voyage, and to the merciless cupidity of land-sharks the moment he has touched the opposite shore. But the Mormon ship is A Family under strong and accepted discipline, with every provision for comfort, decorum, and internal peace. On his arrival in the New World the wanderer is received . . . [and] he is passed on from friend to friend, till he reaches the promised home."

European immigrants were met by a Church agent in New Orleans, or other ports, then sent by boat to campgrounds in Missouri and Iowa where additional agents had "fit-outs" (usually one wagon, two yoke of oxen, and two cows) waiting. The wagons had usually been purchased in Cincinnati or St. Louis and transported to the point of departure by steamboat. The cattle were purchased from western dealers and driven to the campgrounds, or taken by cattle cars on the boats. Some immigrants chose to buy their own outfits.

This practice of agents making all of the arrangements, which started with immigrant convert companies in Liverpool, England, contributed greatly to the Mormon success of transporting thousands of such converts from Europe to Utah. Some immigrants could not afford to go straight through to Utah and laid over in various cities to earn money—especially in New Orleans, St. Louis, and Council Bluffs, Iowa—where, in the beginning, agents and local Church leaders helped them get jobs. One small group of "seventeen souls" from Germany who migrated in 1853 stayed in St. Louis to work; but when only three remained active in the Church, the agents began to urge everyone to go directly to Zion.

The Perpetual Emigrating Fund was set up to help poor Saints, but people in foreign countries also supported it. Between 1850 and 1869, about 50,000 converts gathered from Europe, but only a fraction relied 100 percent on the fund. Those who benefited were expected to pay it back with interest. That did not happen, and many were delinquent in paying back their advances, as well as the interest. By 1877, the fund was $1 million in debt, much of it written off during the Jubilee Year of 1880. By that date, about one third had paid the loan back, one third paid in part, and one third not at all. By 1890, the Perpetual Emigrating Fund was dissolved. George Q. Cannon told the *New York Times* about the discontinued policy of gathering: "We really urge our missionaries to dissuade them in any way they can. It is not to our advantage to have any come who are not thoroughly grounded in the faith."

Aboard Ship

Although much of the success at sea hinged on the rules and regulations demanded by the Mormon company presidents, the weather and the captain's personality were also significant factors. Some of the emigrants were restive with the rules and wondered why "the Church" was so much different on the ocean than on land.

264 Villages on Wheels

Some of them rebelled and abandoned Mormonism. Some single women found husbands among the crews. Leaders wrote disparagingly of those who resisted the rules: "Apostates on board."

Everyone was affected by the weather. William Clayton was a passenger aboard the *North Atlantic*, the second ship to take passengers to Nauvoo in 1840, and his detailed record painted a grim picture:

> The wind blew hard, the vessel rock[ed] and many were sick all night. This was a new scene. Such sickness, vomiting, groaning and bad smells I never witnessed before and added to this the closeness of the births [sic] almost suffocated us for want of air. . . . This A.M. Elder Turley ordered all the company on deck to wash as the weather was a little more calm.

> Conditions got worse before they got better. At night Elder [Theodore] Turley spoke considerable on cleanliness and afterwards went round the births to see if all the company undressed. Some was found with their cloths on and some had never pulled their cloths off since they came on deck and had done their dirt in the cloths [and] in the corner of their birth. . . . Elder Turley undressed and washed them and ordered the place cleaned out.

The captain was not cooperative and asked Elder Turley if he "understood the laws of mutiny." He also said he would like to kill about a dozen of the Mormon passengers, and "someone was stealing water," already in short supply. About a week later on October 4, Clayton wrote with relief: "We have our full allowance of water again. We have only had 1 ½ quarts since September 20th." Presumably, the passengers also suffered from lice, bedbugs, and rodents. Seven of the passengers died. It was with great relief and prayers of thanks that the passengers finally disembarked in New York on October 11.

A pleasant contrast was the voyage of the *International* in February 1853. Elder Christopher Arthur presided over the 425 emigrants, divided into eight wards of about fifty-five people apiece, each with its own presidency. David Brown, the vessel's captain, was kind, respectful, and interested in the teachings of the Church. Forty-eight were baptized, including Brown, his two mates, and sixteen sailors.

Brown also allowed the missionary leaders to prepare a pageant on April 6 to celebrate the founding of the Mormon Church. Twelve men robed in white and twelve young women in pale dresses carried beribboned scrolls inscribed "Utah's rights." Older men carrying Bibles and Books of Mormon followed in procession. After the administration of the sacrament, four marriages were solemnized, songs, recitations and speeches were presented, and "we tripped the light fantastic toe until late," wrote Arthur. The voyage ended in peace and unity.

If the passengers were treated with respect, they often showed their appreciation, which is how the 321 Saints aboard the *Golcondo* reacted. When they reached New Orleans, they gave "three cheers" for Captain George Kerr.

Another voyage which proved inspirational was that of the *Olympus* in 1851. Captain Horace A. Wilson, seeing a squall blowing over the water, sent two sailors to lower the sails. A gale of hurricane force blew, and the passengers were ordered below. Water in the hold climbed to a depth of four feet. Trunks, boxes, and beds, slid around the cabin. Passengers prayed, cried, and moaned. Hour after hour the ship was tossed about like a "cork on a lake." The captain asked William Howell to "pray to the God of the Mormons and see if he can do anything to save the ship and the people." Elder Howell led the ship's company in prayer and, according to fellow Mormon Wilson G. Nowers:

> While he was still engaged in prayer, I noticed a material change in the motion of the ship; for instead of rolling and pitching as she had been doing, she seemed to tremble as one suffering from the affects of a severe cold. . . . At the close of the prayer of President Howell, all responded with a hearty Amen, and we arose from our position. President Howell then remarked: "You may all retire to your beds." I returned to the deck to find the storm had miraculously ceased . . . while in the distance the billows were still raging.

As a result of this inspirational experience, a "religious fervor" swept the ship. The Saints were allowed to preach to the other passengers, and fifty asked for baptism, conducted from a platform over the ocean. One convert baptism took place near New Orleans, and another after they had docked. Another odd event with spiritual overtones in the company was a young boy named "MacKensie" who had to be exorcised several times of his "many devils."

Another ship assaulted by storm was the *Yorkshire* in 1843. According to Thomas Bullock: "The entire rigging, masts, jib, spanker, and sixteen sails and studding poles—was swept overboard with a great splash." The sailors patched them back together, and the ship limped into New Orleans with its eighty-four LDS passengers.

In 1853 English artist Frederick Piercy boarded the *Jersey* to visit Mormon sites, paint the leaders in the Valley, and write a narrative of his experiences. His departure on February 5 for New Orleans brought poignant thoughts of home: "Soon the land grew less distinct, and as it became more and more grey, there rose above all other sounds the voices of men and women sweetly mingling, 'Yes, my native land, I love thee.' Then the deck became deserted, as the motion of the ship began to affect the heads and stomachs of men and women, hitherto used only to steady Terra Firma.... During the whole of the voyage the weather was charming."

Piercy commended the company's president, George Halliway, and his two counselors:

> They made sure the ship was cleaned out every morning and that all lights except ship lights were put out at eight o'clock at night, and never on any account to permit a naked or uncovered light to be in the ship ... to prevent fire.... The married men and women had been placed in the centre of the ship, the unmarried portion of the two extremities—the males at the bow and the females at the stern.... Sickness disappeared, and was only remembered to be laughed at. Merry groups assembled on deck, and, sitting in the sunshine, told stories, sang songs, and cracked jokes by the hour together, and generally with a propriety most [admirable].

The only passenger who died was an elderly lady who was already feeble when the ship sailed.

Richard Ballantyne was in charge of an emigrant company aboard ship in 1855. The passengers manufactured "twenty-one tents and twenty wagon covers for the trip across the plains." They also had schools for children, attended to sewing and other domestic chores and in general "improved the shining moments." Ballantyne prohibited "grumbling, flirting, [and] sexual improprieties" and strongly encouraged cooking, sanitation, and religious observations. Darker notes were two excommunications, friction with non-Mormons, the death of a little boy who got caught in the deck ropes and was thrown overboard, severe food shortages, and a passage of fifty-six days. But Ballantyne was given a first-class cabin and was invited to eat with the captain.

John Jaques summarized his 1856 voyage with wry good humor:

> Well, I like the beginning and end of a sea voyage better than any other part of it. . . . Ship life is to me a dull and fusty life. It wants the charming variety and freedom, and the exquisite freshness and sweetness of life among the fields, and woods, and hills. I like sailing on such a river as the great "Father of Water" a vast deal more than on the ocean. . . . Who wishes to be forced into a gait as unsteady, staggering, and uncertain as the drunkards? Who admires treading on a platform that seems the plaything of an everlasting earthquake? I have no great taste for these things.

Elder Charles W. Penrose had unexpected company on his return from England in 1861. When he dressed one morning, he discovered that a rat had given birth to her litter in his shoe. Roaches scuttled boldly across the plank floors; bedbugs hatched endless eggs in the bunks; and lice lay in wait for victims. B. H. Roberts reached America at age nine so infested with lice that one of the men in camp chopped off his hair with sheep shears.

Sixteen-year-old Gustave Louis Henroid was probably the first French convert to emigrate but commented only briefly about his voyage in 1853 on the *Commodore*: "The Irish Channel completely upset what there was of me. . . . Father had very thoughtfully . . . provided us with oranges, lemons, claret, brandy, but the sailors . . . could tell more about what became of their distribution than I can."

Separated Families

Mothers sometimes sent children alone. In 1852, seven-year-old Nicolean Marie Bertlesen's parents told her to "wait on yourself, and don't cry" as she embarked ahead of them. An early French convert, Louis Bertrand, left his wife and children in France in 1855; even though he returned to France as mission president in 1859, he again failed to persuade them to accompany him to the Valley. Others came with just part of the family and waited in faith to rescue children who were often left with indifferent relatives or friends in the homeland.

Harry [B. H.] Roberts's parents, Benjamin and Ann, found the gospel divisive, since "the wife loved her faith more than she did her husband" and, in fact, was baptized in secret. Although Benjamin reluctantly joined the Church later, he never matched her in fervor and resisted the concept of gathering. Ann "and her two children would take the long journey and trust to the Providence of God to bring her two remaining children, my sister and I." She left B. H. and Mary with distant relatives and acquaintances, their father abandoned them, and it was five years before the two children could come to the Valley.

John Lingren emigrated from Sweden in 1863. Rather surprisingly, the strict gender segregation of other companies was not observed:

> My berth was down in the hold, 3rd deck in the ship where all single people above 18 years and under 40 were huddled together, male and female. I and my bunk fellows slept alongside of two young ladies on the right and left of us. The weather was favorable all the way. We saw icebergs and a few whales. . . . We landed in New York, June 1, 1863 after a voyage of 30 days. . . . On our journey through the states we saw railroad wrecks and destruction in many places. The Civil War was about to terminate. . . . Winter Quarters . . . [relics] were of different natures; a house that Brigham Young had lived in, a well that Heber C. Kimball had dug . . . and other sacred memories of gone-by times.

John's seventeen-year-old brother Lars started a year later but died en route. John later wrote courageously: "Our motto was forward, onward. . . . We camped at Devil's Gate for the night. I will here give a description of the beautiful country, as I had a brother who died and was buried there September 13, 1864, whose bones were dug up and carried off by the wolves. Let this be as it may; he died a faithful member of the Latter-day Saint Church and was obeying the commandment to gather in Zion."

Missionaries' Painful Partings

The sorrow of parting was not only borne by the converts who heeded the missionaries' message but also by the missionaries themselves who had to leave their families behind, often in dire circumstances. Many elders served repeated missions, while their wives and children heroically shouldered a double burden.

Ann Rogers Taylor and husband, James Taylor, left Great Britain in about 1850. On the voyage, Ann nursed and gave motherly comfort to a sick sailor. Restored to health, he told her how to earn some money in New Orleans. Following his advice, she hired a local woman and applied to do the laundry of passengers on sea-going vessels. She was hired and earned enough in a few weeks to buy a wagon and oxen which took them across the plains. They settled in Lehi; and five years later, James was called to serve a mission to England and Wales. He left Ann with four children and fifty pounds of flour. She and the oldest son plowed and planted a crop of corn, only to have the grasshoppers consume it all but a small patch. She harvested the corn, ground it in a coffee mill, and baked the first bread they had tasted in a long time. She was able to catch some fish in a nearby lake, which added some protein to their diet. The children were without shoes, so she asked a neighbor for a dead ox. She skinned it, tanned the hide, and made moccasins for the children. From the fat, she made candles. Her children had no clothing, so she walked from Lehi to Salt Lake—at least twenty miles—to buy a spool of thread, which cost 50 cents. From a wagon cover, she made shirts, pants, and dresses. Ann dug potatoes on shares; and when smallpox invaded the town, she went from neighbor to neighbor to vaccinate the children to prevent this dreaded disease. She was provider, mother, nurse, seamstress, farmer, and cook. These were women to match the mountains who also inspired writer Wallace Stegner's admiration.

Louisa Barnes Pratt was another woman who staunchly coped with the absence of a missionary husband. When Addison was sent to the Sandwich Islands in 1843 from Nauvoo, Louisa had four small daughters and little else. She mobilized her creativity and resources to provide herself with a "fit-out" in 1848 and headed for the Valley. Though she began the journey worn and weary, she regained her health en route, writing, "I am a different woman than the one who left." Her journal glows with excitement and awe at the country. She remained cheerful and got the family to the Valley where Addison joined them soon afterwards. A few years later she and the four daughters accompanied Addison on another mission to Hawaii.

Mississippi convert John Brown went on five missions between 1843 and 1860, meaning that he was absent from his family about half of the time during those years. Hosea Stout left in October 1852 for China. He had to wait so long for a ship that he spent only about seven weeks in the Hong Kong area before deciding to return home. There were no baptisms and the journey cost $135 in ship fares, most of it donated by members in California. In fact, most of the missionaries depended on the Saints near seaports like New York City and San Francisco for travel funds. (Parley P. Pratt, bound for Chile, got a nice donation from the Mormon Battalion soldiers in the fall of 1846.) Stout returned to his valley home on December 8, 1853, to discover his wife and baby dead and strangers living in his home. He didn't know where his three children were:

> This fore noon I arrived at home or what more properly might be said where once was my house. Here, not 14 months since was concentrated all my earthly happiness. Here, the confiding Louisa, the dearest object of my heart, the solace in all my troubles and my inocent [sic] prattling children, was left, in the most perfect enjoyment of earthly bliss.... Louisa was no more, the scource of my happiness was beneath the cold sod ... by the side of which rests my son who I never saw.... I gazed upon the sad wreck of all my hopes in silence while my heart sank within me & those around could not refrain from mingling their tears with mine.

However, despite his heartache, the resilient Stout, only a few weeks later, had a new wife, another house, and his children restored to him.

Richard Ballantyne was sent out in the fall of 1852 for three years without purse or scrip to become the first Saint to travel the globe westward on his mission to India. His wife and son were left nearly destitute. He suffered from smallpox and seasickness during much of the ocean voyage that lasted nearly six months. His fellow missionaries on board tenderly nursed him; but even after reaching Madras, India, his health was not good. After a year, feeling tired and unsuccessful, Ballantyne returned, having made only a few converts. When he reached the Valley again in September 1855, "he saw at a glance that his sacrifices had been no greater than those of his wife.... While she had tried in every way to disguise her poverty, he noticed that she was thinner and tired [with] hollows under her large black eyes."

Young congratulated him on his historic journey and said: "The Saints here need preaching to more than the world, and I want you to go among them and preach the gospel of repentance and tell them the laborer is worthy of his reward." Young spelled out Ballantyne's "reward": "You have been faithful . . . and now you may have two more wives." Ballantyne obeyed and eventually moved to Ogden where he prospered.

Zebulon Jacobs, a young husband and father, was full of sorrow and tears when he left on a mission for England in 1867. Jacobs wrote: "Then came the parting, it seemed to me as though I should choak in spite of all my exertions to keep up a cheerful face. . . . [I] was kissed and [I] kissed my darling boy [and] the thought of leaving those beings that wound themselves . . . round the heart of a loving husband and father very nigh over came me, the feelings were such as I never experienced before, and never want to again."

Going Upriver

Some of the scenery inspired some Saints to wrestle with their poetic muse. The journey up the Mississippi River to St. Louis, St. Joseph, and Kanesville was a chance to reflect on their surroundings, and the variety of scenery along the banks made a pleasant change from the featureless ocean. Joseph Curtis left a record in sometime-verse of his 1854 trip from New Orleans to St. Louis:

> We Was Crowded
> Now we are traveling up the river
> Crowded in that little Steamer
> But still we felt to ask the Lord
> For to protect us all on board.

The steam boat a puffing and snorting and pushing hard against the streem, but oh, what a durty watter for us to use. We dip it up for to settle it, but don't get much better. Never mind, we will do the best we can with it. I must drink it, anyhow, because I am very thirsty.

And what a rackety noise, it made me shudder. The Captain a shouting and the watter a splashing and the band a playing and some of us singing and some of the sisters a washing and the babies a crying and the sailors a talking and many of them smoking. And all of us trying to do something and the boat a tuging and snorting when traveling up the Missouri river, also the Mississippi. Indeed it was a great sight to us to see such forests of timber and land.

What a wonderful stream this is going in such a force taking down some very large logs.

They some times strike the boat with tremendous blows, but we got through all right. We got to St. Louis about the 10th of April 1854.

And was glad to get there. But what a durty looking place this is to be sure.

Ann Ward King describes the discomfort of her voyage aboard the sidewheeler *Hannibal*, that set off upriver on April 14, 1857, with 110 Mormon families, bound for Genoa, Nebraska:

These people came with weak bodies half starved from their voyage and hope to rest and recuperate in Genoa before continuing their journey to Utah. . . . The Saints were transported for only $4.00 each, and other passengers paid $8.00 each. It was very difficult to obtain a place to sleep . . . as there were not enough berth accommodations. . . . The boat often stopped to "wood" taking on great quantities for fuel. Rarely were the passengers able to replenish their scanty food supply. Some days there was little or no bread and my stomach grumbled. One night the *Hannibal* struck a sandbar and the captain was unsuccessful in getting her afloat. Finally he had to hire the boat *Sultan* to move the Hannibal off the bar, which cost the captain $400. . . . The boat averaged three miles per hour. . . . Measles broke out. . . . The Saints were very humble fasting often and holding prayer meetings daily. . . . Some nights the temperature dropped and the strong northeast wind arose and continued all night, rendering it very uncomfortable for the deck passengers. . . . Snow fell and the decks became icy. . . . Florence [Nebraska] was reached 19 days and almost 800 miles after leaving St. Louis.

Shipwreck

Conway W. Sonne estimated that in 1840–41, 557 ships were reported wrecked, and 28 reported missing. About 650 lives were lost. Most of the ships carrying Saints were blessed and dedicated by the leaders before they left the harbor. The *Julia Ann*, carrying Mormon emigrants from Australia to California, wrecked on a reef; but only five lives were lost. (See Chapter 11.) No Mormon emigrant ship traveling in the Atlantic went down. Whether one believes in miracles or not, this record speaks for itself.

Although deaths by accident or illness were an ever-present danger, a shipwreck was mercifully rare. The worst was the explosion on the Mississippi River of the *Saluda* in 1852. (See also Chapter 11.) The group of 333 Saints emigrated from Liverpool on the *Kennebec*, an uneventful journey except that some Irish emigrants were suspected of stealing rations. "Peace and harmony and good health prevailed." However, the Church officials in St. Louis chartered "an old delapidated steamboat, the *Saluda*." It exploded at Lexington, Missouri, killed about a hundred passengers, and injured and wounded many more. Henry Ballard had been eating breakfast when the explosion occurred and "found the piece of bread I held in my hand when the explosion occurred, and the tin cup from which I was in the act of taking a drink of coffee . . . ; it was mashed flat as a dollar. . . . The people of Lexington were kind to us [but] I left with what clothing I had on my back, without a hat and only one extra sock [and] no extra money [but] kind strangers . . . gave me sufficient money to buy provisions."

While Missouri is known for the early wrongs against the Saints, Lexington can certainly lay claim to this major act of kindness. Many accounts comment on the generosity the town showed to the sick and wounded from this disaster.

Conclusion: Miracles

Thomas D. Giles, a blind man in the Edward Bunker Welsh Handcart Company of 1856, was dying. They were camped near Fort Bridger where his grave was dug; and the company had waited for two days thinking he would join those the grim reaper had snatched. Captain Bunker reluctantly pulled out and left two men to bury the sick man. There were miracles along the trail, however, and Giles was one of the miracles. Giles shared a tent with Thomas D. Evans with a wooden leg, another man with only one arm, and another blind man. Parley P. Pratt, who had known Giles in Wales, came by on his way east and gave Giles a "remarkable blessing" promising he would get to the Valley and live a long life. (Ironically it was Pratt who was on his way to his death in Arkansas a year later.)

While providence might be accused of giving Giles more than his share of burdens, others would claim that he was more than equal to the challenge. Giles recovered, and rejoined his company. On October

2, ninety-five days after picking up his handcart, thirty-five-year-old Giles and his two young sons, Joseph and Hyrum, reached the Valley. His wife, Margaret, and daughter Maria were among the scores who died in those companies. Giles became a noted harpist, gave concerts and played for dances and other events. Giles left a musical legacy as his gift to the Saints, and lived until 1895. (His harp is in the Daughters of Utah Pioneers Museum in Salt Lake City.)

Haven of Hope

The doctrine of gathering came to an end in 1890, but for nearly sixty years, the Saints heard and obeyed the call. Missionaries still go forth to preach; but the call to gather is no longer a part of the discussions. The concept of gathering will always evoke strong emotions in the Mormons who honor their forebears, both those who gathered to Zion and those whose bones lie in unmarked graves on the ocean floor or along the wagon ruts. To many of the pioneers, Zion was worth the cost; it became a place of refuge, and offered chances for financial security to many.

William Wood Sr. was full of gratitude after reaching Zion, and echoes Patty Sessions's sentiments: "Imagine if it is possible, our feelings of joy and thanksgiving to God whom we acknowledge as the means of our safe arrival to the haven of our hope."

To discover the real trail story, one needs to walk along the ruts, see the splendors of the sunsets, climb Independence Rock, help get wagons across the Platte or Sweetwater River, swat a hundred mosquitoes, sleep on the hard ground or in a wet wagon, pick up some buffalo chips and cook with them, hear the cow bells at Devil's Gate at dawn, try to digest a cold breakfast or none at all, and eat at least a pint of dust. These experiences would only be a hint of the difficulty of the real journey.

Today a few new Saints and a lot of Gentiles settle in the modern Zion among the splendors of the Wasatch Mountains, Zion's National Park, and the color country of southern Utah. The modern concept of Zion has changed to include any place in the world that will shelter "the pure in heart" and where the Saints can live and worship. Zion was, and is, a place in one's heart and mind, "a haven of hope."

Index

in Brigham Young Company, 243
lamb, 124
mules, 116, 123, 243, 248–49
oxen, 16, 123–24, 210, 232, 243–44
pigs, 23, 123, 243
purchase of, 262–63
sheep, 23, 65, 123–24, 256
stampedes, 253–55
stolen by Indians, 250–52
treatment of, 252–53
Loader, Patience, 123, 224, 231
Loader, Sarah, 59
Loba, Jean Frederick, 207
Love, Nancy Maria, 43
Lowe, Howard D., xi
Ludlum, Sarah Ann, 178
Lyman, Albert, 89
Lyman, Amasa M., 30, 52, 69, 190, 200
Lyman, Amasa M., Jr., 200
Lyman, Carolina Partridge, 52
Lyman, Eliza Maria Partridge Smith, 52, 54, 56, 69
Lyman, Francis M., 106
Lyon, Christina Enoch, 123

M

MacIntyre, Thomas, 118, 132
Mackensie (twelve-year-old), 46, 268
"Madonna of the Trail" statues, 18
"Maid of Judah, The," 76
mail, 19–20, 89, 162–63
malaria. *See* disease/illness.
malnutrition, 8
mammoth bones, 89
Mammy Chloe, 192
Manning, Isaac, 189, 191
Manning, Peter, 190
Margetts (1856), 185
Margetts, Phillip, 78

Maricope (tribe), 172
Markham, Stephen, 95, 100
Markle, John, 154
marriage
courtship, 131–36
on the trail, 136–38
wife purchased, 142
with mountain men, 231
with Indians, 181–83
Marsden, William, 188
Martin Handcart Company, 18, 41, 59, 65, 115, 119, 122–23, 198, 212, 224–25, 233, 236–38
Mary, 208
masonry, 69–70
Mathews, William, 32
Mattes, Merrill, xxiii–xxv, 176, 193, 219
Matthews, Amanda M., 80
Maughan, Mary Ann Weston, 121–22, 177
Maughan, Peter, 121
May, Ruth, 112, 117
Mayhew, Elijah, 93, 103
McAllister, John Daniel Thomas, 77, 178
McArthur, Daniel D., 119, 241
McArthur Handcart Company, 119–20
McBride, Heber Robert, 75, 112, 233
McBride, Henry, 119
McBride, Peter, 119
McClellan, George, 123
McClellan, Jenny, 123
McIntyre, Margaret, 142
McIntyre, Peter, 142
McIntyre, Thomas, 20, 239
McKee, William, 194
McNeil, Charles Collins Thornton, 123
McNeil, Christena, 132
McWilliams, Jo, 182

Also available from
GREG KOFFORD BOOKS

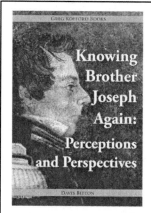

Knowing Brother Joseph Again: Perceptions and Perspectives

Davis Bitton

Paperback, ISBN: 978-1-58958-123-4

In 1996, Davis Bitton, one of Mormon history's preeminent and much-loved scholars, published a collection of essays on Joseph Smith under the title, *Images of the Prophet Joseph Smith*. A decade later, when the book went out of print, Davis began work on an updated version that would also include some of his other work on the Mormon prophet. The project was only partially finished when his health failed. He died on April 13, 2007, at age seventy-seven. With the aid of additional historians, *Knowing Brother Joseph Again: Perceptions and Perspectives* brings to completion Davis's final work—a testament to his own admiration of the Prophet Joseph Smith.

From Davis Bitton's introducton:

This is not a conventional biography of Joseph Smith, but its intended purpose should not be hard to grasp. That purpose is to trace how Joseph Smith has appeared from different points of view. It is the image of Joseph Smith rather than the man himself that I seek to delineate.

Even when we have cut through the rumor and misinformation that surround all public figures and agree on many details, differences of interpretation remain. We live in an age of relativism. What is beautiful for one is not for another, what is good and moral for one is not for another, and what is true for one is not for another. I shudder at the thought that my presentation here will lead to such soft relativism.

Yet the fact remains that different people saw Joseph Smith in different ways. Even his followers emphasized different facets at different times. From their own perspectives, different people saw him differently or focused on a different facet of his personality at different times. Inescapably, what they observed or found out about him was refracted through the lens of their own experience. Some of the different, flickering, not always compatible views are the subject of this book.

Excavating Mormon Pasts: The New Historiography of the Last Half Century

Newell G. Bringhurst and Lavina Fielding Anderson

Paperback, ISBN: 978-1-58958-115-9

Special Book Award - John Whitmer Historical Association

Mormonism was born less than 200 years ago, but in that short time it has developed into a dynamic world religious movement. With that growth has come the inevitable restructuring and reevaluation of its history and doctrine. Mormon and non-Mormon scholars alike have viewed Joseph Smith's religion as fertile soil for religious, historical and sociological studies. Many early attempts to either defend or defame the Church were at best sloppy and often dishonest. It has taken decades for Mormon scholarship to mature to its present state. The editors of this book have assembled 16 essays addressing the substantial number of published works in the field of Mormon studies from 1950 to the present. The contributors come from various segments of the Mormon tradition and fairly represent the broad intellectual spectrum of that tradition. Each essay focuses on a particular aspect of Mormonism (history, women's issues, polygamy, etc.), and each is careful to evenhandedly evaluate the strengths and weaknesses of the books under discussion. More importantly, each volume is placed in context with other, related works, giving the reader a panoramic view of contemporary research. Students of Mormonism will find this collection of historiographical essays an invaluable addition to their libraries.

On the Road with Joseph Smith: An Author's Diary

Richard L. Bushman

Paperback, ISBN 978-1-58958-102-9

After living with Joseph Smith for seven years and delivering the final proofs of his landmark study, *Joseph Smith: Rough Stone Rolling* to Knopf in July 2005, biographer Richard Lyman Bushman went "on the road" for a year, crisscrossing the country from coast to coast, delivering addresses on Joseph Smith and attending book-signings for the new biography.

Bushman confesses to hope and humility as he awaits reviews. He frets at the polarization that dismissed the book as either too hard on Joseph Smith or too easy. He yields to a very human compulsion to check sales figures on Amazon. com, but partway through the process stepped back with the recognition, "The book seems to be cutting its own path now, just as [I] hoped."

For readers coming to grips with the ongoing puzzle of the Prophet and the troublesome dimensions of their own faith, Richard Bushman, openly but not insistently presents himself as a believer. "I believe enough to take Joseph Smith seriously," he says. He draws comfort both from what he calls his "mantra" ("Today I will be a follower of Jesus Christ") and also from ongoing engagement with the intellectual challenges of explaining Joseph Smith.

Praise for *On the Road With Joseph Smith*:

"The diary is possibly unparalleled—an author of a recent book candidly dissecting his experiences with both Mormon and non-Mormon audiences . . . certainly deserves wider distribution—in part because it shows a talented historian laying open his vulnerabilities, and also because it shows how much any historian lays on the line when he writes about Joseph Smith."
-Dennis Lythgoe, *Deseret News*

"By turns humorous and poignant, this behind-the-scenes look at Richard Bushman's public and private ruminations about Joseph Smith reveals a great deal—not only about the inner life of one of our greatest scholars, but about Mormonism at the dawn of the 21st century."
-Jana Riess, co-author of *Mormonism for Dummies*

The Brigham Young University Book of Mormon Symposium Series

Various Authors

Nine-volume box set, ISBN: 978-1-58958-087-9

A series of lectures delivered at BYU by a wide and exciting array of the finest gospel scholars in the Church. Get valuable insights from foremost authorities including General authorities, BYU Professors and Church Educational System instructors. No gospel library will be complete without this valuable resource. Anyone interested in knowing what the top gospel scholars in the Church are saying about such important subjects as historiography, geography, and faith in Christ will be sure to enjoy this handsome box set. This is the perfect gift for any student of the Book of Mormon.

Contributors include: Neal A. Maxwell, Boyd K. Packer, Jeffrey R. Holland, Russell M. Nelson, Dallin H. Oaks, Gerald N. Lund, Dean L. Larsen, Joseph Fielding McConkie, Richard Neitzel Holzapfel, Truman G. Madsen, John W. Welch, Robert J. Matthews, Daniel H. Ludlow, Stephen D. Ricks, Grant Underwood, Robert L. Millet, Susan Easton Black, H. Donl Peterson, John L. Sorenson, Monte S. Nyman, Daniel C. Peterson, Stephen E. Robinson, Carolyn J. Rasmus, Dennis L. Largey, C. Max Caldwell, Andrew C. Skinner, S. Michael Wilcox, Paul R. Cheesman, K. Douglas Bassett, Douglas E. Brinley, Richard O. Cowan, Donald W. Parry, Bruce A. Van Orden, Kenneth W. Anderson, Leland Gentry, S. Kent Brown, H. Dean Garrett, Lee L. Donaldson, Robert E. Parsons, S. Brent Farley, Rodney Turner, Larry E. Dahl, Mae Blanch, Rex C. Reeve Jr., E. Dale LeBaron, Clyde J. Williams, Chauncey C. Riddle, Kent P. Jackson, Daniel K. Judd, Neal E. Lambert, Michael W. Middleton, R. Wayne Shute, John M. Butler, and many more!

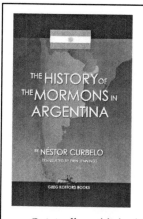

The History of Mormons
in Argentina

Néstor Curbelo

English, ISBN: 978-1-58958-052-7

Originally published in Spanish, Curbelo's The History of the Mormons in Argentina is a groundbreaking book detailing the growth of the Church in this Latin American country.

Through numerous interviews and access to other primary resources, Curbelo has constructed a timeline, and then documents the story of the Church's growth. Starting with a brief discussion of Parley P. Pratt's assignment to preside over the Pacific and South American regions, continuing on with the translation of the scriptures into Spanish, the opening of the first missions in South America, and the building of temples, the book provides a survey history of the Church in Argentina. This book will be of interest not only to history buffs but also to thousands of past, present, and future missionaries.

Translated by Erin Jennings

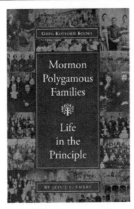

Mormon Polygamous Families:
Life in the Principle

Jessie L. Embry

Paperback, ISBN: 978-1-58958-098-5
Hardcover, ISBN: 978-1-58958-114-2

Mormons and non-Mormons all have their views about how polygamy was practiced in the Church of Jesus Christ of Latter-day Saints during the late nineteenth and early twentieth centuries. Embry has examined the participants themselves in order to understand how men and women living a nineteenth-century Victorian lifestyle adapted to polygamy. Based on records and oral histories with husbands, wives, and children who lived in Mormon polygamous households, this study explores the diverse experiences of individual families and stereotypes about polygamy. The interviews are in some cases the only sources of primary information on how plural families were organized. In addition, children from monogamous families who grew up during the same period were interviewed to form a comparison group. When carefully examined, most of the stereotypes about polygamous marriages do not hold true. In this work it becomes clear that Mormon polygamous families were not much different from Mormon monogamous families and non-Mormon families of the same era. Embry offers a new perspective on the Mormon practice of polygamy that enables readers to gain better understanding of Mormonism historically.

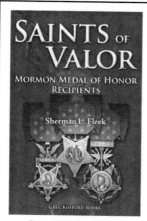

Saints of Valor: Mormon Medal of Honor Recipients

Sherman L. Fleek

Hardcover, ISBN: 978-1-58958-171-5

Since 1861 when the US Congress approved the concept of a Medal of Honor for combat valor, 3,457 individuals have received this highest military decoration that the nation can bestow. Nine of those have been Latter-day Saints. The military and personal stories of these LDS recipients are compelling, inspiring, and tragic. The men who appear in this book are tied by two common threads: the Medal of Honor and their Mormon heritage.

The purpose of this book is to highlight the valor of a special class of LDS servicemen who served and sacrificed "above and beyond the call of duty." Four of these nine Mormons gave their "last full measure" for their country, never seeing the high award they richly deserved. All four branches of the service are represented: five were Army (one was a pilot with the Army Air Forces during WWII), two Navy, and one each of the Marine Corps and Air Force. Four were military professionals who made the service their careers; five were not career-minded; three died at an early age and never married. This book captures these harrowing historical narratives from personal accounts.

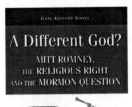

A Different God?
Mitt Romney the Religious Right and the Mormon Question

Craig L. Foster

Paperback, ISBN: 978-1-58958-117-3

In the contested terrain of American politics, nowhere is the conflict more intense, even brutal, than in the territory of public life also claimed by religion. Mitt Romney's 2007–08 presidential campaign is a textbook example.

Religious historian (and ardent Republican) Craig L. Foster revisits that campaign with an astute focus on the never-quite-contained hostility that Romney triggered among America's religious right. Although few political campaign are known for their kindness, the back-stabbing, mean-spirited attacks, eruptions of irrationalism, and downright lies exploded into one of the meanest chapters of recent American political history.

Foster readjusts rosy views of America as the tolerant, pluralistic society against the context of its lengthy, colorful, and bruising history of religious discrimination and oppression against many religious groups, among them Mormonism. Mormons are now respected and admired--although the image hasn't tilted enough to work for Romney instead of against him. Their turbulent past of suspicion, marginalization, physical violence, and being deprived of voting rights has sometimes made them, in turn, suspicious, hostile, and politically naive. How much of this pattern of mutual name-calling stems from theology and how much from theocratic ideals?

Foster appraises Romney's success and strengths—and also places where he stumbled, analyzing an intriguing pattern of "what-ifs?" of policy, personality, and positioning. But perhaps even more intriguing is the anti-Romney campaign launched by a divided and fragmenting religious right who pulled together in a rare show of unity to chill a Mormon's presidential aspirations. What does Romney's campaign and the resistance of the religious right mean for America in the twenty-first century?

In this meticulously researched, comprehensively documented, and passionately argued analysis of a still-ongoing campaign, Craig Foster poses questions that go beyond both Romney and the religious right to engage the soul of American politics.

Penny Tracts and Polemics: A Critical Analysis of Anti-Mormon Pamphleteering in Great Britain, 1837–1860

Craig L. Foster

Hardcover, ISBN: 978-1-58958-005-3

By 1860, Mormonism had enjoyed a presence in Great Britain for over twenty years. Mormon missionaries experienced unprecedented success in conversions and many new converts had left Britain's shores for a new life and a new religion in the far western mountains of the American continent.

With the success of the Mormons came tales of duplicity, priestcraft, sexual seduction, and uninhibited depravity among the new religious adherents. Thousands of pamphlets were sold or given to the British populace as a way of discouraging people from joining the Mormon Church. Foster places the creation of these English anti-Mormon pamphlets in their historical context. He discusses the authors, the impact of the publications and the Mormon response. With illustrations and detailed bibliography.

The Gift and Power: Translating the Book of Mormon

Brant A. Gardner

Hardcover, ISBN: 978-1-58958-131-9

From Brant A. Gardner, the author of the highly praised *Second Witness* commentaries on the Book of Mormon, comes *The Gift and Power: Translating the Book of Mormon*. In this first book-length treatment of the translation process, Gardner closely examines the accounts surrounding Joseph Smith's translation of the Book of Mormon to answer a wide spectrum of questions about the process, including: Did the Prophet use seerstones common to folk magicians of his time? How did he use them? And, what is the relationship to the golden plates and the printed text?

Approaching the topic in three sections, part 1 examines the stories told about Joseph, folk magic, and the translation. Part 2 examines the available evidence to determine how closely the English text replicates the original plate text. And part 3 seeks to explain how seer stones worked, why they no longer work, and how Joseph Smith could have produced a translation with them.

Second Witness: Analytical and Contextual Commentatry on the Book of Mormon

Brant A. Gardner

Second Witness, a new six-volume series from Greg Kofford Books, takes a detailed, verse-by-verse look at the Book of Mormon. It marshals the best of modern scholarship and new insights into a consistent picture of the Book of Mormon as a historical document. Taking a faithful but scholarly approach to the text and reading it through the insights of linguistics, anthropology, and ethnohistory, the commentary approaches the text from a variety of perspectives: how it was created, how it relates to history and culture, and what religious insights it provides.

The commentary accepts the best modern scholarship, which focuses on a particular region of Mesoamerica as the most plausible location for the Book of Mormon's setting. For the first time, that location—its peoples, cultures, and historical trends—are used as the backdrop for reading the text. The historical background is not presented as proof, but rather as an explanatory context.

The commentary does not forget Mormon's purpose in writing. It discusses the doctrinal and theological aspects of the text and highlights the way in which Mormon created it to meet his goal of "convincing . . . the Jew and Gentile that Jesus is the Christ, the Eternal God."

Praise for the *Second Witness* series:

"Gardner not only provides a unique tool for understanding the Book of Mormon as an ancient document written by real, living prophets, but he sets a standard for Latter-day Saint thinking and writing about scripture, providing a model for all who follow. . . . No other reference source will prove as thorough and valuable for serious readers of the Book of Mormon."

-Neal A. Maxwell Institute, Brigham Young University

1. 1st Nephi: 978-1-58958-041-1
2. 2nd Nephi–Jacob: 978-1-58958-042-8
3. Enos–Mosiah: 978-1-58958-043-5

4. Alma: 978-1-58958-044-2
5. Helaman–3rd Nephi: 978-1-58958-045-9
6. 4th Nephi–Moroni: 978-1-58958-046-6

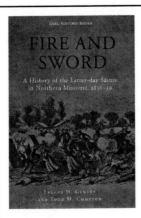

Fire and Sword: A History of the Latter-day Saints in Northern Missouri, 1836-39

Leland Homer Gentry and Todd M. Compton

Hardcover, ISBN: 978-1-58958-103-6

Many Mormon dreams flourished in Missouri. So did many Mormon nightmares.

The Missouri period—especially from the summer of 1838 when Joseph took over vigorous, personal direction of this new Zion until the spring of 1839 when he escaped after five months of imprisonment—represents a moment of intense crisis in Mormon history. Representing the greatest extremes of devotion and violence, commitment and intolerance, physical suffering and terror—mobbings, battles, massacres, and political "knockdowns"—it shadowed the Mormon psyche for a century.

Leland Gentry was the first to step beyond this disturbing period as a one-sided symbol of religious persecution and move toward understanding it with careful documentation and evenhanded analysis. In Fire and Sword, Todd Compton collaborates with Gentry to update this foundational work with four decades of new scholarship, more insightful critical theory, and the wealth of resources that have become electronically available in the last few years.

Compton gives full credit to Leland Gentry's extraordinary achievement, particularly in documenting the existence of Danites and in attempting to tell the Missourians' side of the story; but he also goes far beyond it, gracefully drawing into the dialogue signal interpretations written since Gentry and introducing the raw urgency of personal writings, eyewitness journalists, and bemused politicians seesawing between human compassion and partisan harshness. In the lush Missouri landscape of the Mormon imagination where Adam and Eve had walked out of the garden and where Adam would return to preside over his posterity, the towering religious creativity of Joseph Smith and clash of religious stereotypes created a swift and traumatic frontier drama that changed the Church.

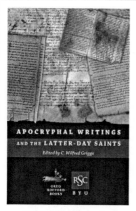

Apocryphal Writings
and the Latter-day Saints

Edited by C. Wilfred Griggs

Paperback, ISBN: 978-1-58958-089-3

This sought-after volume of essays takes an in-depth look at the apocrypha and how Latter-day Saints should approach it in their gospel study. With notable LDS authors such as Stephen E. Robinson, Joseph F. McConkie, and Robert L. Millet, this volume is an essential addition to any well-rounded Mormon studies library. Essays include: "Whose Apocrypha? Viewing Ancient Apocrypha from the Vantage of Events in the Present Dispensation," "Lying for God: The Uses of Apocrypha," and "The Nag Hammadi Library: A Mormon Perspective."

"Swell Suffering": A Biography of Maurine Whipple

Veda Tebbs Hale

Paperback, ISBN: 978-1-58958-124-1
Hardcover, ISBN: 978-1-58958-122-7

Maurine Whipple, author of what some critics consider Mormonism's greatest novel, *The Giant Joshua,* is an enigma. Her prize-winning novel has never been out of print, and its portrayal of the founding of St. George draws on her own family history to produce its unforgettable and candid portrait of plural marriage's challenges. Yet Maurine's life is full of contradictions and unanswered questions. Veda Tebbs Hale, a personal friend of the paradoxical novelist, answers these questions with sympathy and tact, nailing each insight down with thorough research in Whipple's vast but under-utilized collected papers.

Praise for *"Swell Suffering"*:

"Hale achieves an admirable balance of compassion and objectivity toward an author who seemed fated to offend those who offered to love or befriend her. . . . Readers of this biography will be reminded that Whipple was a full peer of such Utah writers as Virginia Sorensen, Fawn Brodie, and Juanita Brooks, all of whom achieved national fame for their literary and historical works during the mid-twentieth century"
—Levi S. Peterson, author of *The Backslider* and *Juanita Brooks: Mormon Historian*

Modern Polygamy and Mormon Fundamentalism:
The Generations after the Manifesto

Brian C. Hales

Paperback, ISBN: 978-1-58958-109-8

**Winner of the John Whitmer Historical Association's
Smith-Pettit Best Book Award**

This fascinating study seeks to trace the historical tapestry that is early Mormon polygamy, details the official discontinuation of the practice by the Church, and, for the first time, describes the many zeal-driven organizations that arose in the wake of that decision. Among the polygamous groups discussed are the LeBaronites, whose "blood atonement" killings sent fear throughout Mormon communities in the late seventies and the eighties; the FLDS Church, which made news recently over its construction of a compound and temple in Texas (Warren Jeffs, the leader of that church, is now standing trial on two felony counts after his being profiled on America's Most Wanted resulted in his capture); and the Allred and Kingston groups, two major factions with substantial membership statistics both in and out of the United States. All these fascinating histories, along with those of the smaller independent groups, are examined and explained in a way that all can appreciate.

Praise for *Modern Polygamy and Mormon Fundamentalism*:

"This book is the most thorough and comprehensive study written on the sugbject to date, providing readers with a clear, candid, and broad sweeping overview of the history, teachings, and practices of modern fundamentalist groups."
—Alexander L. Baugh, Associate Professor of Church History and
Doctrine, Brigham Young University

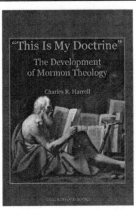

"This is My Doctrine":
The Development of Mormon
Theology

Charles R. Harrell

Hardcover, ISBN: 978-1-58958-103-6

The principal doctrines defining Mormonism today often bear little resemblance to those it started out with in the early 1830s. This book shows that these doctrines did not originate in a vacuum but were rather prompted and informed by the religious culture from which Mormonism arose. Early Mormons, like their early Christian and even earlier Israelite predecessors, brought with them their own varied culturally conditioned theological presuppositions (a process of convergence) and only later acquired a more distinctive theological outlook (a process of differentiation).

In this first-of-its-kind comprehensive treatment of the development of Mormon theology, Charles Harrell traces the history of Latter-day Saint doctrines from the times of the Old Testament to the present. He describes how Mormonism has carried on the tradition of the biblical authors, early Christians, and later Protestants in reinterpreting scripture to accommodate new theological ideas while attempting to uphold the integrity and authority of the scriptures. In the process, he probes three questions: How did Mormon doctrines develop? What are the scriptural underpinnings of these doctrines? And what do critical scholars make of these same scriptures? In this enlightening study, Harrell systematically peels back the doctrinal accretions of time to provide a fresh new look at Mormon theology.

"This Is My Doctrine" will provide those already versed in Mormonism's theological tradition with a new and richer perspective of Mormon theology. Those unacquainted with Mormonism will gain an appreciation for how Mormon theology fits into the larger Jewish and Christian theological traditions.

LDS Biographical Encyclopedia

Andrew Jenson

Hardcover, ISBN: 978-1-58958-031-2

In the Preface to the first volume Jenson writes, "On the rolls of the Church of Jesus Christ of Latter-day Saints are found the names of a host of men and women of worth—heroes and heroines of a higher type—who have been and are willing to sacrifice fortune and life for the sake of their religion. It is for the purpose of perpetuating the memory of these, and to place on record deeds worthy of imitation, that [this set] makes its appearance."

With over 5,000 biographical entries of "heroes and heroines" complete with more than 2,000 photographs, the *LDS Biographical Encyclopedia* is an essential reference for the study of early Church history. Nearly anyone with pioneer heritage will find exciting and interesting history about ancestors in these volumes.

Andrew Jenson was an assistant historian for the Church of Jesus Christ of Latter-day Saints from 1897 to 1941.

A House for the Most High: The Story of the Original Nauvoo Temple

Matthew McBride

Hardcover, ISBN: 978-1-58958-016-9

This awe-inspiring book is a tribute to the perseverance of the human spirit. *A House for the Most High* is a groundbreaking work from beginning to end with its faithful and comprehensive documentation of the Nauvoo Temple's conception. The behind-the-scenes stories of those determined Saints involved in the great struggle to raise the sacred edifice bring a new appreciation to all readers. McBride's painstaking research now gives us access to valuable first-hand accounts that are drawn straight from the newspaper articles, private diaries, journals, and letters of the steadfast participants.

The opening of this volume gives the reader an extraordinary window into the early temple-building labors of the besieged Church of Jesus Christ of Latter-day Saints, the development of what would become temple-related doctrines in the decade prior to the Nauvoo era, and the 1839 advent of the Saints in Illinois. The main body of this fascinating history covers the significant years, starting from 1840, when this temple was first considered, to the temple's early destruction by a devastating natural disaster. A well-thought-out conclusion completes the epic by telling of the repurchase of the temple lot by the Church in 1937, the lot's excavation in 1962, and the grand announcement in 1999 that the temple would indeed be rebuilt. Also included are an astonishing appendix containing rare and fascinating eyewitness descriptions of the temple and a bibliography of all major source materials. Mormons and non-Mormons alike will discover, within the pages of this book, a true sense of wonder and gratitude for a determined people whose sole desire was to build a sacred and holy temple for the worship of their God.

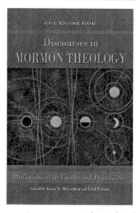

Discourses in Mormon Theology: Philosophical and Theological Possibilities

Edited by
James M. McLachlan and Loyd Ericson

Hardcover, ISBN: 978-1-58958-103-6

A mere two hundred years old, Mormonism is still in its infancy compared to other theological disciplines (Judaism, Catholicism, Buddhism, etc.). This volume will introduce its reader to the rich blend of theological viewpoints that exist within Mormonism. The essays break new ground in Mormon studies by exploring the vast expanse of philosophical territory left largely untouched by traditional approaches to Mormon theology. It presents philosophical and theological essays by many of the finest minds associated with Mormonism in an organized and easy-to-understand manner and provides the reader with a window into the fascinating diversity amongst Mormon philosophers. Open-minded students of pure religion will appreciate this volume's thoughtful inquiries.

These essays were delivered at the first conference of the Society for Mormon Philosophy and Theology. Authors include Grant Underwood, Blake T. Ostler, Dennis Potter, Margaret Merrill Toscano, James E. Faulconer, and Robert L. Millet

Praise for *Discourses in Mormon Theology*:

"In short, *Discourses in Mormon Theology* is an excellent compilation of essays that are sure to feed both the mind and soul. It reminds all of us that beyond the white shirts and ties there exists a universe of theological and moral sensitivity that cries out for study and acclamation."
                    -Jeff Needle, Association for Mormon Letters

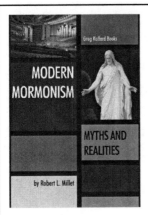

Modern Mormonism: Myths and Realities

Robert L. Millet

Paperback, ISBN: 978-1-58958-127-2

What answer may a Latter-day Saint make to accusations from those of other faiths that "Mormons aren't Christians," or "You think God is a man," and "You worship a different Jesus"? Not only are these charges disconcerting, but the hostility with which they are frequently hurled is equally likely to catch Latter-day Saints off guard.

Now Robert L. Millet, veteran of hundreds of such verbal battles, cogently, helpfully, and scripturally provides important clarifications for Latter-day Saints about eleven of the most frequent myths used to discredit the Church. Along the way, he models how to conduct such a Bible based discussion respectfully, weaving in enlightenment from LDS scriptures and quotations from religious figures in other faiths, ranging from the early church fathers to the archbishop of Canterbury.

Millet enlivens this book with personal experiences as a boy growing up in an area where Mormons were a minuscule and not particularly welcome minority, in one-on-one conversations with men of faith who believed differently, and with his own BYU students who also had lessons to learn about interfaith dialogue. He pleads for greater cooperation in dealing with the genuine moral and social evils afflicting the world, and concludes with his own ardent and reverent testimony of the Savior.

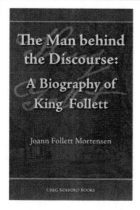

The Man behind the Discourse: A Biography of King Follett

Joann Follett Mortensen

ISBN: 978-1-58958-036-7

Who was King Follett? When he was fatally injured digging a well in Nauvoo in March 1844, why did Joseph Smith use his death to deliver the monumental doctrinal sermon now known as the King Follett Discourse? Much has been written about the sermon, but little about King.

Although King left no personal writings, Joann Follett Mortensen, King's third great-granddaughter, draws on more than thirty years of research in civic and Church records and in the journals and letters of King's peers to piece together King's story from his birth in New Hampshire and moves westward where, in Ohio, he and his wife, Louisa, made the life-shifting decision to accept the new Mormon religion.

From that point, this humble, hospitable, and hardworking family followed the Church into Missouri where their devotion to Joseph Smith was refined and burnished. King was the last Mormon prisoner in Missouri to be released from jail. According to family lore, King was one of the Prophet's bodyguards. He was also a Danite, a Mason, and an officer in the Nauvoo Legion. After his death, Louisa and their children settled in Iowa where some associated with the Cutlerities and the RLDS Church; others moved on to California. One son joined the Mormon Battalion and helped found Mormon communities in Utah, Idaho, and Arizona.

While King would have died virtually unknown had his name not been attached to the discourse, his life story reflects the reality of all those whose faith became the foundation for a new religion. His biography is more than one man's life story. It is the history of the early Restoration itself.

Exploring Mormon Thought Series

Blake T. Ostler

IN VOLUME ONE, *The Attributes of God*, Blake T. Ostler explores Christian and Mormon notions about God. ISBN: 978-1-58958-003-9

IN VOLUME TWO, *The Problems of Theism and the Love of God*, Blake Ostler explores issues related to soteriology, or the theory of salvation. ISBN: 978-1-58958-095-4

IN VOLUME THREE, *Of God and Gods*, Ostler analyzes and responds to the arguments of contemporary international theologians, reconstructs and interprets Joseph Smith's important King Follett Discourse and Sermon in the Grove, and argues persuasively for the Mormon doctrine of "robust deification." ISBN: 978-1-58958-107-4

Praise for the *Exploring Mormon Thought* series:

"These books are the most important works on Mormon theology ever written. There is nothing currently available that is even close to the rigor and sophistication of these volumes. B. H. Roberts and John A. Widtsoe may have had interesting insights in the early part of the twentieth century, but they had neither the temperament nor the training to give a rigorous defense of their views in dialogue with a wider stream of Christian theology. Sterling McMurrin and Truman Madsen had the capacity to engage Mormon theology at this level, but neither one did."

—Neal A. Maxwell Institute, Brigham Young University

The Incomparable Jesus

Grant H. Palmer

Paperback, ISBN: 978-1-58958-092-3

Distilled from his personal experiences in teaching Jesus to the hard-to-reach, this professional educator has produced a tender testament to the incomparable Jesus. It describes a Savior who walked with him through the halls of the county jail where he served as chaplain, succoring those in need.

In this slim volume, Palmer sensitively shares his understanding of what it means to know Jesus by doing his works. He lists the qualities of divine character attested to by the Apostles Peter and Paul, and also those that Jesus revealed about himself in his masterful Sermon on the Mount, particularly in the beatitudes.

With reverence Palmer shares personal spiritual experiences that were life-changing assurances of Jesus's love for him—a love poured out unstintingly in equally life-changing blessings on prisoners whose crimes had not stopped short of sexual abuse and murder. Reading this book offers a deeper understanding of the Savior's mercy, a stronger sense of his love, and a deeper commitment to follow him.

Hugh Nibley:
A Consecrated Life

Boyd Jay Petersen

Hardcover, ISBN: 978-1-58958-019-0

Winner of the Mormon History Association's Best Biography Award

As one of the LDS Church's most widely recognized scholars, Hugh Nibley is both an icon and an enigma. Through complete access to Nibley's correspondence, journals, notes, and papers, Petersen has painted a portrait that reveals the man behind the legend.

Starting with a foreword written by Zina Nibley Petersen and finishing with appendices that include some of the best of Nibley's personal correspondence, the biography reveals aspects of the tapestry of the life of one who has truly consecrated his life to the service of the Lord.

Praise for *A Consecrated Life*:

"Hugh Nibley is generally touted as one of Mormonism's greatest minds and perhaps its most prolific scholarly apologist. Just as hefty as some of Nibley's largest tomes, this authorized biography is delightfully accessible and full of the scholar's delicious wordplay and wit, not to mention some astonishing war stories and insights into Nibley's phenomenal acquisition of languages. Introduced by a personable foreword from the author's wife (who is Nibley's daughter), the book is written with enthusiasm, respect and insight. . . . On the whole, Petersen is a careful scholar who provides helpful historical context. . . . This project is far from hagiography. It fills an important gap in LDS history and will appeal to a wide Mormon audience."
    —Publishers Weekly

"Well written and thoroughly researched, Petersen's biography is a must-have for anyone struggling to reconcile faith and reason."
    —Greg Taggart, Association for Mormon Letters

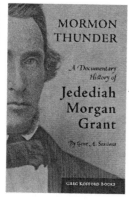

Mormon Thunder:
A Documentary History of Jedediah Morgan Grant

Gene A. Sessions

Paperback, ISBN: 978-1-58958-111-1

Jedediah Morgan Grant was a man who knew no compromise when it came to principles—and his principles were clearly representative, argues Gene A. Sessions, of Mormonism's first generation. His life is a glimpse of a Mormon world whose disappearance coincided with the death of this "pious yet rambunctiously radical preacher, flogging away at his people, demanding otherworldliness and constant sacrifice." It was "an eschatological, premillennial world in which every individual teetered between salvation and damnation and in which unsanitary privies and appropriating a stray cow held the same potential for eternal doom as blasphemy and adultery."

Updated and newly illustrated with more photographs, this second edition of the award-winning documentary history (first published in 1982) chronicles Grant's ubiquitous role in the Mormon history of the 1840s and '50s. In addition to serving as counselor to Brigham Young during two tumultuous and influential years at the end of his life, he also portentously befriended Thomas L. Kane, worked to temper his unruly brother-in-law William Smith, captained a company of emigrants into the Salt Lake Valley in 1847, and journeyed to the East on several missions to bolster the position of the Mormons during the crises surrounding the runaway judges affair and the public revelation of polygamy.

Jedediah Morgan Grant's voice rises powerfully in these pages, startling in its urgency in summoning his people to sacrifice and moving in its tenderness as he communicated to his family. From hastily scribbled letters to extemporaneous sermons exhorting obedience, and the notations of still stunned listeners, the sound of "Mormon Thunder" rolls again in "a boisterous amplification of what Mormonism really was, and would never be again."

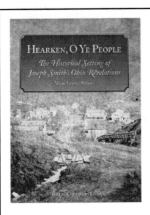

Hearken, O Ye People:
The Historical Setting of Joseph Smith's Ohio Revelations

Mark Lyman Staker

Hardcover, ISBN: 978-1-58958-113-5

2010 Best Book Award - John Whitmer Historical Association

2011 Best Book Award - Mormon History Association

More of Mormonism's canonized revelations originated in or near Kirtland than any other place. Yet many of the events connected with those revelations and their 1830s historical context have faded over time. Mark Staker reconstructs the cultural experiences by which Kirtland's Latter-day Saints made sense of the revelations Joseph Smith pronounced. This volume rebuilds that exciting decade using clues from numerous archives, privately held records, museum collections, and even the soil where early members planted corn and homes. From this vast array of sources he shapes a detailed narrative of weather, religious backgrounds, dialect differences, race relations, theological discussions, food preparation, frontier violence, astronomical phenomena, and myriad daily customs of nineteenth-century life. The result is a "from the ground up" experience that today's Latter-day Saints can all but walk into and touch.

Praise for *Hearken O Ye People*:

"I am not aware of a more deeply researched and richly contextualized study of any period of Mormon church history than Mark Staker's study of Mormons in Ohio. We learn about everything from the details of Alexander Campbell's views on priesthood authority to the road conditions and weather on the four Lamanite missionaries' journey from New York to Ohio. All the Ohio revelations and even the First Vision are made to pulse with new meaning. This book sets a new standard of in-depth research in Latter-day Saint history."
-Richard Bushman, author of *Joseph Smith: Rough Stone Rolling*

"To be well-informed, any student of Latter-day Saint history and doctrine must now be acquainted with the remarkable research of Mark Staker on the important history of the church in the Kirtland, Ohio, area."
-Neal A. Maxwell Institute, Brigham Young University

"Let the Earth Bring Forth"
Evolution and Scripture

Howard C. Stutz

Paperback, ISBN: 978-1-58958-126-5

A century ago in 1809, Charles Darwin was born. Fifty years later, he published a scientific treatise describing the process of speciation that launched what appeared to be a challenge to the traditional religious interpretation of how life was created on earth. The controversy has erupted anew in the last decade as Creationists and Young Earth adherents challenge school curricula and try to displace "the theory of evolution."

This book is filled with fascinating examples of speciation by the well-known process of mutation but also by the less well-known processes of sexual recombination and polyploidy. In addition to the fossil record, Howard Stutz examines the evidence from the embryo stages of human beings and other creatures to show how selection and differentiation moved development in certain favored directions while leaving behind evidence of earlier, discarded developments. Anatomy, biochemistry, and genetics are all examined in their turn.

With rigorously scientific clarity but in language accessible to a popular audience, the book proceeds to its conclusion, reached after a lifetime of study: the divine map of creation is one supported by both scientific evidence and the scriptures. This is a book to be read, not only for its fascinating scientific insights, but also for a new appreciation of well-known scriptures.

The Wasp

Hardcover, ISBN: 978-1-58958-050-3

A newspaper published in Nauvoo from April 16, 1842, through April 26, 1843, *The Wasp* provides a crucial window into firsthand accounts of the happenings and concerns of the Saints in Nauvoo. It was initially edited by William Smith, younger brother of Joseph Smith. William was succeeded by John Taylor as editor and Taylor and Wilford Woodruff as printers and publishers. Some of the main stories covered in the newspaper are the August 1842 elections where local candidates endorsed by the Mormons easily won against their opponents, the fall from grace of John C. Bennett, the attempt by the state of Missouri to extradite Joseph Smith as an accessory in the attempted murder of Lilburn W. Boggs, and the Illinois legislature's effort to repeal the Nauvoo charter.

With a foreword by Peter Crawley putting the newspaper in historical context, this first-ever reproduction of the entire run of the *The Wasp* is essential to anyone interested in the Nauvoo period of Mormonism.

CPSIA information can be obtained at www.ICGtesting.com
Printed in the USA
BVOW032348180612

293007BV00003B/5/P